COACHING VOLLEYBALL SUCCESSFULLY

The USVBA Coaching Accreditation Program and American Coaching Effectiveness Program Leader Level Volleyball Book

William J. Neville

Head Coach of the Women's Volleyball Team at the University of Washington, and Former USA Men's Team Head Coach

Leisure Press

Library of Congress Cataloging-in-Publication Data

Neville, William J.
   Coaching volleyball successfully : the USVBA Coaching
Accreditation Program and American Coaching Effectiveness Program
level 1 volleyball book / William J. Neville.
     p.   cm.
  Bibliography: p.
  Includes index.
  ISBN 0-88011-362-6
  1. Volleyball--Coaching. I. United States Volleyball
Association. II. Title. III. Title: USVBA Coaching Accreditation
Program. IV. Title: American Coaching Effectiveness Program level 1
volleyball book.
  GV1015.5.C63N48   1990
  796.325'07--dc20   89-32987
                                               CIP

ISBN: 0-88011-362-6

Some illustrations in this volume are modeled from those that appear in *Pass, Set, Crush* by Jeff Lucas.

Developmental Editor: Linda Anne Bump, PhD; Copyeditor: Barbara Walsh; Assistant Editor: Julia Anderson; Proofreader: Karin Leszczynski; Production Director: Ernie Noa; Text Design: Keith Blomberg; Typesetter: Sandra Meier; Text Layout: Kimberlie Henris and Denise Lowry; Cover Design: Jack Davis; Cover Photo: Dave Black and Darrell Miho; Interior Art: Ranee Rogers, David Gregory, and William Pardy; Printed By: Versa Press

Printed in the United States of America   10 9 8 7 6 5

Leisure Press
A Division of Human Kinetics Publishers
Box 5076, Champaign, IL 61825-5076
1-800-747-4457

Canada: Human Kinetics Publishers, Box 24040, Windsor, ON N8Y 4Y9
1-800-465-7301 (in Canada only)

Europe: Human Kinetics Publishers (Europe) Ltd., P.O. Box IW14, Leeds LS16 6TR, England
0532-781708

Australia: Human Kinetics Publishers, P.O. Box 80, Kingswood 5062, South Australia
618-374-0433

New Zealand: Human Kinetics Publishers, P.O. Box 105-231, Auckland 1
(09) 309-2259

Dedication

This Level I manual is dedicated to Dr. Jim Coleman. In a word, Jim Coleman was, is, and always will be my guru. No one in the United States has been more dedicated to bringing our national teams to world prominence than Jim Coleman. Doug Beal, Carl McGown, Marv Dunphy, Terry Liskevych, and countless others have been inspired by Jim's relentless pursuit of excellence. He has taught all of us to be creative, to explore new ways, to always ask "why not?," to keep going when facing seemingly insurmountable odds. There can not be enough said to honor Jim Coleman's contribution to the development of the USA teams internationally. When I was a young, cocky, unruly college kid, he saw I had potential and made me believe it in order to maximize my abilities.

Now, as an old, still cocky, still unruly college graduate, I think of Jim Coleman with deep gratitude and fondness. I hereby take a writer's privilege and honor him with this book. Anyone who knows volleyball understands that he is one of the most creative, most knowledgeable volleyball people in the world. Thanks, Jim.

Series Preface

Coaching Volleyball Successfully is part of the American Coaching Effectiveness Program (ACEP) sport-specific series. The decision to produce this series evolved after the release of the ACEP Leader Level sport science course. In that course, local youth sport administrators were encouraged to apply the information presented to the specific sports in their program. They were asked to identify the skills to be taught and the proper progression in teaching these skills. They were also asked to develop a seasonal plan and sample practice plans for their coaches.

The task seemed easy enough, but it wasn't. Considerable time is needed to carefully identify the skills to be taught and then to integrate them into a seasonal plan from which daily practice plans can be derived. As a result, ACEP staff members were encouraged to develop this information for various sports, which we now have done.

The ACEP Leader Level sport-specific series is unique in several ways:

1. The emphasis is on teaching skills to athletes, not on learning the skills yourself as in most other books.
2. The emphasis is also on teaching basic skills to beginning athletes. Often, beginners are very young children, but not always. Therefore, the books in this series are developed for coaches who teach the basics to players from 6 to 18 years old.
3. Careful consideration is given to the proper progression for teaching these skills. Information from the field of motor development is combined with the practical experience of veteran coaches to ensure that the progressions maximize learning and minimize the risk of injury.
4. Seasonal plans for teaching basic skills are presented along with daily practice plans. Coaches will find these plans very helpful.
5. Drills or exercises appropriate for beginning athletes are also included.

Other helpful features appear in each book in this series: a short history of the sport to help you appreciate its evolution, a glossary of terms, and the rules of the sport (not available in volleyball).

Keeping the information practical, basic, and accurate was the guiding principle in preparing this series. The content had to be practical for beginning coaches yet equally useful for more experienced coaches. Coaches did not need another treatise on the sport; many of those are already available.

Keeping this series basic was perhaps the most difficult task. Including more information about the skills to impress coaches with all the knowledge available was a constant temptation. However, we resisted because this is not what coaches of beginning athletes need.

Finally, accuracy was essential; thus, many expert coaches and sport scientists reviewed the content of this book to confirm its accuracy.

To achieve maximum benefit, you cannot just read a book in this series in an evening and then put it aside. It must be used like a reference book, a dictionary, or a working manual. Read the book thoroughly, then refer to it often during the season.

This book and ACEP are dedicated to improving the quality of youth sports. We hope you find the books in the series useful to you in achieving that goal. Enjoy your coaching, and thanks for helping young people learn to play sports better.

Rainer Martens, PhD
ACEP Founder

Contents

List of Drills and Activities

Preface

Welcome to the United States Volleyball Association's Coaching Accreditation Program! The welcome is also extended to those of you who have purchased this ACEP Leader Level sport-specific manual to add to your library.

It is the goal of the United States Volleyball Association Coaching Accreditation Program (CAP) to provide a logical progression of information, experiences, and opportunities. Obviously, we encourage you to take part in the program. If you would like more information about CAP, please write or call the United States Volleyball Association, 3595 E. Fountain Blvd., Suite I-2, Colorado Springs, CO 80910-1740, (800) 275-8782.

An important aspect of the program is our desire to involve coaches in the evolution of the game. The program is dynamic. If coaches learn how to harness their own strengths and apply the information gleaned here in their own individual styles, then the program is on track.

Although the information included in this manual is based on thoroughly researched principles, the techniques, drills, and tactics presented here are not the only ways to approach volleyball. The wise coach will continue to collect as much information as possible from different sources.

Coaches and teachers should provide opportunities for young people to explore what they can do. Though some cultural and societal limitations are assumed and implied (especially for females in athletics), there are seldom any scientific studies to support these claims. The purpose of this program is to assist coaches and teachers in teaching young athletes in a manner that encourages them to explore their limitless potential, pursue great goals, reap the benefits of team membership and healthy competition, and explore their individuality through cooperation.

Coaching Volleyball Successfully is divided into two guides—a coaching guide and a planning guide. The coaching guide includes descriptions of each skill, general principles of execution, tactical applications, keys to effective teaching, and a variety of drills. Basic tactics, such as offensive and defensive playing systems and their strengths, weaknesses, selection, and tactical applications, are also covered. The planning guide highlights unique volleyball coaching concerns, keys for developing a program, ways to design practices and drills, a sample seasonal plan, and selected practice plans.

Finally, the information contained in this manual is designed to stimulate creative thought. We hope you find the guidelines for program development valuable. The manual is not intended to be a recipe book with exact measurements of ingredients. Great coaches, like great chefs, create, explore, learn from others, and write their own recipes.

Acknowledgments

Many great people contributed to the concepts found in this book and to the development of the Coaching Accreditation Program (CAP) of the United States Volleyball Association (USVBA). Dr. Doug Beal, coach of the 1984 USA men's Olympic gold medal–winning team, is one of the founders of the USVBA coaching education program. His insightful, creative thinking permeates this book and the program it represents. He is one of the foremost authorities in the world of volleyball.

Dr. Carl McGown, Brigham Young University professor of motor learning, former USA national team coach, and current adviser to CAP and the national team program, is key in the design of effective teaching methods based on thorough research done specifically with volleyball. His contributions are invaluable.

The coaches in the first year of CAP who consented to be the charter cadre of instructors in 1988 became directly involved on the front lines, presenting a program that had no tradition. Based on their commitment to volleyball and their trust in their colleagues, they took the risk of being identified with an unknown program. These coaches have been fabulous, and I am proud to call them colleagues and friends.

The coaches responsible for getting the program off to a great start include Jerry Angle, Kathy DeBoer, Carol Dewey, Mike Fleming, Dave Gantt, Sue Gozansky, Gerald Gregory, Mike Hebert, John Kessel, Laurel Kessel, Scott Luster, Oleg Moiseenko, Pam Parks, Marlene Piper, Geri Polvino, Ken Preston, Tom Read, Cecile Reynaud, Russ Rose, Brad Saindon, Dick Scott, Tom Shoji, Fred Sturm, Tom Tait, Bill Walton, and Farley Warshaw.

The USVBA professional staff have been and continue to be extremely supportive of the Coaching Accreditation Program. Dick Powell, director of recreational programs, initiated the United States Olympic Fund grant that grubstaked the program and has provided ongoing inspiration. Al Monaco, the USVBA's first executive director, encouraged the formulation of a coaching education program. Dr. Cliff McPeak, the former executive director, is committed to the continuing success of the program. Dr. Kerry Klostermann, senior director of management, wrote the original outlines of the program and continually provides professional guidance. Terry Liskevych, USA women's coach and Marv Dunphy, USA men's coach 1984 and 1988, provide very identifiable role models for coaches.

To all of these colleagues and very close friends, I say thank you—which, upon reflection, seems insufficient recognition of their contributions.

A special acknowledgment goes to Kristina Watson, my first secretary and assistant, whose debut assignment was typing the original manuscript from my handwritten scrawl. Not only has she typed and retyped every word of this book (including this acknowledgment), she has been the primary organizer of the program's logistics. She is a key to the program's success.

Dr. Linda Bump, my relentless editor, has provided me with an education on attention to detail and organization. Linda, ACEP, and

Human Kinetics Publishers, Inc., have provided superb guidance in preparing this text.

My three kids, Cory Jo, Russell, and Ramsey have done proofreading, given honest feedback, and organized the photographs for illustrations. They are great inspirations, providing me great joy and making me an extremely proud father.

Finally, I want to acknowledge my wife, Barbara. The profession of coaching is so specifically measured in the eyes of the public by wins and losses that coaches often begin to evaluate their own success and failure by the same standard. It is important to have a spouse who understands coaching and its inherent emotional ebb and flow. Barbara keeps life in perspective and, for me, makes it all worthwhile.

The Volleyball
Coaching Guide

Welcome to volleyball! Your interest in coaching athletes will be rewarded in many ways throughout the volleyball season. You will experience the joy of seeing players learn and develop skills, establish new friendships, develop confidence, win games, and thoroughly enjoy playing volleyball. However, you also will need to discipline players from time to time and deal with parents who may become too emotionally involved in their child's activity. You may need to check your own emotions on occasion. The information presented in this coaching guide will help you understand how to teach volleyball skills and playing strategies effectively so that you maximize your joy and minimize your frustration. If you are determined to help the players on your team have a positive and successful volleyball experience, and if you take the time to study *Coaching Volleyball Successfully* then you are on your way to a successful season.

Before you jump into learning how to teach volleyball, however, take some time to consider how you will approach the players on your team and the general atmosphere you want to create during practices and games. As a coach, establishing your coaching philosophy before the season begins is very important. You need to decide your program's goals and how you will accomplish them. You may want to consider one of two major coaching philosophies: emphasizing winning as the most important objective, or stressing participation, fun, and skill development.

The philosophy advocated by the American Coaching Effectiveness Program is *Athletes First, Winning Second*. This means that every decision you make as a coach should first reflect the best interest of your athletes, and second, the desire to win. We hope that helping young people to develop physically, psychologically, and socially will always be more important to you than defeating the other team.

Athletes First, Winning Second does not mean that winning or striving to win is unimportant. You should instill in your players a desire to win, to do their best, to pursue excellence. However, the outcome of the game—the winning or losing—is not the most important objective. The most important objective is that your players try to win, that they try their best. If they do their best, they will be successful regardless of the outcome of the contest.

This philosophy also will be reflected in how you present yourself to the players on your team. As a coach, you are in an influential position. How you teach will be as important as what you teach. To implement the ACEP philosophy, consider the following points:

Be a good role model. Present a model for the behavior you want your athletes to emulate. Set positive examples at practices and games.

Everyone is important. Treat each player as an important human being. Each player has a different personality and different needs. Be sensitive to these differences and show interest and concern for each team member.

Consider the ages and skill levels of your players. Your athletes will be full of energy and eager to try many skills. You must approach your athletes at their level; do not expect them to come up to yours.

Consider individual differences. Teach volleyball skills according to the ability of each player. Some players will be fast learners who will progress rapidly. Other players will not learn as quickly, so you will need to proceed more slowly with them.

Keep everyone active. Organize your practices and games so that each player is able to participate as much as possible. Players want to play volleyball for many reasons; one of the most important is to have fun participating. If they are neither kept active in practices nor allowed to play in games, they will quickly lose interest.

Include athletes in the decision-making process. Athletes should have input as to what skills they practice and how they practice them. Ask your players what they need to work on, how they want to be grouped for practice, and what positions they would like to play. Naturally, athletes should not control the entire practice, but do consider their interests and ideas when designing practices and playing games.

Be patient. You will need patience, especially with beginning players who are learning volleyball. Volleyball skills require coordination and timing that can be developed only through repeated practice. Encourage your players to develop their skills, and positively reinforce their effort and skill development. When players learn new skills, both you and your players should be proud.

Part I: Basic Skills

The six basic skills of volleyball, along with their basic movements and postures, are included in this segment of the text. Each of the skills chapters include the following six elements:

- Introduction to the skill
- Basic principles
- Description of the skill
- Teaching keys and coaching points
- Teaching progressions
- Tactical applications

Where appropriate, examples of drills for each skill complete the chapter.

When teaching skills, it is important not to overteach. Learners can assimilate only a small amount of information at one time. The detailed descriptions contained in these chapters are designed to help you understand each skill. When you present the skills to your players, focus on the keys, progressions, and drills.

For example, before outlining specific movement patterns for specific circumstances, allow the players the opportunity to react naturally to those situations. A good teaching principle to follow is allowing your players to *explore* movements needed to attain a specific physical goal. As a player requires more information to execute efficient movements successfully, provide a crisp cue word or phrase that triggers the appropriate response.

Too much "by the numbers" instruction can bring about very mechanical movements in your athletes, ultimately impairing the free-flowing, spontaneous reactions inherent in the game of volleyball. In addition, your players will become more fully vested in learning if you give them a more active role in their learning experiences.

Teaching and learning skills should be fun for you and your players. The more confident you are in your knowledge of the skills, the easier it is to point out the keys and effectively guide the learning process.

The following key will assist you in interpreting the drill diagrams throughout the text:

- ●   Ball
- ⟶   Direction of player movement
- ⇢   Path of ball from tosser or coach
- ⤏   Path of ball from player

Bucket of balls

 Coach

 Blocker

 General player

(P) Passer

(D) Defensive player

(TA) Target

(TO) Tosser

(S) Setter

(H) Hitter

MB Middle back

MF Middle front

LF Left front

LB Left back

RF Right front

RB Right back

[Player position relative to ball

 Alternate positions

Chapter 1: Basic Movements and Postures

Each volleyball skill has its own unique movement. It is important that both the player and the coach understand the related movement principles.

Footwork is an integral part of each skill and is paramount to successful execution. Floor defense, attack, and occasionally blocking require dramatic and specific footwork patterns. Serving, forearm passing, and overhead passing require less active movement but still demand precise execution.

Basic footwork patterns specific to each skill are described as part of the individual skill chapters. Further, the subtleties of balance and the related body movement are detailed relative to each skill. In this chapter, general principles of movement and posture are considered.

It is important for you and your players to understand that volleyball differs from other team-ball sports. To control the rebound angle effectively, the player must arrive at the point of contact and be set up in good precontact posture before the ball arrives. In other team-ball sports, the player and the ball can arrive simultaneously; the player can gain control of the ball by catching or dribbling it before sending it off to its next destination. In volleyball, only spiking (discussed in chapter 5) provides the luxury of simultaneous arrival.

Movement Principles

Some general movement principles can be applied at all levels of volleyball skill. Consider the following guidelines:

- Move through the ball to the target.
- When moving, keep the body weight between the feet.
- When moving, keep the ball between your floor position and the net. *Exception:* The designated setter should be between the ball and the net.
- Track the ball at all times when moving.
- Move into position to play the ball *before* it arrives.
- Initiate controlled movement to the ball with the feet.

Posture Principles

Volleyball is played in three different posture ranges (see Figure 1-1). In the *low range* the player must dive, collapse, or roll on the floor to retrieve an opponent's attack. *Middle range* postures must be assumed to serve, forearm pass, and overhead pass effectively. *High range* postures are used when jumping to attack, block, and jump set.

Fig. 1-1

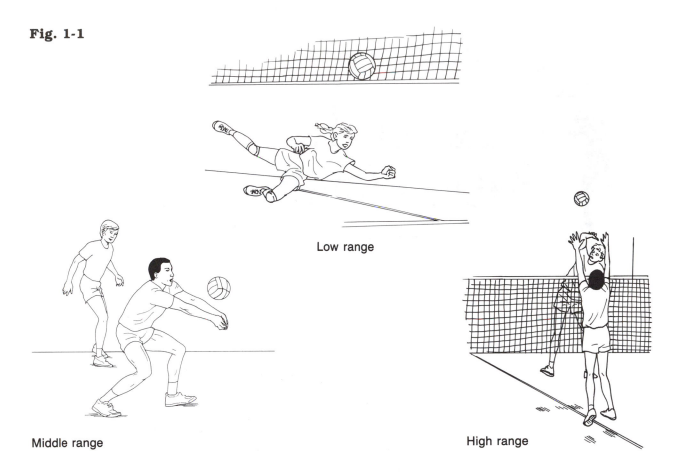

Low range

Middle range

High range

The posture principles represent what the player is attempting to achieve in the course of playing the ball. The nature of the game forces players into off-balance, uncontrolled postures. This underscores the critical importance of training athletes to make controlled movements and postures when playing the game.

Coaching Points

1. In volleyball, a player must arrive at the point of contact *before* the ball arrives in all skills except spiking.
2. The posture assumed prior to contact must be *balanced*, allowing the player to move through the ball to the target with control.
3. John Wooden, former UCLA basketball coach, said, ''Be quick, but don't hurry.'' This concept applies to volleyball movements as well.
4. Be effective and efficient by designing warm-up drills that use volleyball-

specific movements. For example, during the jogging phase of warm-up, have players practice footwork patterns for blocking, spiking, and moving into position to contact the ball. During the stretching phase, use the floor movements required in floor defense such as collapses, sprawls, rolls, and dives.

Effective learning theory tells us that movements and postures are best taught specific to the skill in which they are required. Therefore, there are no specific drills designed solely for movements or postures.

When designing a prematch or practice warm-up routine, consider requiring movements specific to the skills of volleyball. For example, when players are jogging, have them go through a three-step accelerated spike approach, dive, or roll. When teaching movements and postures, though, use the skill the players are required to execute successfully.

Chapter 2: Serving

The serve initiates play, is the only skill completely within the control of an individual player, and is the only skill that can be replicated with no adjustments in technique on all occasions. Successful serves can force opponents into a difficult attack position, reducing their attack options and enabling the serving team to react more effectively in setting up the defense. In addition, a server can score a point by serving the ball in such a way that the opponent is unable to return it. This is known as an ace.

Serve variations include the underhand, overhead float, roundhouse float, standing spike, roundhouse spin, jump, sky ball, and sidespin serves. Only the underhand and overhead float serves are covered in this chapter. More advanced serves will be presented in future levels of *Coaching Volleyball Successfully* manuals.

General Principles

To ensure consistent service, present the following principles to your athletes as they learn the skill:

- Duplicate the same skill mechanics each time you serve.
- The flight of the ball is determined by how close to the net and how high the ball is contacted. For example, a shorter player who wants to hit a flat serve must stand further away from the net. This relationship is illustrated in Figure 2-1.
- Hold the ball so that the valve is pointing either downward or toward the target. A horizontal panel, preferably the one with the label, should be facing the server. Failure to position the ball

Fig. 2-1

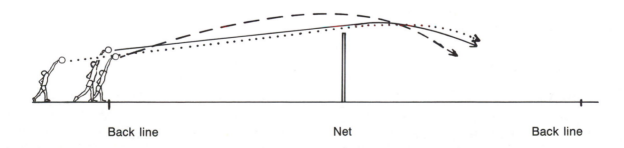

Back line   Net   Back line

properly can result in an uncomfortable point of contact.

- Contact the ball with the "meat" part of the hand as shown in Figure 2-2.
- Continue moving through the ball and toward the target after contact.

Fig. 2-2

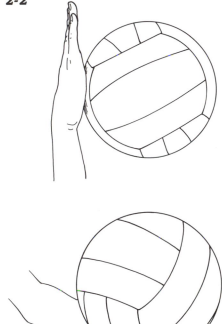

The Underhand Serve

The simplest of the serving techniques, the underhand serve is excellent for young players and for those just beginning their involvement in volleyball. It is also a starting point for developing other serves because it teaches the concept of comfortable contact and familiarizes the player with the amount of force required to get the ball over the net. The underhand serve can easily evolve into a sidearm or overhead technique.

Preparation

In preparing to serve, the player should stand in a semicrouched position with the lead toe pointing toward the target and the weight predominantly on the back foot (see

Figure 2-3). The nonserving "shelf arm" should be bent 90 degrees at the elbow and held comfortably so that the ball is approximately in front of the navel when placed on the "shelf" (hand).

Fig. 2-3

The hitting arm should hang comfortably at the player's side. The hitting hand can be held in a variety of forms: fist, paddle hand, or open hand. In any case, the contact point will be the same—the meat part of the hand.

Precontact Movement

All serving techniques use a two-count rhythm. On the count of one, the ball is tossed from the shelf, the hitting arm is cocked, and weight is transferred from the back foot to the front. On the count of two, the hips are turned toward the target, and the ball is contacted.

A creative way to present this two-count rhythm is the "oompah" method. The rhythm can be described as the familiar sound of a tuba. As your young players practice the two-count movement, have them vocalize with gusto, "Oom . . . pah!" (A successful serve will then be followed with an "Ahhh . . .")

The toss is critical in this and in all other serving movements. In the underhand technique, the ball must be tossed from the shelf hand before contact is made. Rules on this vary from one association to another. Often the rules of the National Federation of State

High School Associations (NFSHSA) are different from those of the United States Volleyball Association (USVBA), the National Association of Girls and Women in Sports (NAGWS), and the Fédération Internationale de Volleyball (FIVB). The service toss is a case in point: NFSHSA rules allow for the ball to be hit directly off the hand. USVBA and FIVB rules require that the ball be clear of the tossing hand before it is contacted. I strongly encourage teaching players to toss the ball prior to contact because most of their careers will be governed by the USVBA, NAGWS, and FIVB rules. The ball should be tossed approximately 2 to 4 inches off the shelf by the shelf hand, which then drops out of the way of the hitting hand. Simultaneously, the hitting arm is swung back and forward in a pendulum-type movement.

Contact

Contact should be made with the meat part of the hitting hand as the weight shifts to the front foot. It is important that the player swing his or her arm in line with the intended trajectory of the ball. In addition, the server must focus on the ball during the hitting motion. To complete an effective serve, the hitting hand should accelerate approximately 6 inches from the point of contact, creating a "punching" effect.

The terms *coaching points* and *teaching keys* are used throughout the skills chapters. Coaching points are principles of execution or points of tactical application. They are pieces of information the coach and players must clearly understand. Teaching keys are cue words or short phrases used to trigger memory responses in the learner. They are reference points to use in the verbal feedback phases of teaching.

Coaching Points for the Underhand Serve

1. The ball must be tossed from the shelf hand.
2. Players should contact the ball with the meat part of the hand.
3. The precontact swing of the arm should be in line with the desired trajectory of the ball.
4. Accelerate the contact hand just prior to contact.
5. Use teaching keys: "Oom . . . pah!"

Teaching Progression for the Underhand Serve

1. Briefly explain the purpose of the serve. (To begin the game. To make it as difficult as possible for the opponent to receive.) These purposes can be accomplished only by getting the ball over the net. (1 to 2 minutes)
2. Demonstrate or have an assistant demonstrate several good serves.
3. Have players focus on the weight transfer from back foot to front foot. (1 to 2 minutes for Steps 2 and 3)
4. Have players try the total skill, but focus on weight transfer. (6 to 8 minutes)
5. Players return. Ask players what they were focusing on as they served. (1 to 2 minutes)
6. Demonstrate again. Have players focus on toss and contact. Emphasize that it is the same every time. The arm swing is back and forth in line with the intended trajectory. (1 to 2 minutes)
7. Players serve, but focus on toss and contact. Players should continue to use weight transfer. (6 to 8 minutes)
8. Players return to the group. Ask the players to review weight transfer, consistent toss, and contact. (1 to 2 minutes)
9. Demonstrate serving again. Have players focus on a combination of movements. Note that the movements are compact, efficient, and consistent. (1 to 2 minutes)
10. Begin serving drills.
11. Develop key descriptive words that you feel efficiently and effectively convey the desired message. The "oompah" method is an example.

The Overhead Float Serve

The overhead serve is designed to produce a "floating" ball that has no spin. Air currents, the ball being not perfectly round, the humidity, and the altitude can influence such a ball's path, making its trajectory unpredictable. Conversely, a spinning ball balances itself and cuts its way through the air in a predictable manner.

The floating serve's final destination is also unpredictable. The ball bobs, weaves, dips, rises, and fades. In addition, the receiver has difficulty determining the speed of the serve because there is no spin to read. In short, the float serve is similar to the knuckleball in baseball.

The overhead serving technique described in the following sections is the standard method of delivering the float serve. Stylized variations can emerge with experience; however, it is important that each player clearly understand and follow the basic principles described here.

Preparation

The server should take a position behind the serving line with the leg on the hitting arm side facing away from the court, locked at the knee. The front leg should be flexed with the toe pointing toward the target. Most of the body weight is on the back leg.

The shelf arm should be held comfortably flexed at a 90-degree angle at the elbow, enabling the server to maintain the compact posture necessary for consistent, controlled serves. The hand holding the ball should be approximately at the player's neck level.

The hitting arm should be positioned so that the elbow is as high and as far from the shoulder as possible. This positioning will reduce wind-up movements and insure consistent and high contact. The hitting hand should be in line with the lead toe and the wrist locked with the fingers pointing over the top of the held ball at the target. Figure 2-4 illustrates the preparation position for the overhead float serve.

The correct starting position can be likened to the position William Tell would take prior to shooting his arrow at the apple on his son's head. Present that image to your athletes and encourage them to work with it.

You will know if the server is in the correct starting position if he or she can turn the head toward the hitting arm and look directly into the inside of the elbow. When the player looks straight ahead, the eyes should be level with the top of the ball. As a final check, you should be able, without warning, to move the player's lead foot with little or no resistance because the bulk of the player's weight should be on the back leg. If you stub your toe during this test, instruct the player to shift his or her weight more to the back leg.

Fig. 2-4

Precontact Movement

Again, the serving motion has a two-count rhythm initiated by the toss, the hitting arm being drawn back, and the lead foot stepping forward. On the count of two, the weight is transferred, and the ball is contacted.

The toss is the key to a successful serve. During the toss, the ball should never be more than 12 to 18 inches above the shelf hand. The player should think of the ball as simply an extension of the shelf hand's movement.

Two additional considerations mark a well-executed toss. First, the ball should have no spin as it is being tossed. The horizontal panel should still squarely face the server. Second, if the ball were to drop to the floor after the toss, it should land directly on or slightly in front of the lead toe (see Figure 2-5).

Fig. 2-5

12-18 inches

Contact

On the second count of the serving rhythm, the player should transfer weight from the back foot to the lead foot. The back foot drags on the toes and does not pass the lead foot. This allows for body stability and insures that the force of contact is directed at the selected target.

The hitting arm's forward motion is initiated by the shoulder and elbow. By leading with these body segments, the player propels the hand forward in a whipping motion. The hitting hand remains locked at the wrist and is extended to contact the ball as high and as far in front of the head as possible.

Contact is again made with the meat part of the hand. The hitting arm accelerates approximately 6 inches prior to contact to

initiate the punching effect, which should cause the arm to appear to bounce off the ball.

You can check to see if the force of the serve is directed through the ball to the target by allowing the arm to follow through. If force is directed properly, the arm should hit the trailing leg on the thigh (see Figure 2-6).

Fig. 2-6

Coaching Points for the Overhead Float Serve

1. The lead leg should be comfortable with the toe directed at the target.
2. The hitting arm should be drawn back with the elbow at shoulder level or higher.
3. The hitting hand should be locked at the wrist.
4. Players should hit through the ball with the meat part of the hand.
5. Accelerate the contact hand just prior to contact to achieve the punching effect.
6. You can tell how the ball was hit by watching the spin produced. If the ball spins to the left, contact was made on the right side of the ball; if the ball spins to the right, contact was

on the left side of the ball. Backspin indicates contact under the ball with a flexed wrist, whereas topspin indicates contact over the top of the ball allowing the wrist to break. No spin means the ball was contacted dead center. Figure 2-7 illustrates these situations.

7. Use the teaching keys: step, toss, hit in the "oom . . . pah!" rhythm ("Step-toss . . . hit!").

Teaching Progression for the Overhead Float Serve

1. Briefly explain the advantages of the overhead float serve (hard serve, flat trajectory, unpredictable course, difficult for receiver to handle). Remind players that a serve is effective only if it goes over the net and into play. (1 to 2 minutes)

2. Demonstrate or have an assistant demonstrate several good serves. (1 to 2 minutes)

3. Point out the bow-and-arrow ready position, and have players focus on weight transfer. Refer to the teaching key, "step-toss." (1 to 2 minutes)

4. Have players try the overhead serve, focusing on a good ready position and weight transfer. (6 to 8 minutes)

5. Players return. Ask players to review preparation and weight transfer ("step-toss"). (1 to 2 minutes)

6. Repeat the demonstration. Have players focus on the toss and contact. Emphasize that the toss and contact should be the same every time. A locked wrist and contact with the meat part of the hand through the center of the ball toward the target is what makes the serve float. Refer to the teaching key, "hit." (1 to 2 minutes)

7. Players serve while focusing on the toss and contact. (6 to 8 minutes)

8. Players return. Ask them to review the key points: step-toss and hit, weight transfer, consistent toss, locked wrist, and contact with meat part of hand. (1 to 2 minutes)

9. Demonstrate the serve again. Have players focus on total movement. (1 to 2 minutes)

10. Begin drills.

If players have difficulty serving the ball over the net from the back line, allow them to move closer. As they get comfortable at the shortened distance, gradually move them back until they are in the legal service area.

Tactical Applications

The first and foremost application of the serve for the young or beginning player is to get the ball into the opponent's court.

Fig. 2-7

There are no tactics, nor is there play, if the serve is into the net or out of bounds.

Once a player can consistently serve into the opponent's court, encourage him or her to vary the trajectory, velocity, and target of the serve. Consistent serving means that the player is able to place the served ball into the opponent's court with confidence and control 80% of the time.

Varying Trajectory

The server should be able to control the flight of the ball. The most effective servers use a variety of trajectories ranging from flat serves to lobs. This allows for flexible targeting. The trajectory can be varied by changing the distance behind the end line from which the server contacts the ball, or the height of the ball at contact (review Figure 2-1, p. 9). Such variation, coupled with a change in velocity, can wreak havoc on the opponent's ability to receive the serve effectively.

Varying Velocity

The server must learn to harness the force that controls the speed of the serve. Each player must learn (through experimentation) how much energy is required to get the ball to the intended target. The accomplished server will mask the amount of force utilized by appearing to use a particular motion, but increasing or decreasing acceleration just prior to contact.

Varying Targets

It is important that your athletes learn to serve to a variety of locations on the court. No nook or cranny of the opponent's court should be immune to a server's aim. As servers become more adept at positioning the ball, incorporate drills that pinpoint a location for each serve.

Varying Techniques

Ideally, as the player develops his or her skill in volleyball, he or she should develop several kinds of serves. At the beginning level, however, we suggest that players learn either the underhand serve, the overhand serve, or both well enough to use in competition.

Serving is a weapon. It is one of the four ways of scoring in volleyball. If you teach your players to be tough servers, you can guarantee that points will be scored.

Drills and Activities for Serving

In this chapter and the ones that follow, a particular format has been selected in which to present drills. You will find in-depth coverage of each of the components in chapter 12, "Practice and Drills Design."

(2.1) Contact Progression

Purpose. To develop serving rhythm and control

Classification. Player-centered

Category. Teaching

Equipment. Ideally, there is one ball for every two players and one net and court for every six players. Modification can be made to adapt to existing equipment.

Personnel. At least two players and one coach

Description. Players face each other on opposite sides of the net. The players start at their respective 3-meter lines. They serve back and forth, controlling the direction and distance of the ball using either the underhand or overhead serve. After a specified number of successful repetitions, the players move back to midcourt and then to the back line (see Figure 2-8).

Measurement. A specified number of repetitions must be completed before moving back.

(2.2) Target Progression

Purpose. To develop accuracy for tactical application; to continue work on the serving rhythm

Classification. Player-centered

Category. Teaching

Equipment. Ideally, one ball for each player and six players to a court. If necessary, two players may share a ball.

Fig. 2-8

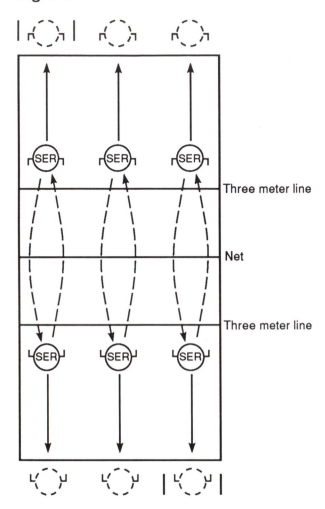

Three meter line

Net

Three meter line

Measurement. Players must hit a specified number of successful serves into an area before targeting the next.

Fig. 2-9

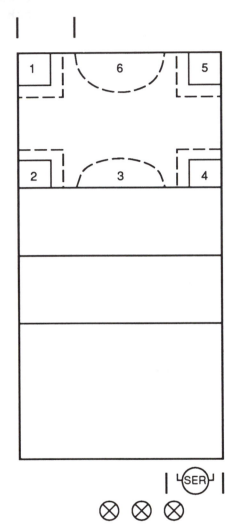

Personnel. A minimum of one player to a court

Description. Tape areas approximately 1-1/2 meters square to be used for targets (hula hoops are also good targets). Set targets in areas into which it is progressively more difficult to serve. The first target is deep position 5. The second is deep position 1, the third is short position 4, the fourth is deep position 6, the fifth is short position 3, and the sixth is short position 2. Players serve from the service area using either the underhand or overhead serve and must attain a specified number of successful serves into specified areas in a progressive order (see Figure 2-9). If the players are working by themselves, they must chase their own balls. If players are working with partners, the player not serving retrieves the served ball.

(2.3) Hula Hoop/Elastic

Purpose. To practice controlled trajectory and relative velocity; to add variety to a repetitive activity

Classification. Player-centered

Category. Teaching

Equipment. One ball per two players and three hula hoops per court

Personnel. At least two players and one coach

Description. One, two, or three players hold hula hoops above the net at designated "corridors" where serves should cross the net. The server serves through the hoops into the opponent's court using either the underhand or the overhead serve (see Figure 2-10). Instead of hula hoops, elastic can be strung between the tops of the net antennae to present a trajectory "ceiling" above the net. If the players are working in pairs, the server's partner retrieves the ball. The server working alone must retrieve his or her own ball.

Measurement. Players must hit a specified number of successful serves through the targets.

Variation.

Target Practice. Floor targets added to the aerial targets increase difficulty. Add variety! Use inflatable, bottom-weighted clown dolls as targets.

Fig. 2-10

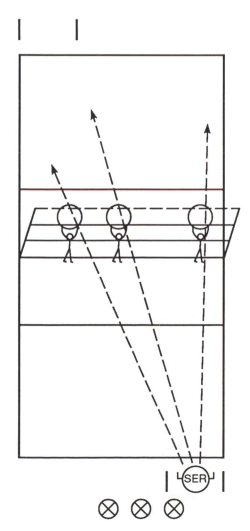

(2.4) Horse I

Purpose. To combine the serving technique with competitive pressure; to "play" with the serve

Classification. Player-centered

Category. Teaching

Equipment. One ball per two players on one court

Personnel. At least two but no more than six players per court

Description. The court is laid out as for the Target Progression drill (see Figure 2-9). This drill is played like the game of "horse" in basketball. One player selects and serves at a target. If the ball lands in the target, the other players must duplicate the serve. If a subsequent player misses, he or she gets an "H." If the player successfully duplicates the serve, no letter is given. When the lead player misses a target, the next player takes over and so on until someone hits a target. Then the others must duplicate the serve or get a letter. If a player successfully hits a target, forcing the others to follow suit, he or she cannot select the same target in the next round. If a player has accumulated "HORS," the lead player hits another target, and the player with "HORS" fails to duplicate the serve, that player has two options: he or she can try again or can challenge the lead player to hit the target again. If the lead player does, then the challenger gets tagged with an "E," spelling "HORSE," and the game is over. If the lead player misses, the game continues until one player or the other finally gets an "E."

Measurement. Play continues until one player has "HORSE."

(2.5) Team Serving

Purpose. To provide the server with live targets in game positions; to practice serving tactics

Classification. Player-centered

Category. Teaching (game-related)

Equipment. A bucket of 24 balls and one court

Personnel. Six players in an assigned server-reception pattern. One or more players serve.

Description.   Set up players in your desired serve-reception pattern. Direct the server(s) to serve to specific areas and receivers, explaining the tactical reasons for the serve. This drill should be used in conjunction with serve receive practices. Each player who receives the serve attempts to return the ball to the player marked "TA" in Figure 2-11.

Measurement.   Require a specified number of repetitions or a specified number of successful serves in a row. You may also use progressive targeting with a required number of successes at each target.

Fig. 2-11

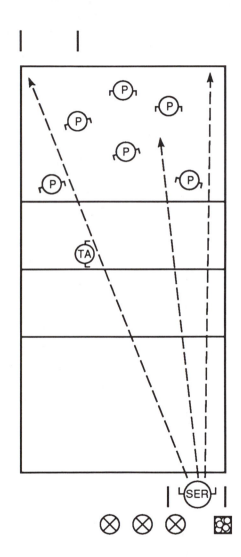

Chapter 3: Forearm Passing

Forearm passing is self-descriptive: The ball is contacted on the forearms and is passed to a designated target. It appears to be an easy skill because few movements are involved. However, because controlled forearm passing is an *intermediate contact*, one of the first two of the three allowable contacts per side, it is significantly influenced by the trajectory, velocity, and location of the incoming ball.

Forearm passing is unique to the sport of volleyball. Most athletes are trained to handle balls with the hands and feet. Forearm passing requires retooling the usual ball-handling thought processes and controlling the ball with the forearms.

The key to successful forearm passing is getting into a stable, consistent precontact position before the ball arrives. If the ball is coming from the opponent, assume that he or she intends to disrupt the passer's form by forcing some movement to the ball. Your players must be ready to move into position *before* the ball arrives.

Forearm passing is as easy as it looks if a ball is simply tossed in front of a player. A person could hit successfully while sitting comfortably in a rocking chair. However, the ball seldom comes directly to a player. Therefore, movements needed during actual game play must be incorporated as soon as players are familiar and comfortable with forearm contact with the ball.

Forearm Pass Functions

Forearm passing is used in serve reception (serve receive), passing free or down balls, setting, and floor defense.

Serve Receive

The primary function of forearm passing is to pass the serve to initiate the offense. Often, the terms *serve receive* and *forearm passing* are used interchangeably, but serve receive is merely one of the applications of forearm passing. Serve receive can legally be done with the face or with any other body part above the waist, although these alternatives to the forearms are not recommended.

Free and Down Ball Passing

A *free ball* is a ball that is returned in an easy manner to the opponent during a rally. The Japanese translate the term to mean "chance ball." In other words, a ball easily played offers a chance for a controlled offensive response.

A *down ball* is one that is hit by a team back to the opponent with top spin and moderate velocity. Because the attacking player is either standing in or hitting from a deep court position, accuracy and power of the hit are limited.

Setting

Although most setting is done using the overhead pass, sometimes the forearm pass can be used to set the ball. If the first contact is inaccurate, the setter may find it valuable to use the forearm pass to get the ball up and in front of the hitter legally.

Floor Defense

The techniques of floor defense are many. Forearm passing in its most basic form is used to receive direct shots from the opposing attacker. Adaptations of the forearm pass will be explored in chapter 7, "Floor Defense."

General Principles

As you teach the forearm pass, keep the following principles in mind:

- Players should be in controlled, balanced, precontact positions before the ball arrives.
- The ball contact on the forearms should be as far from the hips as the player can control.
- Forearm passing is a skill requiring controlled deflection. The ball's rebound path as it leaves the forearms will correspond to the angle at which the player holds the forearms.

Executing the Forearm Pass

If the passer knows exactly where the ball will be delivered and its velocity and incoming trajectory, forearm passing is fairly routine. What makes forearm passing difficult is that the opponent usually puts the ball in difficult places to access, at different speeds and angles, forcing the passer to move continually in an effort to trip the opponent up.

You must teach your players efficient movements and rebound angle adjustments to respond to various situations. Coaches often tell players to "pass with the feet" to get them to concentrate on moving to the

point of contact before the ball arrives instead of leading with the hands, leaving feet and balance behind. Begin teaching movement patterns and adjustments as soon as your players are comfortable with actual ball contact on the forearms.

One of the keys to consistent forearm passing is stability. Players attain stability by getting their feet balanced at the point of contact. Therefore, you must continually remind players to focus on moving their feet before they try to get their arms in place. Figure 3-1 shows how a player who has gotten to the point of contact before the ball has arrived looks more stable than when he is leading with arms and hands.

Fig. 3-1

Ready

Reaching

Coaches can also tell their players, "Think with your feet!" Although this instruction cannot be obeyed literally, the statement has some value. Players must think about getting their feet in position first. When this is accomplished a major part of the battle is won.

Preparation (The Ready Position)

The player must acknowledge that he or she will have to move and should be ready to do so. A player can assume the desirable ready position by standing with the feet together, then moving one foot forward until the big toe of the back foot is lined up with the arch of the front foot. Keeping that front-to-back alignment, have each player move the back foot laterally away from the front foot (approximately one shoulder width) until he or she feels balanced and comfortable. Next, the player bends at the knees so that the knees are inside and in front of the big toes. If the legs are optimally flexed, the player should be able to reach down, placing the elbows at the insides of the knees, and touch the inside and in front of the big toes with extended fingers. Keeping the hips low and the back straight, the player can raise his or her head and look at the incoming trajectory line (see Figure 3-2). Have players place their hands, heels out, on their upper thighs or dangle them, whichever is more comfortable.

Because the ready position is not comfortable, the player should smoothly and efficiently assume this position *just prior* to the opponent's contacting the ball. Obviously, the lengthy sequence just described need not be employed each time the player gets ready. With practice, each player should be able to assume the ready position quickly and naturally.

The Movement to Precontact Position

Because movement in volleyball is a spontaneous reaction, it is wise to take advantage of natural movements and not inhibit them. Before you teach this movement, see if your players can do it naturally. After all, a person suddenly motivated to make a quick lateral movement by, say, a charging grizzly bear

Fig. 3-2

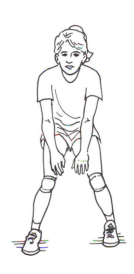

would lead with the head away from the feet. Because this person would naturally want to keep his or her balance, the feet would continually stay under the head, producing a natural cross step. As the slavering silver tip closed in, the person's arms would pump to maintain the necessary rhythm and acceleration. Volleyball players use a similar movement pattern in attempting to get in front of an incoming ball quickly, with control, and before the ball arrives (to be in position to pass). A player must employ the most efficient move to the contact spot, which coupled with a stopping technique results in correct posture. Three techniques are used in getting to the point of contact: the skip or slide step, the cross-step brake step, and the backslide. Notice some similarities to the technique the person in our example used to avoid the grizzly.

The Skip or Slide Step

A player should never make any unnecessary movements, especially when the ball must be controlled with precision. If the ball is not far away or is moving slowly on its journey, the player should use an easy skip or slide step. To accomplish this, simply push off the foot farthest from the intended direction of movement. The hips remain facing the incoming ball (see Figure 3-3). If the player must change direction, turn the foot nearest the intended passing target and balance as described for the brake step (see the next section).

The Cross-Step Brake Step

This is the technique used to get to a ball a significant distance away from the prospective passer. The passer in the ready position assesses the speed, trajectory, and final target of the incoming ball. Leading with the head, the player follows the natural inclination to cross step (that is, turn and run) toward the projected point of contact. The player takes as many steps as required to get to the final precontact position. This is the cross step phase.

Upon arrival, the receiver turns, points his or her crossing foot at the teammate in-tended to be the recipient of the pass, and plants that foot, keeping his or her weight inside that foot. When the foot is planted (called the brake step), the body will swing around into precontact position. The player's weight should remain *over the brake step.* The outside foot is used for balance and for stopping any movement away from the ball. The arms move forward to prepare for a forearm pass as the player brake steps (see Figure 3-4). The player should be in position before the ball arrives.

The Backslide

An incoming ball that is on a direct line to the receiver but is going deep forces the receiver to retreat. It can be difficult to pass under these circumstances. This situation requires the passer to recognize the velocity and trajectory of the ball as soon as possible. Early detection makes the required adjustment much easier.

A passer who recognizes that the ball is coming at him or her fast and deep immediately gets one foot back and opens the stance to accommodate the retreating movement and prepare for contact. Keeping the weight forward, the passer skips back without cross stepping. The desired precontact position is achieved when the back foot stops the retreat, enabling the passer to transfer his or her weight through the ball to the target (see

Fig. 3-3

Fig. 3-4

Brake step

Figure 3-5). As described in the brake step, final positioning adjustments relative to the passing angle are made on the last step with the lead foot.

Fig. 3-5

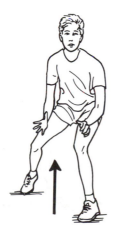

Precontact Position

The precontact position is similar to but not as pure as the ready position. Both require spontaneous adjustments in reacting to the ball. In the ideal precontact position (see Figure 3-6, page 24), the receiver is balanced with the weight forward so that he or she can move through the ball to the target. The receiver's hips are lower than the incoming ball and the intended outgoing trajectory. To accommodate this low posture, the feet are spread wider than in the ready position. The knees are still inside and in front of the big toes. The player's eyes are focused on the ball, with shoulders thrust forward to insure controlled contact away from the body. The arms are in the forearm passing position.

Fig. 3-6

The player's arm position is critical to a symmetrical, smooth rebound surface. Such a surface is prepared by putting the wrists and thumbs together. Players can use one of several methods as long as symmetry of the forearms is maintained and the elbows and wrists are hyperextended, thumbs pointing down. Three of the most common positions are described here.

The Scoop
Put the thumbs together with one hand in the crotch between the thumb and index finger of the other. The advantage of the scoop is that it creates smooth undersurface for taking balls close to the floor. It is easily adaptable to specialized digging techniques (see Figure 3-7a).

Fingers Interlaced
Interlace the fingers at the second knuckle. Thumbs and wrists should be together. The player assuming this position is secure in the knowledge that the hands will not fly apart during ball contact. The interlace method (see Figure 3-7b) is not as adaptable as the scoop to specialized digging techniques. The player cannot play the ball as close to the floor as with the scoop, without sacrificing his or her fingers.

Fist Insert
One hand is formed into a fist and surrounded by the other hand (see Figure 3-7c). The fist insert is quick and easy to form, is comfortable, and is adaptable to specialized digging techniques. It is not, however, as stable as the other techniques. It is also restrictive in performing the J stroke, a technique that will be detailed in chapter 7, "Floor Defense."

Fig. 3-7

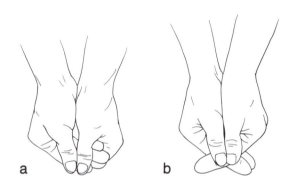

I strongly recommend the scoop method because of its adaptability to all uses of the forearm pass. Regardless of which technique you select, stress to your players the key to forming a good forearm passing platform: *getting the wrists together.*

Contact

The amount of arm motion involved in the contact phase is directly related to the speed of the ball upon its arrival at the passer. The faster the incoming ball is traveling, the less arm movement is required to get the ball to the intended target. The slower the incoming velocity, the more arm movement is required to pass the ball.

The movement of the arms and the body's weight through the ball to the target, the angle of deflection, and the point where the eyes are focused are all important in good ball contact. Players should be taught to use only those movements necessary to get the ball to the target.

Necessary Movements Only

Young players have a tendency to "pray" prior to putting their arms in position to make ball contact (see Figure 3-8). Coach your players to avoid this tendency by simply putting their hands together in one of the methods previously described and making contact. Unnecessary movements waste energy and can disrupt the timing necessary for effective passing.

Fig. 3-8

"Bumping" the Ball

The movement starts with hands below the waist. The ball contacts the arms just above the wrists in an action often described as *bumping*; the player appears to "bump" the ball with his or her forearms. Bumping is easier to say than forearm passing, which is really more descriptive of the total effect. "Bunting" the ball is also a good way to describe the movement to a player who has wielded "the lumber" in baseball or softball.

The Angle of Deflection

This term is related to the position of the forearms at the moment of contact. The angle of deflection determines the trajectory of the pass. If the player cannot face the target (a common situation), he or she should dip the shoulder nearest the target and move through the ball with the forearms in that direction. The dip of one shoulder will raise the other, modifying the angle of deflection or rebound angle (see Figure 3-9a). If the passer wants to pass flat to the target, then the arms must make contact *behind* the ball (see Figure 3-9b). If the passer desires the ball to go up high, the forearms must make contact *under* the ball (see Figure 3-9c).

Have your players experiment with trajectory control by asking them to pass the ball high and low. They will discover that modifying the angle of deflection alters the trajectory.

Force

Your players also must be aware of how much force is required to get the ball to the target. The speed of delivery depends on how much force is applied at contact. Vary the distance the players must pass the ball and change the speed of the ball with each repetition.

Focus

The passer should be focusing on the incoming ball, quickly analyzing and reacting to its characteristics. When the ball is making contact with the player's arms, his or her eyes should be focused between the target and the point of contact. In doing this, the player can still see the ball in the lower segment of the range of vision at contact, as well as the target through the upper range, with minimal head movement.

When athletes play volleyball, they must also see the *big picture*. Certainly their focus is on the ball, but they must also see other significant movements and features taking place around them. To develop this skill, players must practice "seeing" at all times.

Demonstrate the big picture by having the players hold their arms out to their sides at shoulder level. While they look straight

Fig. 3-9

a   b   c

ahead, have them slowly move their hands forward until they can "see" their wiggling fingers without moving their eyes. This will give them a good indication of how much they can see laterally.

Repeat the exercise, but have the players hold one outstretched arm above the head and the other below the waist. This will help them define the vertical limitations of peripheral vision.

Follow-Through

At contact, the player's legs should be flexed. The force to pass the ball comes from the movement of the arms from the shoulders. The legs should remain stable. Only *after* the ball is on its way to the target does the player stand up and move to his or her next assignment.

Coaching Points

1. The preceding description of forearm passing is detailed and correct. Giving this all-encompassing description to your players, however, would probably overload their circuits. The information here is intended for *your* understanding. When you teach your athletes this skill, keep your descriptions limited to the keys. The learning will come when the players discover the details through their actions.

2. Remember, when passing, the ball should be kept in front of the passer, and between him or her and the target.

3. Use teaching keys:
   - Wrists together
   - Face the ball
   - Get to point of contact *before* ball arrives
   - Pass to target

Teaching Progression

1. Gather the players and describe the skill and its uses. (1 to 2 minutes)
2. Demonstrate forearm passing. (1 to 2 minutes)
3. Have players focus on the "wrists together" concept. (1 to 2 minutes)
4. Have players try the skill, focusing on keeping their wrists together. (6 to 8 minutes)
5. Players return. Review the first key: wrists together. Ask players to describe what happens to the forearms. (1 to 2 minutes)

6. Again, demonstrate the skill. Have players focus on facing the incoming ball. (1 to 2 minutes)
7. Players practice the skill, focusing on facing the ball. (3 to 4 minutes)
8. Players return. Ask players to review the first two principles. (1 to 2 minutes)
9. Demonstrate the skill again. Have a tosser move the ball around. Have players focus on movement to the contact point. (1 to 2 minutes)
10. Have players practice, with the tosser moving the ball to different positions. (4 to 5 minutes)
11. Players return. Review keys with players. (1 to 2 minutes)
12. Demonstrate the forearm pass one last time. Have players focus on passing to the target. (1 to 2 minutes)
13. Have players practice the skill, focusing on moving through the ball to target. (3 to 4 minutes)
14. Players return. Have them verbalize the four keys to performing a successful forearm pass. (1 to 2 minutes)
15. Begin drills.

Remember to provide additional information as needed on an individual basis. Let the players discover the details by providing them with a demonstration of the desired end result and the keys to success.

Tactical Applications

The tactical applications of forearm passing are reflected in the trajectory of the ball and the velocity with which it is passed. Forearm passing is an intermediate contact and is used to aid the overall tactical plan. However, a passer can affect the speed on an offensive play by controlling how fast the ball is delivered to the setter. The rules of thumb that govern the serve receiver (or free or down ball passer) are as follows:

- The tougher the play, the higher and slower the pass
- The easier the play, the lower and faster the pass

For example, if a ball coming over the net is difficult to play because it forces the receiver to move a great distance or get into an awkward position, then he or she must concentrate on just getting the ball up high enough for a teammate to play. Trying to be too precise or accurate in these instances often leads to a complete loss of control. If a ball coming over the net is easy to play, allowing the receiver to get into correct position easily, then he or she can focus on accuracy to the target. The receiver can control the velocity and trajectory of the pass with confidence. This rule is a spin-off of one of volleyball's overriding principles: *Attempt tactically only what you can control technically.*

Drills and Activities for Forearm Passing

(3.1) Pass-Off Toss

Purpose. To pass with correct body posture; to sequence ready position, precontact, and contact

Classification. Player-centered

Category. Teaching

Equipment. One ball per two players

Personnel. At least two players and one coach

Description. One player assumes a ready position. The second player stands with a ball 3 to 4 meters in front of the first player, facing him or her. The second player tosses the ball using a two-hand overhead motion, varying the velocity and placing the ball in different positions in front of the receiving player. Using correct techniques and posture, the receiver passes the ball back. Players should strive to vary the trajectory on command from either the coach or the other player. Remember: The passer must face the net. The tosser should have his or her back to the net. Always duplicate correct positions relative to the net (see Figure 3-10).

Measurement. Require a specified number of successful repetitions in a specified amount of time to measure progress.

Fig. 3-10

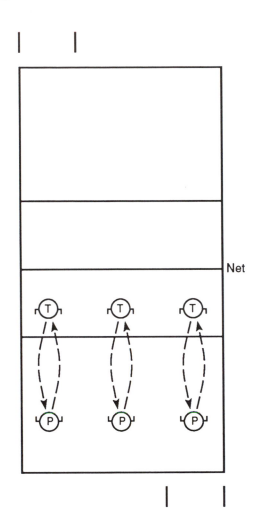

tosser is at the net and the passer is facing the net (see Figure 3-11).

Measurement. A specified number of successful repetitions in a specified time block measure progress.

Fig. 3-11

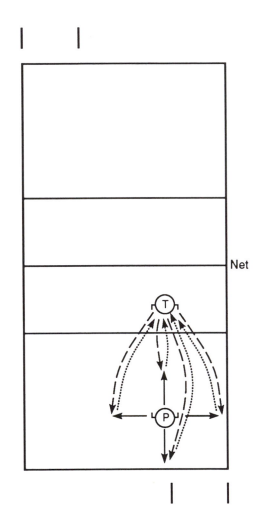

(3.2) Points of the Compass

Purpose. To involve all game-related movements with forearm passing

Classification. Player-centered

Category. Teaching

Equipment. One ball per two players

Personnel. At least two players and one coach

Description. A tosser with a ball faces a receiver 3 to 6 meters away. The tosser, using a two-hand overhead tossing technique, throws the ball in various positions within 2 to 3 meters of the receiver. The receiver, using correct techniques, reacts with the most efficient footwork and passes the ball back to the tosser. It is important for the tosser to vary the height and velocity of the tosses. Orient the players so that the

(3.3) Same-Side Triads

Purpose. To orient the player to the game's angles and required adjustments

Classification. Player-centered

Category. Rapid-fire

Equipment. Two balls for every three players; regular court setup

Personnel. At least three players and one coach. Additional players form triads. One court can handle four sets of triads (12 players).

Description. There is a tosser, a target, and a passer. To begin, the tosser and target each have a ball. The tosser, using a two-hand overhead toss, throws the ball in various places at different velocities, forcing the passer to adjust. The passer passes the ball to the target. As soon as the tosser releases a ball, the target bounces a ball to the tosser, and the drill repeats (see Figure 3-12). After one player has completed the specified goal, the triad rotates: The tosser becomes the passer, the passer becomes the target, and the target becomes the tosser. The drill continues until the three players have completed each station.

Measurement. Measure performance with a specified number of repetitions or time block.

Fig. 3-12

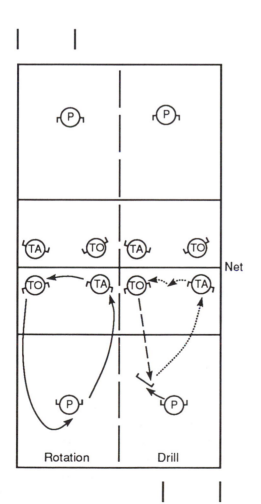

Rotation   Drill

(3.4) Diamond Bump Setting

Purpose. To practice movements and techniques required to set the ball with the forearms

Classification. Coach-centered

Category. Rapid-fire

Equipment. Full-court setup with a bucket of at least 12 balls

Personnel. 12 players and one coach

Description. This is a station-type drill. Players handle two balls at the points of the diamond and one ball at the sides. The coach bounces a ball low and away from setter A. Setter A bump sets the ball in the direction opposite that of the bounced ball. As soon as A bump sets, the coach bounces a ball in the other direction. Player A bump sets the other way. Player B or D attacks the ball using the skill best fitted to the quality of the set. They should never catch the ball. After A sets two balls, he or she rotates to the left. After B and D attack one ball, they rotate left. After C shags two balls and hands them to the coach, he or she rotates left (see Figure 3-13). The coach bounces another ball as soon as the attacker contacts the previous ball. Make sure the setter gets the ball high and between the net and the attacker.

Measurement. This drill is timed.

(3.5) Butterfly Serve Receive

Purpose. To review the movements required in serve receive; to warm up on one court

Classification. Player-centered

Category. Teaching/warm-up

Equipment. A full-court setup with at least six balls

Personnel. At least 12 players and one coach

Description. Place two players in each position: server, receiver, and target on each side of the net. The servers serve. The passers pass. The targets catch the balls and go to the serving line. Players rotate from server to receiver (passer), to target, to server, and so on. They simply follow the path of the ball; see Figure 3-14. The drill can also be done serving cross-court. I encourage you to develop this skill as well.

Measurement. This drill is timed.

Fig. 3-13

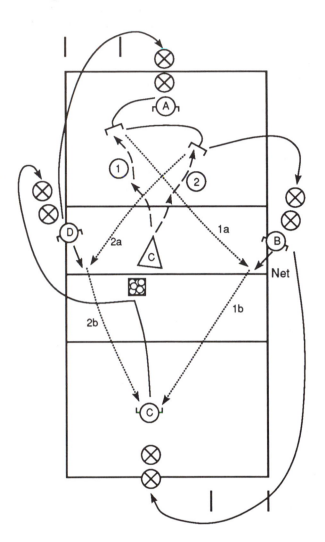

Fig. 3-14

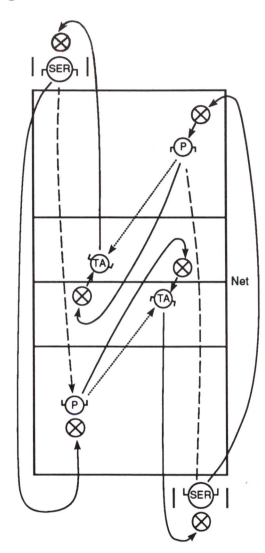

(3.6) Serve Receive Triads

Purpose.   To apply forearm passing specifically to serve reception

Classification.   Player-centered

Category.   Rapid-fire

Equipment.   Two balls per triad; one coach

Personnel.   The optimal situation is one triad per half court.

Description.   This drill is similar to Same-Side Triads (3.3), with a tosser, a passer, and a target, except that the tosser becomes a server. Progress from Drill 3.3 to this drill in this manner: First, the tosser uses a two-hand overhead toss from half court, duplicating a normal serve trajectory. Next, the tosser serves from half court, and final-

ly, the tosser serves from full court (see Figure 3-15). Players rotate from server (tosser) to receiver (passer) to target. You may set up an additional group serving from the opposite service area. Or, if space is limited, make the triads "sixes" by assigning two players to each station.

Measurement.   You can use either a specific time block or a certain number of successful repetitions to measure performance.

(3.7) Three-Point Game

Purpose.   To duplicate the pressure of game serve reception; to practice under competitive pressure

Classification.   Player-centered

Category.   Crisis

Fig. 3-15

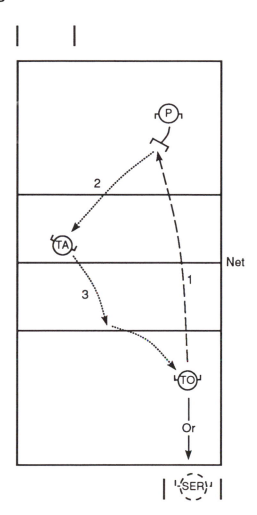

landing either out of bounds or out of the passer's designated area, is a point for the passer. To win, the server or passer must score 3 points in a row. The only time the score is 0-0 is at the beginning of the game. A point is always scored and begins the sequence of 3. The loser stays in position. The winner exchanges places with the target.

For variety, match the best players against each other or run a ladder tournament. The winner from each triad moves up, the second-place finisher stays in the same position, and the loser moves down.

Measurement. Play for a certain amount of time (e.g., 30 minutes). The player with the most "wins" is the winner.

Fig. 3-16

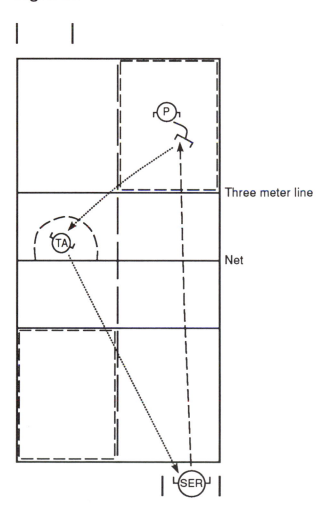

Equipment. One, two, or three balls per triad

Personnel. Groups of at least three players and one coach

Description. Set up in the same way as described in Drill 3.6, with a passer, a target, and a server (see Figure 3-16). Groups may operate from both service areas. Scoring is the key to this drill. The "target" player keeps score. The server serves the ball to the passer, who passes to the target. A ball passed high enough and to within one step of the target is a point for the passer. If the pass is outside that area, is too low, or is completely missed by the passer, it counts as a point for the server. A missed serve,

Chapter 4: Overhead Passing

Virtually everyone involved with volleyball uses the term "setting" to describe overhead passing. It is certainly easier to say, "Let's set a few balls" than "Let's overhead pass a few balls." However, we must make a clear distinction between setting and overhead passing. Setting, which will be covered thoroughly in Level II of the Coaching Accreditation Program, is the tactical skill of putting the ball in a position where a teammate can initiate an attack. Setting can involve any number of technical skills, including forearm passing, overhead passing, and one-handed "knucklers." Some South American players even use their heads to set the ball on occasion.

Overhead passing is by far the preferred skill to use when setting the ball. It can be used for other purposes as well, however, including passing a down or free ball, covering tips, and performing an attack volley. Every player must know how to overhead pass effectively, because *every* player will be called upon to set occasionally in competition. Players identified and trained as setters must develop exceptional overhead skills, along with other ball-handling skills. The setter's skills must ultimately be more specialized. They must be able to jump set, collapse set, back set, quick set, play set, short set, and bump set and use specialized postures and deceptive movements.

All volleyball players, whether or not they are specifically to become setters, need to master basic overhead passing and the application they will most likely use.

The fundamental principles of overhead passing are presented here. If you still find it easier to say, "Let's go set a few balls," instead of "Let's go overhead pass a few balls," by all means do so. Just be sure you and your players understand the difference between overhead passing and setting.

General Principles

- Contact the ball above and as close as possible to the forehead (see Figure 4-1a).
- Be compact and balanced (see Figure 4-1b).
- Get to the point of contact before the ball arrives, and face the target (see Figure 4-1c).

Executing the Overhead Pass

As in all skills, the overhead pass involves several phases of execution that, though taught in a fluid sequence, need to be analyzed separately.

Preparation (The Ready Position)

The ready position for overhead passing is similar to that in passing—a flexed stance with one foot slightly in front of the other.

Fig. 4-1

a

b   c

The arms are held comfortably in front of the body with the weight forward. The only real difference is in the posture: The overhead pass requires a higher stance than the forearm pass, due to the differing functions of the two passes.

The most common function of the overhead pass is setting. Therefore, the setter must be in a flexed position, loading the muscles for necessary adjustments. The setter must not be so tense as to be unable to assess surrounding player movements. Rather, the setter must determine where to set the ball as it approaches, get into position to set the ball accurately, judge the kind of set he or she is capable of delivering, and judge which spiker is ready for the set.

The setter's goal is to get to the spot before the ball arrives and *face* the target. The footwork is the same as used in forearm passing (see chapter 3). In forearm passing, there is some flexibility allowing the passer to pivot on the foot nearest the target while

deflecting the ball onto its outgoing path. Although I do not generally encourage movement, it is sometimes necessary. However, in overhead passing, facing the target prior to contact is critical to consistent accuracy. (There are exceptions to this principle in advanced setting techniques, which will be examined in higher-level manuals.)

Precontact Posture

When the player realizes that the overhead pass will be used, he or she will naturally move into a higher posture than would be used for forearm passing. Obviously, adjustments need to be made according to the height of the ball. The player should move into position and assume a posture similar to the one illustrated in Figure 4-2.

Fig. 4-2

Feet
One foot is in front of the other pointing toward the target. The weight is mostly on the back foot with the feet approximately a shoulder-width apart and 1 to 1-1/2 foot lengths from front to back. (This differs from the foot placement in forearm passing, which is wider and has only half a foot length separation from front to back.) The legs should be flexed with the knees in front of the big toes. The back is straight (see Figure 4-3).

Fig. 4-3

Arms

The arms are brought up as if the player were drawing a pair of six-guns. If the coach provides too much detailed instruction on exact position of the elbows, the player will tend to assume a mechanical posture. The player's elbows will naturally spread as the hands are brought up above the forehead. The player should explore the position. If the player looks horribly uncomfortable and confused, make some suggestions. For example, have the player get his or her hands higher above the head by holding the elbows higher and keeping them bent.

Hands

The hands form a bowl into which the ball will drop (see Figure 4-4). The thumbs are pointed at the eyes, and the fingers are spread but relaxed, as if the player were handling a valuable antique bowl.

Fig. 4-4

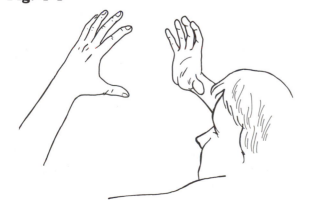

The eyes should look through the bowl at the incoming ball. It should appear to the casual observer that the player is pantomiming the close examination of the bottom of that antique bowl. The hands should be 2 to 5 inches away from the eyes and forehead.

Contact

Overhead passing contact is the most difficult of the volleyball skills to describe accurately. "Touch" is the term used for the overhead passing contact. A "soft" touch can be recognized but is difficult to describe. So visual analogies are employed: "She must have sharpened pencils for fingers, the way she touches the ball." Or, "She touches the ball like Downy touches clothes." And, as an aside, "Does he actually *eat* with those hands?"

The ongoing banter concerning player's touch is traditional and endless. The creative coach and players can always find some levity in trying to describe the often frustrating skill of overhead passing.

Players who wear glasses often try to contact the ball away from the face, instinctively fearing that the ball will hit their glasses and drive them into the bridge of the nose or the eyes. That is really not likely to happen, but players can perceive it as a point of potential pain. Encourage players to contact the ball close to the face.

Hand Position

The ball passes by the little and ring fingers and makes initial contact on the middle finger, forefinger, and thumb (see Figure 4-5). A useful visual analogy is that the ball strikes these fingers like a diver strikes a diving board. When the fingers reach a maximum flexion, the ball begins its move in the direction away from the forehead (see Figure 4-6). This diving board effect constitutes the "touch"; the smoother and quicker the finger flexion transfer, the softer the touch appears.

Wrist Flexion

If a freeze-frame photo were taken of the ball contact at the point of maximum finger flexion (see figure 4-7), you would note that the little and ring fingers are touching the

Fig. 4-5

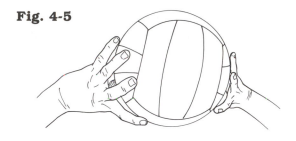

Fig. 4-6

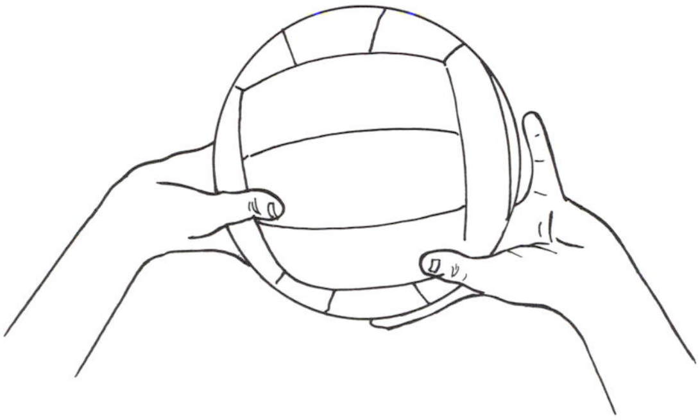

Fig. 4-7

ball but not really involved in the driving force, the hands are on the sides of the ball, and the wrists are ahead of the hands and pointed in the intended trajectory of the pass.

Common Errors

Look for your players to make some common errors when learning this very difficult skill.

- Beginning players have a tendency to stab at the ball instead of letting it come to the hands. Encourage players to contact the ball as close to the head as possible (see Figure 4-8a).
- The player may point the thumbs at the ball instead of at the eyes. It is important to have the thumbs back for the most flexion and force potential. Players run the risk of sprained thumbs if they point them toward the ball (see Figure 4-8b).
- Contact is sometimes made too far away from the head to allow the elbow "levers" to work. The hands may absorb the ball, but if the arms are extended at contact there is no power left to deliver the ball any significant distance (see Figure 4-8c).
- The ball is often contacted too low or too far out front relative to the head. Some players have a tendency to follow the ball with their hands and not with their feet, forcing them to play away from the body and lose control. This is called "water witching." It looks as if the player is pursuing the ball with a divining rod (see Figure 4-8d).

To insure good contact, the player must be trained to get the forehead under and behind the intended trajectory line. Then the player forms the bowl with his or her hands.

The Follow-Through

The follow-through in overhead passing is more premeditated and specific than in other skills and therefore deserves much more attention.

Though there is little variation in thought concerning how the ball should be contacted, the push of the arms and actual follow-though are the focus of continuous debate. The description provided here is based on the general principles of skill execution—compactness, efficiency, and symmetry. The key is to apply force constantly, symmetrically, and in the exact line of trajectory.

As the ball springs off the hands, the body's weight is transferred from the back foot in a straight line through the hands. The hands follow the ball, quickly reacting to the flexion in the fingers and keeping actual contact with the ball to a minimum. The player builds a pyramid behind the ball on release. In a full follow-though the bottoms of the thumbs touch each other as the hands turn over. The hands are retracted to the hairline, in a praying position in line with the nose, and are then relaxed. When the hands are retracted, it appears that they are rebounding off the ball (see Figure 4-9).

Fig. 4-8

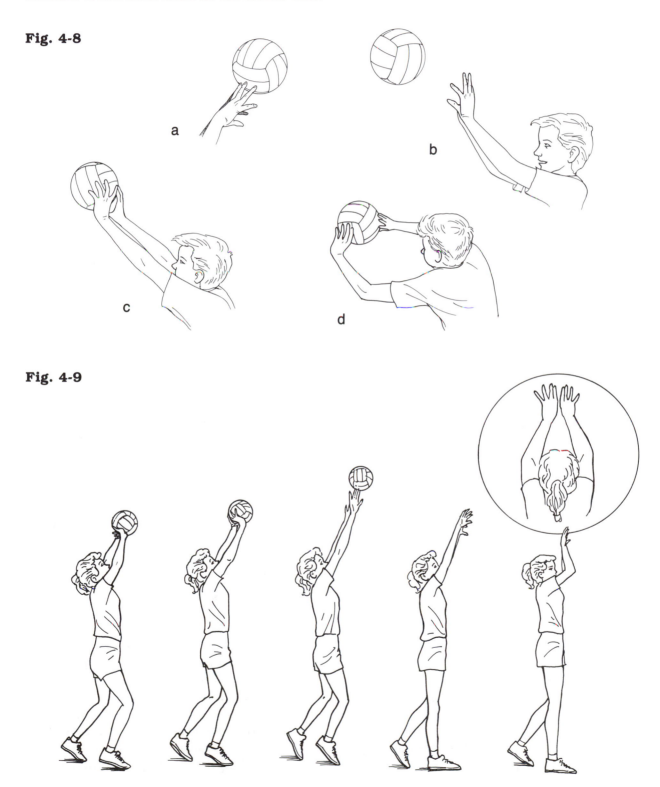

Fig. 4-9

In the course of a game, passes of varying heights and distances may be needed to complete a play. If greater height, distance, or both is required, the player has a tendency to "swim" with the hands at full arm extension. The hands will pronate away from the intended trajectory line, compromising accuracy (see Figure 4-10a).

Another common error involves dropping the hands with arms extended after the release (see Figure 4-10b). Similar to "swimming," the force is pulled away from the ball and consistent control is jeopardized.

Fig. 4-10

a

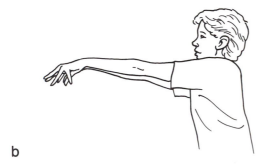

b

Coaching Points

1. To be successful, all players must develop consistent overhead passing skills.
2. Make sure that all players use overhead passing in game-like situations and clearly understand the functions of overhead passing.
3. Players must understand the varying heights and distances required for each function of a pass or set.
4. Use teaching keys:
   - Hands up early
   - Bowl-shaped hands
   - Face the target
   - Extend and pray

Teaching Progression

1. Demonstrate the skill of overhead passing. Focus on getting the hands up early in a bowl shape. Describe the diving-board effect. "Hands up early" and "bowl-shaped hands" refer to positions assumed. (3 to 4 minutes)
2. Pairs of players face each other 3 to 4 meters apart. One player tosses the ball to the other using a two-handed underhand toss. The receiving player then overhead passes back to the tosser. Each player passes 5 to 10 balls before switching roles. (8 minutes)
3. Players return. Again demonstrate the overhead pass. Have players review the first two keys. Now focus on the flexed, ready position, and the extension of the arms toward the target ("Face the target/Extend and pray"). (2 minutes)
4. Have the players toss and pass while focusing on posture and extension. (6 minutes)
5. Players return. Have players review the key points: Hands up early, bowl-shaped hands, face the target, and extend and pray. Again demonstrate the skill. In the demonstration have the tosser move you or your demonstrator two or three strides from side to side and from front to back. Focus attention on footwork, stopping, and facing the target before the ball arrives. Demonstrate this technique. Then emphasize the importance of

position: Have your hands up early and bowl shaped. Prior to contact, spread your hands and let the ball hit your head. If you are in the correct position, the ball will bounce toward the target. This "head" drill emphasizes the need to get to the point of contact and face the target before the ball arrives. (3 minutes)

6. In pairs, one player tosses to the other, making him or her move two or three strides. The passers focus on correct footwork, getting to the point of contact before the ball arrives, and facing the target. Have them try the whole skill first, then have them try the "head" drill to understand the importance of position. (5 minutes)

7. Players return. Demonstrate overhead passing as used in setting, focusing on the general principles described on page 33. The ball should be set high and should look at its peak like it's coming off a waterfall. Demonstrate setting from the setting position in your offense, but emphasize that a set can come from anywhere on the floor and needs to be placed high, between the hitter and the net. (3 minutes)

8. Players pair off and practice focusing on high sets. (6 minutes)

9. Players return and review all overhead passing keys. Have players reiterate that overhead passing is the primary technical skill used in the tactical skill of setting. (1 minute)

10. Go to the overhead pass drills in combination with forearm passing and attack.

Tactical Applications

Like forearm passing, overhead passing is an intermediate contact. Most often, forearm passing is used in the first contact (serve receive) and overhead passing in the second (setting). Consistent with the nature of volleyball, though, seemingly predictable conditions can change. For example, handling a free ball overhead can be the first contact. Setting a low, errant pass is best handled on the forearms. An attack volley is an overhead pass and the third, terminating contact.

If overhead passing is used to handle a free or down ball, the tactical application is exactly like that in forearm passing. In this situation, overhead passing can get the ball to the setter more quickly.

The tactical application of overhead passing in setting defines the team's offense. All the planned trajectories and velocities combined with the attacker's timed approaches integrate specific application of overhead passing into the total offensive scheme. However, every player at every level of competition must understand some basic tactical principles:

- The tougher the play, the higher the pass.
- When setting, make the simplest play you can. Set the ball to the closest attacker who is in front of you. It is imperative that the attacker get a good swing at the ball.
- Keep the ball off the net.
- Stop prior to contact. A player must be situated so that he or she can move through the ball to the target. A player backing away must compensate with the hands, losing rhythm and control.

Principles of Setting

- *Set the ball high between the attacker and the net.* The ball does not need to be pinpointed; it needs to be high. It needs to be 1 to 2 meters back from the net. At its apex, the ball should look like it's coming off a waterfall.
- *The ball should be set inside.* This principle refers to players who are not designated setters. The most important objective is to provide the attacker with a good swing at the ball. If it is set too wide or too tight to the net, the attacker cannot get an effective swing.

• *Set the ball to the easiest option.* Each player should make the highest percentage play, because coaches, teammates, and fans alike will hold their collective breath when a player other than a setter jump sets, back sets, or attempts a difficult variation. Each player should be instructed to set the closest, easiest option in front. If a front option is not available, then and only then should a player launch a back set.

Variations of the Overhead Pass

Overhead passing is the primary skill used in setting. However, setting is only one of the functions of overhead passing. All players and coaches must understand this distinction to understand overhead passing.

The variations of the overhead pass really apply only to the setter: Jump setting, back setting, collapse setting, and setting various heights are all required in offensive patterns. The general player uses the front overhead pass skill most of the time, although he or she does need some skill in back setting and collapse setting. Jump setting for the general player occurs only in desperation.

Drills and Activities for Overhead Passing

Most of the general forearm ball-handling drills can also be used for overhead passing.

(4.1) Two Targets
Purpose.   To react and adjust to required angles and pass the ball accurately
Classification.   Player-centered
Category.   Rapid-fire
Equipment.   Two balls for every three players and a full-court setup
Personnel.   At least three players and one coach

Description.   Two target-tossers are stationed, one at each side of the court (see Figure 4-11). The passer begins at middle back. Using a two-hand underhand throw, the tossers alternate tosses to move the passer laterally, away from the target-tosser. The passer, using correct movements, passes the ball back to the tosser and prepares for the next ball from the other tosser. *Measurement.*   The drill can be timed, or a successful number of repetitions can be used to rate performance.

Fig. 4-11

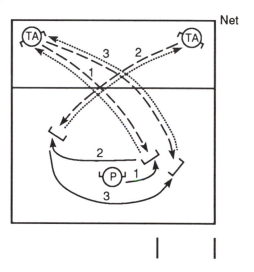

(4.2) Free-Ball Passing
Purpose.   To combine correct movements and postures specific to overhead (or forearm) passing
Classification.   Coach-centered
Category.   Rapid-fire
Equipment.   A full court and a container of balls
Personnel.   Five or more players and one coach
Description.   The coach with the container of balls and a feeder are at midcourt on one side of the net. Three players line up at the end line on the other side of the net. Another player is the "target" (see Figure 4-12). The coach hits or tosses an easy ball to each passer, alternating left and right. Passers

Fig. 4-12

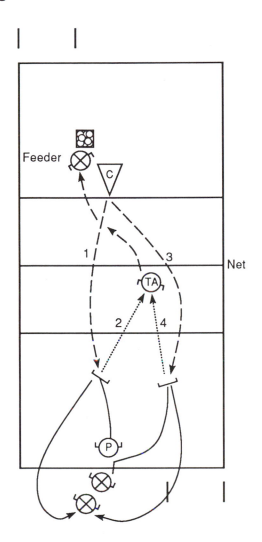

Classification. Player-centered

Category. Crisis

Equipment. A full-court setup and one ball per participating unit

Personnel. Two or more players (this activity can be done without a coach)

Description. The game can be played with one, two, or three players on each side. Up to three contacts may be used on each side. Players can use only overhead passes and may not jump. The serve is initiated by an overhead pass. Boundaries are the 3-meter lines, the sidelines, and the center line (see Figure 4-13). Score this game normally or use fast score. For details on scoring systems, see chapter 12, "Practice and Drills Design," pages 159-160.

Measurement. This drill can be played to 15 points or can be timed.

Fig. 4-13

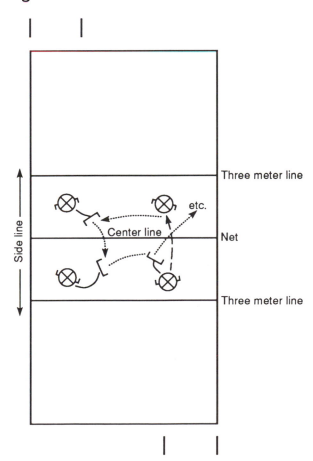

make the correct, necessary moves to play the ball, and pass it to the target. The target player bounces the ball back to the feeder. After each hit, the passers alternate. The coach hits another ball as soon as the passer has released the previous ball. To vary the drill, the target player can set the passed ball to a spiker target who in turn can hit it.

Measurement. To measure performance, this drill can be timed, or a total number of perfect passes, or perfect passes in a row can be specified.

(4.3) Three-Meter Game

Purpose. To develop reactions and control in compact, competitive conditions

(4.4) Two Contact/Narrow Court Game

Purpose.   To develop reactions in compact, competitive conditions

Classification.   Player-centered

Category.   Crisis

Equipment.   A full net setup and one ball per two playing units are needed. Tape a center line perpendicular to the net.

Personnel.   Teams of one, two, or three players

Description.   This is the same game as the Three-Meter Game (4.3), except it is played on a long and narrow court (see Figure 4-14). Only two contacts per side are allowed to force quick reactions with control.

Measurement.   This drill can be played to 15 points or can be timed.

Fig. 4-14

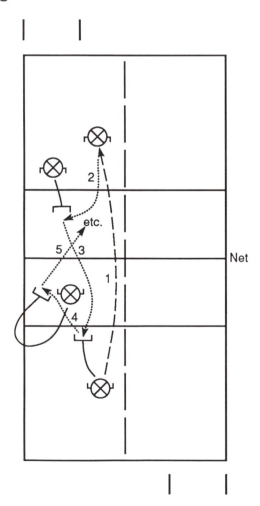

(4.5) Six-Player Rotation

Purpose.   To focus on controlled overhead contact using correct communication and movement skills

Classification.   Player-centered

Category.   Crisis

Equipment.   A full-court setup with a container of balls

Personnel.   12 players and one coach

Description.   Divide the group into two teams of six. They assume coach-assigned positions and movements, depending on which side of the net the ball is on. Each team *must* have three contacts, all overhead. The drill can be competitive, but it should be a cooperative activity. The object is to keep the ball going. After a team sends the ball over the net, that team rotates one position (clockwise). As soon as a ball is unplayable, the coach throws in another ball.

Measurement.   Designate a time block to maintain control of the ball (e.g., 15 minutes). Be sure to have 20 balls in a container next to the coach. The key is to keep a ball in play for as long as possible. Once a ball is unplayable, it is out. If the players can get through the time block without using the designated number of balls, they "win."

(4.6) The Setting Game

Purpose.   To develop overhead pass accuracy and reaction; to integrate competition and fun while working on performing the overhead pass correctly

Classification.   Player-centered

Category.   Crisis

Equipment.   Basketball hoops and one ball for two players

Personnel.   At least two players

Description.   The game begins with one player standing at either the free-throw line or the top of the key. He or she tosses to him- or herself and sets the ball to the basket. If the ball goes in, it counts as 1 point if the shot was taken from the free-throw line, and 2 points if taken from the top of the key. If the ball careens off the basket or board, play continues as each player alternates attempting to score using the overhead pass technique. Play pauses if there is a score or if the ball is unplayable. If a player's set misses the apparatus entirely, the opponent can option to play or to start the next series from the line or the top of the key (see Figure 4-15). The ball can bounce once on the floor before a player attempts a set. Scoring is as follows:

- From the top of the key on the initial shot: 2 points
- From the free-throw line on the initial shot: 1 point
- Any "basket": 1 point

Measurement. The first to score 21 points "wins."

Fig. 4-15

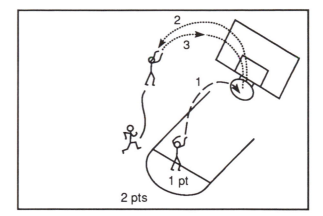

Chapter 5: Attack

Spiking is the predominant skill used in a team's attack. Despite its number of components, spiking is relatively easy to teach. The movements involved are similar to those found in other popular sports (e.g., baseball, tennis). Spiking is a *terminal* contact. Positive feedback generated by the skill itself is specific and easily identified.

Spiking is motivational. Just as shooting and making a basket in basketball is a rewarding terminal contact, so is a successful spike hammered at the opponent. All "real" volleyball players want to be able to smack the ball and score. Fans and teammates applaud the spike, and a sense of power flows through the triumphant attacker. Though fleeting, the awesome glory of the moment keeps volleyball players aching to blast one more ball.

The motivation for players to learn the comparatively dull intermediate contacts is the sobering fact that without ball control, there would be no spiking. Unlike in basketball, where a player can score points more or less independently, spikers don't get the chance to score unless their teammates are able to control the first two contacts. On a poor ball-handling team, the spikers must be satisfied with getting in their blasts during prematch warm-ups.

General Principles

A general principle governing spikers, or hitters as they are sometimes called, is that of making oneself available to hit by moving off the net so the setter can set the ball between the attacker and the net. This movement *must* occur *every* time. Young players often stand at the net during a rally. Once the ball is on your team's side of the net, attackers must get back so they have room to approach, jump, and hit.

During serve receive, you can put spikers in a ready position before the play begins. During long rallies where the ball crosses the net several times, front-row players must alternate from blocking (when the opponent has the ball) to attacking (when their team has the ball). This is the principle of transition, which must be followed every time the ball crosses the net. Figure 5-1 diagrams the paths of spikers and setters in transition.

Executing the Spike

Principles of execution are given for each of the four phases of spiking; preparation (ready position), approach, jump, and arm swing.

Preparation (The Ready Position)

The spiker must move away from the net so that he or she can approach with as many steps of the designed pattern as required. It is the spiker's responsibility to adjust the ready or starting position so the setter can get the ball into an approachable, hittable position.

Fig. 5-1

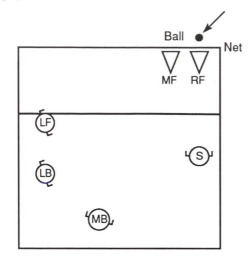

Standard defense

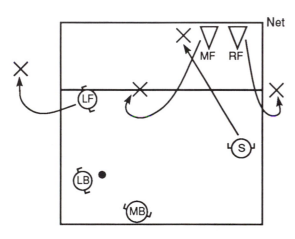

Ball is dug by the left back—
Team transition to offense

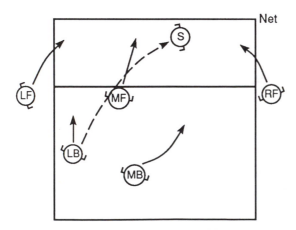

Positions and routes of players as
the ball is being passed to setter

The spiker should be in a flexed position with one foot forward, leaning toward the approved direction. The *arms* are dangling from the shoulders. The body weight is balanced but ready to move over the lead foot (see Figure 5-2). The eyes should be focused on the setter and the situation he or she is facing.

The key is to be ready to move quickly but to stay relaxed. The ready position will be individualized through experience to accommodate each player's movement idiosyncrasies.

Fig. 5-2

The Approach

There is considerable discussion as to the correct method of approach in spiking. Certainly, several methods are common. Further, as the offensive aspects of volleyball have become more sophisticated, approach routes have become more specialized. In these paragraphs, I describe the basic four-step approach. Within the four steps, of course, are the two- and three-step variations.

The "step close" approach is featured here. Studies have shown that it is more efficient and produces greater heights in jumping than the pure prejump or hop technique. In the four-step approach, right-handed hitters start on the right foot and left-handed hitters start on the left.

Arm movements are extremely important to the approach and jumping process. However, give your players very little specific guidance about arm movement other than to be relaxed and natural. A baby learning to walk is not instructed to swing one arm opposite the leading foot. It happens because of the natural balance required in the body. This concept also holds true in the first two steps of the spike approach.

The arm position in the last two steps is not quite as natural. The spiker wants to generate as much force in the jump as possible. When the foot reaches out on the third step, both arms reach as far back and as high as physically possible. The arms should be straight and the hands relaxed (see Figure 5-3).

As the fourth step is being initiated, the arms come forward. In a full sweeping motion, the arms swing through in a direct line with the approach, next to the knees (see Figure 5-4). If the prelaunch position could be frozen, it would appear that the spiker is grabbing a bar behind the knees. The hands, however, should be relaxed.

Many coaches prefer to teach a three-step approach because in advanced levels of play, most tactical approach patterns focus just on the last three steps. If you want to teach

Fig. 5-3

Fig. 5-4

the three-step approach, simply use the last three steps as the focal point. Three-step approaches are found in more advanced Coaching Accreditation Program manuals.

I strongly suggest that you allow each player to explore how to coordinate the arm swing with the approach. If you try to specifically teach the arm swing, players will tend to use very mechanical and rigid arm movements. If an athlete has difficulty coordinating the movement, provide assistance as needed.

The Jump

The basic spike jump should be as vertical as possible. It is ludicrous, though, to assume that a moving body can make an accelerating horizontal approach, jump and hammer a ball in the direction of travel, and return directly to the launch pad. It is simply not possible. Therefore, players must allow for a degree of horizontal journeying.

The angle at which the knees and ankles are flexed varies with the player and his or her individual physical characteristics. However, too little flexion is preferable to too much. Being too high means little or no preloading of the quadriceps, hamstrings, and hip flexors, which provide the force for the jump, and being too low means a slower exchange of power, causing the loss of momentum (see Fig. 5-5).

Fig. 5-5

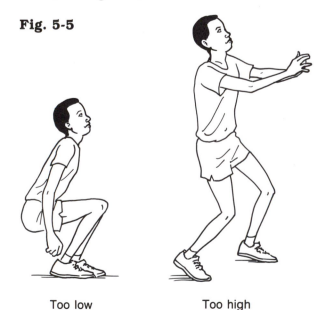

Too low   Too high

The forward lifting movement of the arms should be coordinated with the straightening of the legs. If the arms swing too fast and get to approximately chest level before the legs straighten, a braking effect occurs, inhibiting the height of the jump. You can easily see if the player is coordinating movement of the arms and legs with the natural straightening of the torso.

If a spiker with a light attached to his or her hip approached and jumped in a dark room, the light would trace a check mark ✓. If the light traced a hump before the bottom of the mark ✓, it would indicate that the spiker was raising the center of gravity prior to lowering it. This means the jumper loses acceleration and quickness, two commodities essential to a good jump. As you watch your players, look for the check mark approach.

To be comfortable with jumping, athletes need practice. Engage them in activities that require jumping. To learn spike jumping, athletes must repeatedly jump and spike a ball. The best way to teach the use of arms in the approach and jump is to have the players focus on throwing their arms upward as they jump. Watch for too much tension. The players must be powerful but relaxed. Following the procedure just outlined can help you avoid the mechanical movements that result from overteaching the approach.

The Arm Swing and Contact

Most Americans play throwing games. The motion of spiking is similar to that of throwing overhand, but there are two major differences. First, the spiker uses a *throwing* motion but *hits* the ball; second, the spiker is in the air hitting a moving target.

It is often helpful to think of the arm as a whip and the hand its tip. The snap of the whip begins with the shoulder. Because of the body torque created by the foot plant, the hitting shoulder is *away* from the intended flight path of the ball.

The elbow should be drawn back, high and away from the shoulder. The hand should be open and relaxed. The shoulder moves toward the point of contact, followed quickly by the elbow, then by the hand. The hips should rotate with the shoulders (see Figure 5-6).

The player should try to contact the ball as high and as far in front of the head as can be controlled, keeping the hand open and loose (see Figure 5-7). The hand contacts the

Fig. 5-6

Fig. 5-7

top of the ball, heel first, and spreads out over the ball. If the movement could be frozen just after the ball explodes off the hand, it would appear that the spiker is hitting over a barrel (see Figure 5-8).

The follow-through will be natural because gravity controls it. The player must control the landing point and the finishing arm position. If the player touches the net, the official will issue a penalty.

The player must always be aware of how close he or she is to the net when contacting the ball yet must not be intimidated by the net. Spikers need to practice the adjustments required to attack a ball close to the

Fig. 5-8

net—a shortened arm swing, a slowed or standing jump, a rotation along the net. You can teach these adjustments by putting players in specific situations, giving them limitations, and having them explore the adjustments necessary to control the situation.

Coaching Points

1. Accelerate into the jump.
2. The back arm swing should be as high and as far back as possible with relaxed, open hands.
3. The foot plant should preset body torque.
4. Lift-off is a coordinated effort of forward arm swing, leg extension, and torso straightening.
5. The arm swing is like a whip originating in the hitting shoulder and snapping through the elbow to the open, relaxed hand.
6. The hand hits the top and back of the ball, heel first, and snaps.
7. Follow-through is adjusted to avoid fouling.
8. Use teaching keys:
   - *Run*—Accelerate to the jump
   - *Jump*—Jump off both feet and throw your hands up
   - *Hit*—Contact the ball at a point high and in front of you

Teaching Progression

Spiking is the most motivational individual volleyball skill. Every player likes to smack the ball, and every player should get the chance to do so during every practice, even defensive specialists and setters. Work it in somehow. It's fun!

1. Demonstrate spiking. Have players focus on the approach footwork. Then ask them to describe it. (Teaching key: "Run.") (3 minutes)
2. Players get into a line. Tell players, "You go, I throw." As each player approaches the net, you throw the ball

high enough in front of the player so he or she can hit it over the net. (6 to 8 minutes)

3. Demonstrate spiking again. Have the players focus on the jump. They should be able to describe what the arms are doing. Also have them take note of the foot position. (Teaching key: "Jump.") (2 minutes)

4. Go back to the "You go, I throw" exercise. This time, have players focus on the jump. (6 minutes)

5. Demonstrate spiking again. Have the players focus on the hit. Ask: What are the arms doing? What does the hitting hand do? Where is the ball being contacted? (Teaching key: "Hit.") (2 minutes)

6. Continue "You go, I throw." Have the players focus on hitting the ball. (6 minutes)

7. Demonstrate spiking a set ball. Have players focus on timing, when to begin the approach, and when to make related adjustments. (2 minutes)

8. Players form a spiking line to hit a set ball. Players should focus on when and where to approach. Figure 5-9 illustrates how to organize this learning activity. (6 minutes)

9. Have players return and review the keys to spiking. (1 minute)

10. Begin drills.

Fig. 5-9

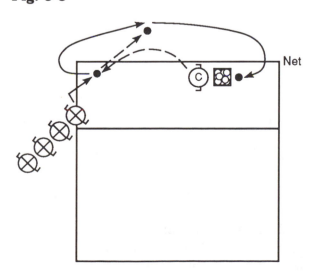

Functions

Spiking has one primary function: to put the ball down on the opponent's court. A secondary function is to keep the ball in play. A spiker must be able to distinguish between a situation best suited to an aggressive swing and one that calls for a controlled shot. The inability to recognize what should be done and when to do it is the downfall of many mechanically excellent spikers. For example, a ball set too low cannot be hit hard because it will be buried in the net. If a ball is set too wide or too deep, a hard swing will send the ball long and out of play. Each spiker must learn his or her own limitations in any given situation. As you teach spiking, create situations that allow players to expand but also teach them to understand their limits. Discretion must be taught along with mechanics.

Even though the function of spiking is virtually singular, the ways of getting the job done are many. The crisp, forceful shot that intimidates the opposition may be spectacular, but well-spaced, well-placed tips and off-speed shots can be equally effective. Additional variations will be covered in higher levels of *Coaching Volleyball Successfully*.

Different timing patterns, deceptive setting, and disguised spike approaches are variations used at advanced levels of play. Combining individual variations with changing locations makes for a potent and effective attack. Team offensive tactics are also covered in more advanced levels of *Coaching Volleyball Successfully*.

Tactical Applications

Spiking tactics, both team and individual, are the most sophisticated strategies in volleyball. *Team tactics* always finish with one player employing individual tactics. They are designed to free the lone attacker by confusing the block. Theoretically, team tactics, which include a wide range of deceptive approach patterns of two or more players in coordination with each other, make it easier to carry out individual tactics. In reality, players concentrating on elaborate fakes often end up in a poor position to get a good swing at the ball.

Individual tactics can be employed only if the hitter has the ability to hit the ball where he or she wants to with controlled velocity. The player's shot selection is a reaction to the unfolding situation—the opponent's defensive scheme, the quality of the set, and the game conditions.

Tactical Principles

- Attack at the defensive weakness, such as a small or inept blocker; a lumbering, lazy, or out-of-position back-row defender; or a predetermined weakness in the opponent's defensive system.
- When in doubt of where to hit, be sure to hit the ball in, not out!
- Be more aggressive in point-making plays (a mistake results in a side out) and be safer in side-out plays (a mistake results in a point for the opponent).
- Develop a variety of shots. Be able to adjust to the situation.

Drills and Activities for Attack Skills

The drills included here have spiking as their focus. However, because spiking never occurs by itself, several other skills are incorporated. In these drills, strive to require the same movement patterns and spiking approach as used in actual game situations.

(5.1) Pairs Bounce/Self-Hit

Purpose. To adjust to a moving ball and hit it with control over the net; to have players be able to hit realistically without the benefit of a setter

Classification. Player-centered

Category. Teaching

Equipment. One ball for every two players and a full-court setup

Personnel. An even number of players, and a coach

Description. Players in pairs face each other on either side of the net, each standing about 5 meters from the net. One player bounces the ball so it goes up in front of him or her. The player then makes the appropriate approach and spikes the ball to the player on the other side of the net. The spiker does what he or she can control. If the spiker is able to jump and spike, that is preferable. If not, then he or she should use the spiking motion from a standing position. Multiple pairs may work at one net (see Figure 5-10).

Measurement. Success in this drill is measured by completing a given number of successful spikes in a specified time period.

Fig. 5-10

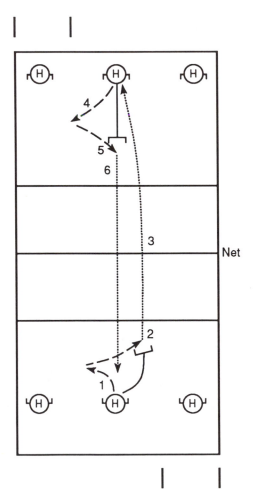

(5.2) Rhythm Hitting

Purpose. To focus on the complete skill without an accurate setter; to practice a variety of shots; to get maximum repetitions in a short time

Classification. Coach-centered

Category. Rapid-fire

Equipment. A container of balls, a chair, and a full-court setup

Personnel. 2 to 12 players and one coach

Description. There are two player lines, one ready to spike and the other handing balls to the coach at his or her hip. After a player hits, he or she shags the ball and goes to the end of the handing line. After a player hands a ball, he or she goes to the end of the spiking line. The coach tosses the ball with a two-hand underhand toss to a spot a meter back from the net and as high as desired. Spikers move to hit the ball. The rhythm should be fast (see Figure 5-11).

The coach can designate where he or she wants the ball hit and can control where

Fig. 5-11

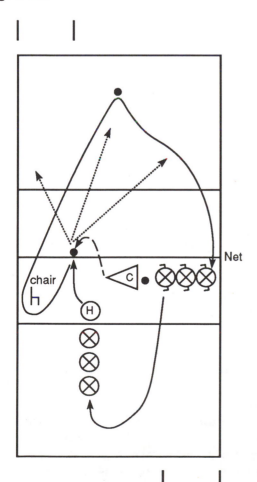

along the net and at what depth the ball is to be contacted. The coach can require each hitter to go around a chair on his or her side of net after hitting to discourage going under the net after contact. For variety, the coach can require a player to hit a specified number of balls in a row at various heights and positions before shagging. The player then shags the same number of balls he or she hit.

Measurement. This drill can be measured by time or a specified number of successful repetitions to a target.

(5.3) Setter Initiates

Purpose. To set and hit from a simulated serve receive; to warm up

Classification. Player-centered

Category. Teaching

Equipment. One ball per player with a full net setup

Personnel. At least six players

Description. Set the group up with a setter and a spiking line (see Figure 5-12). The setter underhand serves to the first player in line, who passes back to the setter and gets into approach position. The setter sets to that player who attacks, shags, and returns to the end of the spiking line.

Measurement. Simply keep this drill going for a specified time period. Rotate setters as necessary.

Variation.

Coach Initiates. Align players in separate passing and spiking lines (see Figure 5-13). The coach half serves to the passing line. The first player in that line passes to the setter positioned near the net, who sets to the first player in the spiking line. The spiker hits the ball, shags it, puts it in the container next to the coach, and goes to the end of the passing line. The passer goes to the end of the spiking line after passing. An important tip: Start the spiker in the position where he or she would most likely be placed in an actual game.

(5.4) Setter Chase

Purpose. To have attackers work with a setter under game-like adjustment conditions; to have setters work on position and setting

Classification. Coach-centered

Fig. 5-12

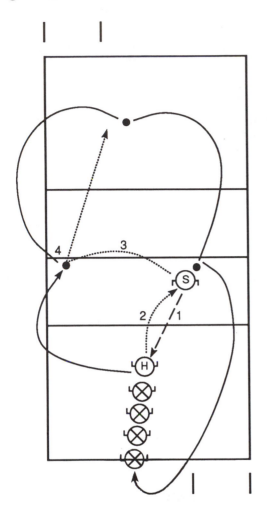

Fig. 5-13

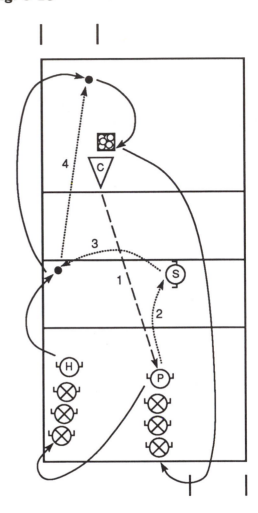

Category. Rapid-fire

Equipment. A container of at least 15 balls, and a full-court setup

Personnel. At least six players and one coach

Description. Form two spiking lines, one on each side of the same court. One setter begins at the target. The coach is near the back of the court with the container of balls. The coach bounces the ball, forcing the setter to move and get into position facing the spiker. The setter sets to alternating hitting lines or selects the easiest set to execute based on the contact position. After the spiker hits, he or she shags, puts the ball in the container, and goes to the end of the other line (see Figure 5-14). As soon as a hitter makes contact, the coach bounces the next ball. To make this drill more challeng-

ing, add blockers and restrict the spiker's shot selection. You may also add targets for the spiker.

Measurement. You can either time this drill or require a specific number of successful repetitions.

(5.5) Horse II

Purpose. To work on hitting accuracy and variety of shots

Classification. Player-centered

Category. Crisis

Equipment. Full-court setup

Personnel. A minimum of three players and one coach

Description. Spikers pair off and play "horse" as described in Drill 2.4 (p. 17), matching shots into selected targets. The hitter calls for a type of set and position

Fig. 5-14

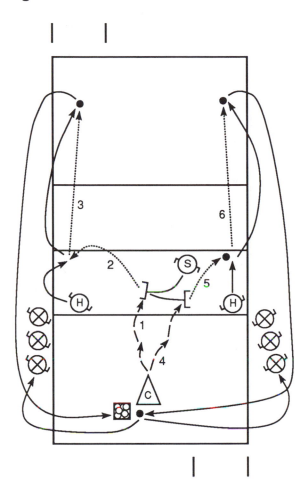

hitting over the net

Classification.   Coach- or player-centered
Category.   Rapid-fire/Teaching
Equipment.   Full-court setup with a container of balls
Personnel.   6 to 12 players and one coach
Description.   Set players up in the formation used for either Rhythm Hitting (5.2), Setter Initiates (5.3), Coach Initiates (5.3), or Setter Chase (5.4). In this drill, contact will be made from behind the 3-meter line. The purpose of this drill is not to teach back-row attack; rather the focus is on timing and player relationships to spiking the ball without the net as a point of reference. The players spike, shag, and return to the spiking line (see Figure 5-16). You can add defenders who play the point out on the receiving side of the net.

Fig. 5-15

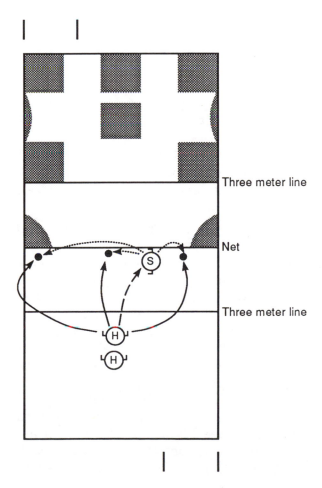

along the net or back-row attack area. He or she must then hit the ball into the specified target, and then his or her partner must match the shot (see Figure 5-15). A letter is assigned to a spiker who is unable to duplicate the spike executed by the "leader." If a player has accumulated "HORS," the lead player hits another target, and the player with "HORS" fails to duplicate the spike, he or she has two options: The player can choose to try again or can require the leader to hit the target again. If the lead player is successful, the "E" is assigned and the game is over. If the leader misses, the game continues until one player has "HORSE."

Measurement.   Play continues until one player has "HORSE."

(5.6) Deep-Court Hitting

Purpose.   To practice controlling body position and timing relative to the ball and to

Measurement. Specify a number of successful repetitions or a time block to measure the drill.

Fig. 5-16

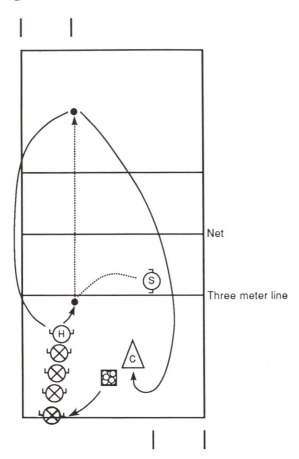

(5.7) Target Practice

Purpose. To develop accuracy and shot variety

Classification. Player- or coach-initiated

Category. Teaching

Equipment. A full-court setup with a container of balls; also, various targets, such as chairs, hula hoops, or bottom-weighted inflatable clowns

Personnel. At least six players and one coach

Description. Using any of the previously described formats, hitters attempt to hit targets set up in areas designated by the coach (see Figure 5-17). It is also wise to practice spiking between the targets, because in a game the hitters should avoid the diggers. As spikers improve, add blockers.

Measurement. Points are awarded for hitting targets. Try a competition to accumulate the most points in a given amount of time.

Fig. 5-17

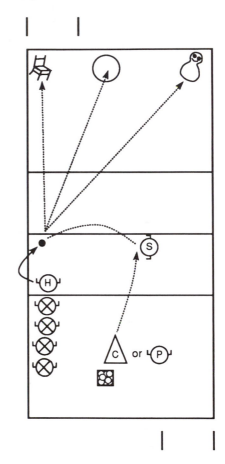

(5.8) Plus/Minus

Purpose. To perform under pressure

Classification. Player-centered

Category. Crisis

Equipment. Full-court setup with a container of balls

Personnel. At least three spikers, one setter, one shagger, and one coach

Description. Assign spikers to groups of three, who will hit in designated positions. Spikers alternate hitting attempts (see Figure 5-18). A ball hit with power in the court scores 1 point. A ball tipped or played in the court safely is a "0." A player who hits the ball out of bounds or into the net or who fouls loses a point. As soon as a player gets a designated number of points, he or she steps out of the three-player rotation and shags balls. The remaining players continue until each player attempts to reach the designated number of points.

The drill can be made more challenging by adding blockers. Any blocked ball is scored a "0."

Measurement.   Play to a designated number of points for each player.

Fig. 5-18

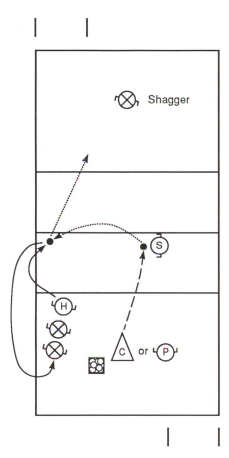

(5.9) Three-Player Rotation

Purpose.   To sequence basic skills with emphasis on precise control

Classification.   Player-centered

Category.   Flow-of-play

Equipment.   Full-court setup, two balls, and tape

Personnel.   6 or 12 players and one coach

Description.   Divide the court in half by taping a line perpendicular to the net.

Players practice in groups of three, each group facing another through the net (see Figure 5-19). The object is to keep the ball in play. When the ball crosses the net, the threesome that "attacked" rotates so the setter becomes the digger, the digger becomes the hitter, and the hitter becomes the setter. The hitter hits to the digger on the other side of the net with control.

Measurement.   The opposing groups of three can be given a specified number of balls to keep in play during a given amount of time. Each time an error is made, the players lose that ball and begin with another. If they run out of balls before time is expired, then they face a negative consequence such as putting away the equipment after practice. If they have balls left, they are rewarded with praise or a small privilege.

Fig. 5-19

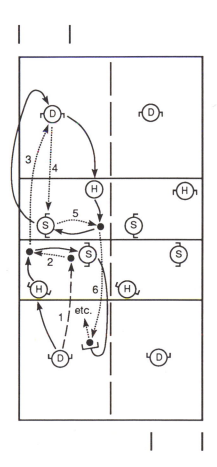

Chapter 6: Blocking

Blocking is the most difficult volleyball skill to teach and to learn. Success is limited by several factors including a player's height and jumping ability and the situation. A blocker's complex, split-second decision-making process is influenced by how high and fast the ball is set; how far off the net the ball is hit; the spiker's arm swing style, jumping ability, timing, and dominant hand; and the player's role in the team offensive pattern.

It is difficult for you as a coach to duplicate specific situations in teaching blocking because of the natural variables that occur the longer the ball is in play. Furthermore, positive feedback resulting from the ultimate goal of a stuff block, in which the ball returns to the attacking team's floor, is rare, especially for shorter players. It is very important that you issue positive feedback to your blockers for good effort, footwork, control, and other mechanical elements of blocking, and not rely solely on result-measured success.

Blocking is the *least important* skill at beginning levels of play. When ball control is inconsistent, the potential for a powerful attack is erratic. Therefore, there is minimal need for blocking. Blocking is needed only when an opposing player can hit the ball harder than your team can control in the back row. At higher levels of play, where the attack comes with frequency and force, blocking becomes extremely important.

Blocking movements are very precise. They require discipline and compact control. Young players must be exposed to these elements even though repeated application will not be necessary until opponents can attack consistently with power.

It is important for players to understand the principles of blocking. Because players will not always see the direct results of their blocking efforts, they must understand their role in the blocking scheme as it affects total team play.

General Principles

- Blockers should *front the hitter*, while lining up in the spiker's attack approach angle and positioning him- or herself so that if the spiker swings directly in line with his or her approach, the hitting arm cuts from the blocker's outside hand to his or her inside shoulder. The blocker must determine where the ball will be contacted to establish this position effectively (see Figure 6-1).
- Outside blockers keep the outside arm above the outside shoulder (see Figure 6-2). Never reach away from the court.
- Keep the eyes open; see the spiker's hand hit the ball (see Figure 6-3).
- Make the hands as "big" as possible (see Figure 6-4).

Fig. 6-1

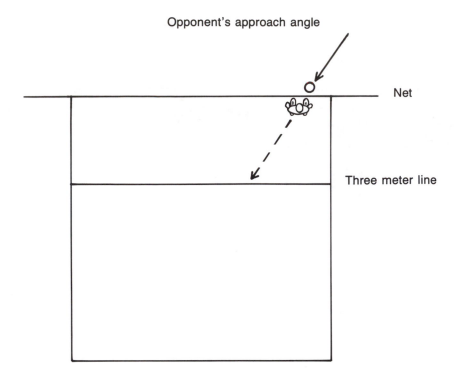

Opponent's approach angle

Net

Three meter line

Fig. 6-2

Fig. 6-3

Fig. 6-4

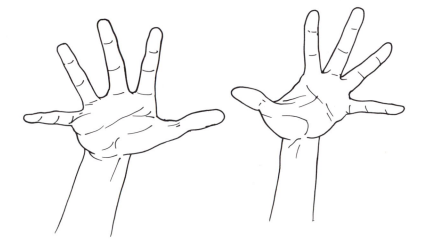

- Begin the block from a stationary position when possible—this is especially applicable to outside blockers (see Figure 6-5).
- When preparing to block, carry the hands high (see Figure 6-6).
- Place the hands on the ball, surrounding it; do not "swing" at the ball (see Figure 6-7).

Fig. 6-7

Fig. 6-5

Execution of the Block

Correct technique is essential to providing an effective block. Even if your players have not yet developed their jumping abilities, refining these basics will improve their attempts at blocking.

Preparation (The Ready Position)

To be ready to block, players should stand with feet side by side, shoulder-width apart. Body weight is shifted slightly onto the foot opposite the predicted direction of movement (see Figure 6-8). The player should

Fig. 6-6

Fig. 6-8

recognize the most probable offensive option as the circumstances unfold and shift accordingly.

The *legs* are flexed slightly at the knees, ready for movement. The *back* is straight, titled slightly forward toward the net. The *hands*, fingers spread, are held in front of the shoulders. The *head* is up; the *eyes* should be focused on the ball as it comes into the opponent setter's hands.

The blockers in the ready position have taken position within a half meter of the net in their respective tactical starting positions. Three basic footwork patterns can initiate a block. To move along the net, players can employ a combination of the patterns or use them individually.

Two-Step

A two-step move is designed to cover 1 to 2 meters. The blocker steps as far as needed with the foot nearest the direction of travel to front the hitter, pushing off the opposite foot. The opposite foot closes with the lead foot. The toes are pointed toward the net during the movement. At the end of the movement, the feet are closer together than in the ready position. It looks like a lateral hop (see Figure 6-9). The key is: *Body weight must be inside the lead foot.* The pelvis and shoulders remain parallel to the net during the movement. The hands are held above the head, in front of the shoulders.

Three-Step

The three-step move is used primarily by middle blockers to cover greater distances (2 to 4-1/2 meters) with control. In this footwork pattern, the blocker pushes off the foot opposite the direction of movement, with the lead toe pointing in the direction of movement. The trailing foot crosses in front of the lead foot, and the toe is planted pointing at the net. The lead foot swings around behind the trailing foot, lining up side by side, toe pointing at the net (see Figure 6-10). The shoulders and pelvis should be parallel to the net in the final position. The hands are carried above the head and in front of the shoulders. Body weight must be inside the lead foot in the final position to insure body control.

Two-Step Cross Step

The two-step cross step is another technique for blockers to use in moving into position. It is not difficult but is specific to the tactical concept of *stack* blocking. As such, the technique will be described in more advanced levels of *Coaching Volleyball Successfully*.

Precontact and Contact

At the completion of any footwork pattern the blocker should be fronting the hitter. Spikers at any level tend to hit in the direction of their approach approximately 80% of the time. For example, a spiker most often

Fig. 6-9

Fig. 6-10

approaches the point of contact at an angle from outside the court toward the opponent's court. This is commonly referred to as the cross-court angle. The spiker usually hits the ball in his or her direction of travel. Therefore, to eliminate as many decisions as possible, the blocker should front the hitter in the cross-court angle to be prepared to deal with the most likely attack.

In the precontact position, the feet are side by side. It is acceptable to have the outside foot slightly closer to the net; however, it is not acceptable to have it any further away. Such a position will naturally cause the player to open up to the incoming attacker, creating a rebound angle that will carry the ball out of bounds. The blocker needs to face the middle of the opponent's court above the net. The ability to assume this position begins with a good foot plant (see Figure 6-11).

Fig. 6-11

The hands drop only to shoulder level in coiling for the jump. It is preferable to keep the hands as high as possible to simplify timing. The more the blocker moves the arms, the more timing is required to contact the ball.

Block position is more important than height of the block jump. As shown in Figure 6-12, the ball seldom crosses the net as high as the spiker contacts the ball; rather, the ball travels downward over the net. Therefore, the blockers do not need to jump as high as the spiker. The blockers must certainly jump high enough to touch the ball, but keeping the hands high during the jump and getting them over the net as soon as possible in good position is more important than having a high jump.

Timing the jump is a significant factor in a successful block. A general rule of thumb is that the blockers should begin to jump when the spiker's hand crosses in front of his or her face during the ascent. This applies when the hitter is contacting the ball within a meter of the net. If the spiker is further than a meter from the net, the blocker should jump as the spiker's hitting arm is being swung toward the ball. Blockers need to make timing adjustments based on the distance from the net at which the ball is being hit.

Each blocker must watch the ball pass from the serve receiver to the setter and must "read" the setter's intentions by understanding the prevailing circumstances and watching the setter set the ball. The blocker watches the ball rise to its peak and makes appropriate positional adjustments. The blocker then focuses on the approaching attacker, keeping the ball within his or her peripheral vision. The blocker should *never* lose sight of the ball but must switch focus to the attacker.

As the spiker's hand crosses his or her face, the blocker jumps vertically, high enough to surround the ball with his or her hands on the opponent's side of the net. The hands are open, trying to catch the ball. There is no waving of the arms or hands. The hands should go after the ball on the other side of the net, trying to smother it as quickly and efficiently as possible. The

Fig. 6-12

shoulders are extended upward, following the arms. There should be no gap between the blocker's arms and the net. The arms should be extended, reaching across the net but not touching it. The angle of deflection is modified by turning the hands toward the middle of the opponent's court. The blocker should see the spiker's contact of the ball and direct the ball back into the spiker's court.

Follow-Through

If the arms going after the ball are controlled, with no flailing, waving, or groping, then the contact or lack of contact will govern the follow-through. The key is to eliminate extra movements by taking an appropriate position in front of the hitter. Place the hands around the ball and extend the shoulders, arms, and hands at the ball simply, quickly, and in straight lines. Block the ball on the opponent's side of the net.

Multiple Blocking

When more than one player is involved in blocking, the problems can multiply. But so can the positive results! You must evaluate the trade-offs between the potency of the opponent's attack and the abilities of your own players. Take inventory of your team's blocking results over a series of matches to determine the value of the blocking scheme you have chosen. The first step has been covered here—the mechanics used in one-on-one blocking. Multiple blocking uses the same mechanics in a coordinated effort. Details of multiple blocking are covered in the Coaching Accreditation Program Level II.

Coaching Points

1. When teaching blocking, be aware of the importance of giving your players positive feedback for good effort and mechanics. It is important that players understand their attempts are correct even though the ultimate goal (a stuff block) may be rare.

2. Alert players that all three functions of blocking (described on page 66) are very important. Too often coaches and players alike view stuffs as the only blocking success.

3. As you lead teaching activities for blocking, remember to help players recognize the situations in which attempting to block would not be beneficial (e.g., a ball set too low, too wide, or too deep; a spiker who is in poor position; etc.).

4. Use teaching keys:

   - Hold hands high
   - Front the hitter
   - Keep eyes open
   - Surround the ball with the hands
   - Press the ball to the middle of the opponent's court

Teaching Progression

1. Demonstrate blocking from a stationary position. Have someone stand on a solid, well-constructed table or box on the other side of the net, simulating an attacker. The person on the box tosses and hits in a predetermined direction. The blocker jumps and blocks. Have the players focus on the hands held high, fronting the hitter. (2 to 3 minutes)

2. Players now block against hitters on boxes. Have them focus on hands held high and fronting the hitter. (6 minutes)

3. Players return. Have them review the first two keys. Again demonstrate blocking. Have players move so they can see how the blocker keeps his or her eyes open throughout the block. (2 minutes)

4. Players again block against hitters on boxes. Have them concentrate on keeping the eyes open. (6 minutes)

5. Players return and review the first three keys. Demonstrate blocking again. Have the players focus on the hands surrounding the ball and on

directing the ball to the middle of the opponent's court. (6 to 8 minutes)

6. Players again practice blocking against hitters on boxes, focusing on surrounding the ball with the hands and directing it to the middle of the court. (6 to 8 minutes)

7. Players return and review the five keys. Demonstrate blocking with the two-step move against the hitter on the box. Make sure to demonstrate movement in both directions. Notice that at the end of the move the blocker is fronting the hitter. (2 minutes)

8. Players practice blocking with a two-step move against the stationary hitter on the box. (6 to 8 minutes)

9. Players return and review the five keys and the two-step move. Demonstrate blocking again. This time use a setter and a regular hitter approaching and jumping. The players focus on reading the setter, watching the ball to its peak, and moving to front the hitter with a two-step move. (3 minutes)

10. Have your players work against a setter and a hitter, focusing on reading the setter and using a two-step move to front the hitter and block. (6 to 8 minutes)

11. If you want to teach the three-step move, use Steps 9 and 10. When incorporating the footwork patterns, make sure your players work in both directions.

12. Involve blocking in as many spiking drills as possible.

Blocking Functions

There are three functions of blocking: stuffing the ball, controlling the ball, and taking a zone. In addition, a well-formed block can force the spiker to tip into the waiting forearms of a back-court defender or smack the ball out of bounds in an effort to prevent the stuff.

A *stuff block* is a *terminal play* in that the ball is blocked back to the attacker's floor.

Such a block results in a direct point if the blocking team has served. A side-out is scored if the blocking team received the serve. Also, a stuff block can cause the momentum of the game to swing in the blocking team's favor.

A *control block* is sometimes called a "soft block." Philosophically, I do not like the term soft block because it implies passive behavior. Blocking in any function is not passive. A control block deflects the ball up and into the blocking team's back row so it can be controlled and converted into an offensive play. A control block is an *intermediate contact*.

A *zone back* forces a spiker to hit the ball in a direction the blocking team desires. If the blockers block cross-court, the spiker must hit down the line to avoid contact. Zone blocking is a function but is also a result of the blockers predicting a spiker's most likely attack angle and trying to stuff the ball. In other words, when the blockers correctly position themselves and attempt to stuff the ball, they create a zone behind the block that cannot be effectively attacked. As a result, the spiker must hit around the blocks to avoid being stuffed. The back-row defenders can then take positions in areas or zones that the attackers can hit. The area of the court behind the block that is protected by the blockers is known as the *block shadow*.

Tactical Applications

Along with the attack patterns found in a team offense, blocking offers the greatest tactical opportunities in volleyball. The tactics are inherent in the blocking functions. For example, a stuff block is usually the result of getting the best blocker in front of the spiker most likely to attack in the particular situation. A control block is the result when a player selects the correct position and timing in a given situation regardless of his or her physical assets and liabilities. A consistent, well-formed block creates zones that the back-row defenders can play with little guesswork. The goals of the block as the first line of defense are to neutralize the opponent's "big guns" (the spikers); to make back-row defensive play easier by limiting the area in which the opponent can attack; and to distract the opponent's setter, forcing him or her to make uncomfortable set selections in an attempt to avoid the block.

As offenses become more sophisticated, so do blocking tactics. In the beginning it is most important to execute the basics, to learn the discipline good blocking requires. The most important tactic in beginning blocking is knowing when *not* to block.

Blocking Pitfalls

The problems blockers can get into often outweigh the benefits. You must consider these common problems before deciding to employ blocking as a major component of your overall playing scheme.

The opponent's poor ball handling results in a shanked serve reception. The setter runs down the errant pass and then delivers a low, deep set to a spiker who has crept too close to the net and has no chance at a decent swing. The hitter launches the ball into the rafters. The block forms and jumps, raking the net on the way up. Even though they ricocheted the ball off the gym ceiling,

the opponents win the play because the block touched the net.

The opponent's spiker is out of position while attempting to swing at the ball. The block jumps. The spiker fluffs the ball, contacting it with so little force that it barely makes it to the net. The block touches it and the ball drifts out of bounds. Point, opponent.

The block, while attempting to stop a hard-driven ball, reaches out toward the in-coming spiker. The block drifts beyond the attack angle and the spiker cracks the ball down easily to the court side of the block. Because the block did not jump up and down, but rather faded laterally, the back-row players had no idea of where to line up. Point, opponent.

The blocking team has a couple of players who, due to their short physical stature and minimal leaping ability, cannot get their first knuckles above the net. Nevertheless, they are expected to block. The only real blocking they do is getting in the way of the back-row defenders' line of sight and restricting the movements of taller teammates.

These are common situations that involve blocking. A wise coach must carefully analyze the value of the block for his or her team and weigh it against the potential disadvantages.

Tactical Principles

- Know the opponent's favorite shot and front it.
- When blocking one-on-one, block cross-court.
- Block outside in, toward the center of the opponent's court.
- Put your best blocker on the spiker most likely to hit in any given situation.
- Go for the stuff. Control and zone blocks will occur naturally.

In beginning levels of play, blocking is more often a hindrance than a help. In advanced levels of play, blocking is one of the most significant factors in winning.

Drills and Activities for Blocking

The two- and three-step blocking moves can be incorporated into warm-ups each day. Have the players move along the net in both directions and practice blocking movements instead of just jogging. Make sure they aren't sloppy but are efficient and balanced every time.

(6.1) Ball Over the Head

Purpose. To make positional and timing adjustments as a situation unfolds; to practice seeing all the elements in a blocking situation

Classification. Coach-centered

Category. Crisis

Equipment. Full-court setup with a container of balls

Personnel. Four or more players and a coach

Description. The coach with the container of balls is positioned on the same side of the net as the blocker(s). Place the remaining players in a hitting line on the other side of the net (see Figure 6-13). The coach lobs a ball up and over but close to the net for the hitter to spike. The blocker(s) adjust when they first see the ball and front the hitter, trying to stuff the ball. The blockers rotate at the coach's discretion.

Measurement. The blocker(s) must score a specified number of points to complete the drill. Points are awarded in this manner:

- Stuff = 3 points
- Control = 2 points
- Hitter error = 1 point
- Blocker error = 1 point

(6.2) Jousting

Purpose. To work on controlling a ball close to the top of the net and making the transition to offense

Classification. Coach-initiated

Category. Flow-of-play

Equipment. A full-court setup and container of balls

Fig. 6-13

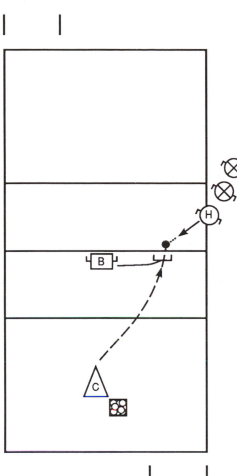

Personnel. Six or more players and a coach

Description. Place three players on each side of the net; two serve as blockers and the third is a cover. The coach tosses the ball with a two-hand underhand motion so that it comes down on top of the net between the opposing blockers. The blockers try to stuff or control the ball. Play continues to its natural conclusion (see Figure 6-14). This drill can also be played with full teams. Players are rotated at the coach's discretion. The back-row players assume the responsibilities required in each situation.

Measurement. Success is measured by a team achieving a specified number of successful plays.

(6.3) Blocking Pin to Pin

Purpose. To develop middle blockers' movement skills and outside blockers' skills to front the hitter

Classification. Coach-centered or coach-initiated

Category. Crisis

Equipment. Full-court setup and a container of balls

Personnel. 10 to 12 players and one coach

Description. Place three blockers on one side of the net. Arrange the remaining players in two hitting lines with a setter on the other side. Either a coach or a passer

Fig. 6-14

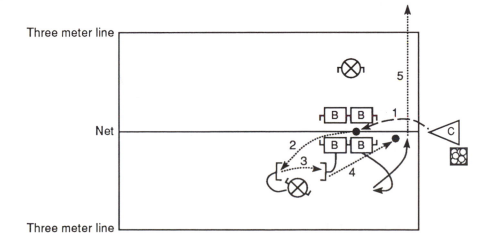

should set up on the side with the hitters and the setter (see Figure 6-15). The setter receives the ball from the coach or passer and sets to either spiker. The blockers react accordingly. A full defensive team can be used and transition can occur naturally. However, using a full defensive team will limit the number of blocks in which each team member is involved. The coach tosses the next ball as soon as the previous play is terminated. Players rotate at the coach's discretion once the specified score is attained.

Measurement.   Blockers must score a specified number of points. Points are scored as follows:

- Stuff = 3 points
- Control = 2 points
- Hitter error = 1 point
- Blocker error = 1 point

(6.4) Block Transition Hit

Purpose.   To develop transitional moves from blocker to hitter to blocker

Classification.   Coach-centered

Category.   Flow-of-play

Equipment.   A full-court setup with two containers of balls

Personnel.   Four to eight players and two coaches

Description.   Arrange each side of the court with a setter, one or two blocker-spikers, and a coach or passer. To begin, a ball is tossed or passed to the setter on court A, who sets to the hitter who hits against the block. As soon as the ball is dead, the coach or passer on court B passes a new ball to the court B setter who sets the transitioning blocker/hitter, who attacks. It continues back and forth until one side wins (see Figure 6-16).

Fig. 6-15

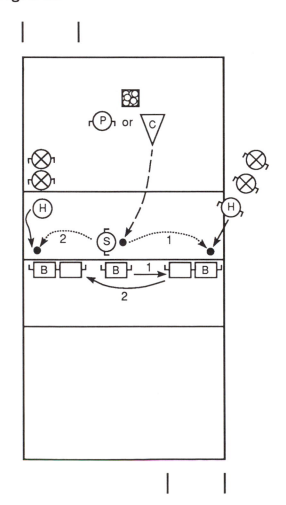

Fig. 6-16

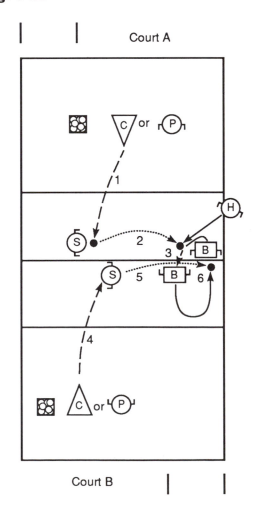

As blockers improve, have two blocker/hitters active on each side of the net.

Measurement.   The total points scored determines the winner. Points are awarded in the following manner:

- Killed spike = 1 point

- Stuff block = 3 points
- Control block = 2 points
- Spiker error = −1 point for spiking team
- Blocker error = −1 point for blocking team

Chapter 7:
Floor Defense

Floor defense is the great equalizer in volleyball. To play good floor defense, the player can be either tall or short, does not have to jump high, does not have to have big hands. It does help to be quick and to have excellent eye-hand coordination. The ingredient required to make a great defensive player is a big heart loaded with determination and saturated with the need for keeping the ball off the floor. A good defensive player is intense, determined, focused, courageous, and technically skilled.

Defense allows the athlete to develop those physical elements he or she can control. Players can't train to increase their height or the length of their arms. But players *can* control and develop *attitude*. Attitude governs the success of a defensive player. Coaches must continually reinforce with word and deed the attitude of relentless pursuit. Drills must be designed to develop the players' attitude.

In volleyball, great defense leads to great points. Even though a defensive play is an intermediate contact, it disrupts the opponent's attempt at a terminal attack and gives the defensive team a chance to counterattack.

Functions

The bottom line for the functional defense is keeping the ball from touching the floor on the defensive side. The specific functions of floor defense include digging hard-hit shots and recovering deflections, tips, and soft shots.

Using a modified version of the forearm technique, the defender must be able to control direct blasts from the opposing spiker. Any ball that ricochets off the block or any other teammate must be kept in play. Any shot that is softly touched and is falling into an open space requires a specific defensive recovery technique to keep the play alive. These are critical plays in any defensive scheme, even though they appear to be less dramatic than the retrieval of a hard-driven shot.

General Principles

- Use the simplest technique required to make the play.
- Stay on the feet if possible.
- Use both hands and arms if possible.
- Keep the ball between the body and the center of the court.

Tactical Principles

- Put the best defenders in the areas most often attacked.
- Place defenders in positions where they can play the ball toward their own court. This is referred to as an *on-help* position.

- The block has back-court responsibility. By virtue of its position, the block eliminates areas of the court for possible attack. Play as many back-row defenders as possible around the block so they have a direct line to the ball.
- Dig the ball as high as possible in the middle of the court.

The Sequence of an Individual Defensive Play

1. The player *establishes floor position* as the ball is set and the block forms.
2. The defensive player establishes *body position*.
3. The opponent's spiker *hits the ball*.
4. The defensive player *retrieves the ball*.

Three defensive activities occur before the fourth and final defensive act. To adjust tactically, therefore, a player must develop skills of analysis to accurately determine where the ball is going to be hit.

Execution

Floor defense is the most spontaneous of the volleyball skills. Each play requires a variation of posture, contact surface, follow-through, and target. Defense is a reactive skill. The opponents are trying to make the attempted retrieval of their attack as difficult as possible. Therefore, as you analyze the components of execution, keep in mind the myriad of possibilities.

Preparation (The Defensive Ready Position)

The ready position described here is specific to defensive play, as opposed to the general ready position a player assumes prior to any ball-handling skill.

Just before the opposing spiker makes contact with the ball, the defender establishes floor position by determining the limited area where the ball can be hit. As the ball is struck, the defender is stationary. The

feet are wide. The knees are inside and in front of the big toes. The hips are level with the knees. The face is in front of the knees. The arms are bent at the elbows and near the thighs. The hands are close together but not attached; they are inside and in front of the knees. The hands are relaxed but ready to be put into the required position. The eyes are on the opponent's hand hitting the ball. The defender is on the balls of his or her feet, lightly bouncing, and ready to make the necessary adjustments (see Figure 7-1). The body weight is such that if all balancing movement stopped, the defender would fall forward on his or her face. The key to this position is that the defender should be leaning into the attack but not rushing it.

Fig. 7-1

On-Help Position

The defender's desired position is facing his or her teammates; this is known as *on help*. To assume this position, a cross-court defender should point the toes across the court with the torso twisted at the waist toward the attacker (see Figure 7-2). When the ball arrives at the defender, the defender will react by twisting back over the toes toward the middle of the court. A player facing directly toward the incoming hard-hit shot tends to dig the ball back over the net. The goal of a good defensive play is to control the ball on your side of the net so your team can go on the attack.

The defensive player playing down the line, known as the line digger, should have

Fig. 7-2

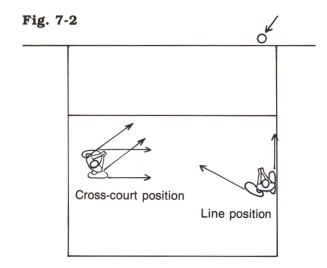

Cross-court position

Line position

his or her outside foot on the line and the inside foot slightly back so the player can dig a direct shot into the middle of his or her court. This position also prevents the defender from having to move to a play on the line side of the body. The player simply plays the ball in front of and inside his or her starting position (see Figure 7-2 for an illustration of the two on-help positions).

The *middle-back* defender does face the attacker directly. This player has not only the bulk of the court between him or her and the net, but his or her teammates as well; therefore, the middle-back player is on help.

Movement to Contact

This is where floor defense can get complicated. Each situation requires slightly different movements. Further, the movements are reactive. The player must adjust immediately as the spiker contacts the ball.

Ideally, the defender is in a position where the ball is hit directly at him or her. The defender's movement involves adjusting the rebound angle of the forearms and how much force the defender needs to apply to pass the ball with control. Any ball hit outside the defender's body line requires a foot adjustment at the very least, and occasionally a complete realignment of posture.

Retrieval Skills

Several skills are used to keep the ball in play defensively. Each skill and its move-

ments are described in the next few pages. Although these skills are described as one-handed contacts, players may use two arms or hands if time allows them to be moved into position.

The Dig

Little footwork is required in digging the ball. The ball is contacted in front of the body on the forearms. The body's angles are modified based on the velocity of the ball. If the ball is coming at the approximate velocity of a serve, then the player uses a normal forearm pass technique. With a hard-hit shot or one with topspin, more cushioning is needed. This can be accomplished by allowing the ball to drive the arms toward the body. Turning the thumbs up and bending the arms at the elbows to absorb the topspin and deflect the ball up is called the *J stroke* (see Figure 7-3). The ball should be played close to the floor to compensate for the its trajectory and velocity. The higher the velocity of the ball, the less movement through the ball is required.

Fig. 7-3

The Collapse

A hard-hit ball within 1.5 meters to the defender's left or right can be played using a collapse. The digger gets his or her body in front of the incoming ball. The ball is contacted on the forearms between the knees. The arms are in the J stroke position and provide as much force as necessary to get the ball high and to the target.

Fig. 7-4

As forearm contact is being made, the defender sits back over the heel of the leading leg. The leading leg's knee is pointed toward the target. The knee should remain up throughout the movement, never touching the floor. The defender should rotate around the lead foot and end up facing the target (see Figure 7-4). The follow-through is a natural rocking back after sitting down. The player returns to his or her feet as quickly as possible.

Low Posture Techniques

The purpose of the low posture techniques—the extension roll, the sprawl, and the dive—is to allow the defender to pursue a ball as close to the floor as possible without hitting any of the corners of the body: that is, toes, heels, ankles, knees, hips, shoulders, elbows, or head. Although the techniques are described for one arm or hand, players can use both arms.

The Extension Roll

The extension roll best illustrates a way to go after a ball and recover without "sanding" any of the body's corners. The ball is usually played with one hand, outside the body line. It is usually used to play deflected or slow-moving balls. There are many exceptions to this guideline, however, so I stress the word "usually" to indicate the highest percentage application.

Hold the contact hand like a maestro holds his or her baton to conduct an orchestra (see Figure 7-5). The ball is contacted on the heel

of the hand and closed fingers. This allows for the wrist and elbow levers to function as needed.

Fig. 7-5

The ball is played close to the floor primarily because the defender has to stretch out quickly to get to the descending ball. The foot on the side of the contact hand reaches out toward the point of contact. The position the defender assumes just before playing the ball looks similar to that of a fencer in the thrusting position. However, the volleyball player is closer to the floor. The player's eyes are on the ball. The hand contacts the ball and follows through toward the target. In turn, the body follows in a twisting motion. The momentum carries both legs in tuck position over the opposite shoulder and onto the feet. The defender should tuck the chin during the twist to avoid hitting the head on the floor. The knees should never hit the floor (see Figure 7-6). The roll described here is similar to a shoulder roll in judo. A barrel roll or a corkscrew roll can also be used.

The Sprawl

The sprawl is an extension roll without the roll and is used as a quick reaction to a tip

Fig. 7-6

over the block or a surprise deflection, when there is no time for stepping into position. As a result, the range of the sprawl is limited to the length of the player's body. The sprawl is easiest going forward, difficult laterally, and virtually impossible backward.

In the sprawl, the player falls to the floor as quickly as possible to get a hand under the ball. The contact hand extends out, palm down. The ball is played on the back of the hand. There is little time for any flexion in the wrist or elbow. Because of its flat appearance, this hand position is commonly re-

ferred to as the *pancake.* The sprawl with a pancake is illustrated in Figure 7-7. The ball simply bounces off the hand instead of the floor. The leg on the opposite side of the contact hand is tucked up and out and the other leg is extended. The player appears to be in a military low crawl position, as if scurrying under barbed wire. The eyes are on the ball.

The Dive

Research has determined that diving is the quickest way to get to a ball a considerable

Fig. 7-7

distance away. The extension roll is effective within 3 to 4 meters; the sprawl, within a body length. The dive's range is limited only by the player's quickness, strength, and desire. Further, it is effective in any direction. The dive can be initiated from a ready position, or it can be the extension of an all-out sprint. It allows for play close to the floor and quick recovery, and when executed properly, it is safe and efficient.

At first glance, the dive looks dangerous. It can be if the player is not strong enough or if the dive is launched from a high posture. Coaches can assist players in attempting this and other emergency retrieval skills by teaching and practicing skills at controllable speeds. That means starting with easy hits in planned locations to avoid injury and fear of injury.

The dive is an extension of a sprinting action toward the ball. The player takes off over the lead foot (opposite the contacting hand). The chest virtually touches the thigh. The hand should be held like a maestro holds a baton; the contact surface is the same as in the extension roll. Closely study the dive sequence illustrated in Figure 7-8.

The player gets the hand between the floor and the ball and thrusts up through the ball from the shoulder, using the levers of the wrist and elbows as needed to get the ball into the air. Both feet are off the floor at the moment the ball is contacted. During flight, the foot on the same side as the contact hand is higher than the head. The opposite leg is straight out, the back is arched, the head is up, and the eyes are on the ball.

The movement of the hand through the ball naturally arches the back. The non-contact hand is palm down on the floor. The body touches down on the lower chest just above the diaphragm. The player slides on the abdomen. The feet remain up until the slide stops, at which point the player gets back up on his or her feet and assumes the ready position again. Should the need arise, the player can contact the ball on the back of the hand as in the sprawl. The maestro position, however, is best for directing the ball accurately.

Be on the lookout for several common dive errors. If you notice any of the following tendencies in your players, work quickly to correct them:

- Players learning to dive sometimes try to stop their forward motion and let themselves down. This technique is known as a *dive and catch*. It doesn't work, nor does it feel very good. The shoulder joints are jolted and the toes bang the floor. The hands should be guides through which the arched body slides.

- Tall players especially like to keep one foot on the ground. They often bring one foot up correctly but drag the other (dropping anchor). This tendency negates the quickness and range of the dive. Some players drop to the floor

Fig. 7-8

with a knee under the stomach. This is not a pleasant experience. In addition, it completely stops any movement toward the ball.
- Still other players, using both hands to contact the floor, complete a *tripod* with the chin. This is painful. Keep the chin and head up, arching the back.

Special Contacts

You must put your players in situations where they have to react. Playing the ball in front of the face with the hands cupped facing the incoming ball, punching a ball out of the net with one hand using the maestro position, and punching the ball upward with the heel of the hand above the head in tight quarters are situations common in volleyball and ones with which players must become comfortable.

The defender never knows what velocity or angle the ball will take and therefore must be prepared to deal with the ball on its own terms. The contact need not be pretty, just effective. The defender must be able to control the ball with every legal contact surface. Although using the face is legal, I do not recommend it as a control surface.

The *knuckler*, a term popularized by Chris Marlowe, captain of the 1984 USA Olympic men's volleyball team, is an overhand technique played in front of the face or above the head when there is no time for a more sophisticated technique. The object is to punch the ball up in the air for a teammate to set (see Figure 7-9).

The *reverse bump* is a two-handed version of the knuckler used when a ball is blasted at the face at short range. The ball is contacted on the little fingers–side of the hands and the arms in front of the face (see Figure 7-10). The object, again, is to get the ball up where a teammate can set it. The rebound angle must be modified to get the ball up by collapsing backward.

Fig. 7-9

Fig. 7-10

A Final Note

Defenders should be taught all the defensive variations. Ideally, they should be able to use the specific technique best suited to any situation that arises. Good defensive players keep the ball from hitting the floor in their assigned area using any technique necessary. Further, they assist teammates in running down deflected balls outside the court. No ball is impossible to play until a maximum effort has been made to retrieve it. No judgment should be made before effort is expended. Great defensive players never, ever give up. Coaches have to teach techniques to the players so their zealous efforts can continue without injury.

Coaching Points for Retrieval Skills

1. When teaching any defensive skill, reinforce the "never quit" attitude. Establish the rule in every drill that a player who does not try for a ball must start the drill over. Maximum effort must become a habit.
2. Remember: As players learn the emergency retrieval skills of diving, rolling, collapsing, and sprawling, they must proceed only as fast as they can control. As their proficiency grows, their execution becomes quicker and more confident.
3. When you teach defensive techniques, always remind players to try to anticipate where the ball is going by reading the opponent's attack situation and the spiker's body language.
4. Use these teaching keys:
   • Get low
   • Stop and lean toward the ball
   • Modify the rebound angle
   • Keep the ball between you and the net

Teaching Progressions for Retrieval Skills

Teach these skills in order, moving progressively closer to the floor. To practice each skill effectively, you must introduce hitting a ball as soon as possible. Use two-hand underhand tosses to put the ball in play.

Players should use emergency skills *only* when normal retrieval skills will not allow an effective play. Therefore, it is critical that your tosses stretch a player's range and simulate actual playing situations as closely as possible.

Remember to move your players in all directions as they learn these skills. And, as with any skill, begin using game-related activities as early in the learning process as possible.

Teaching Progression for the Dig

1. Demonstrate digging a hard-hit ball. Have someone who has good spiking control hit the balls. Have the players focus on getting low, stopping, and leaning toward the ball. (3 minutes)
2. Players practice the dig. One at a time, each player assumes a defensive posture and digs a ball hit by the person running the drill. Each player in turn attempts a dig until the coach calls players back. (8 minutes)
3. Have the players review getting low and leaning toward the ball. Again demonstrate digging. This time have players focus on modifying the rebound angle by using the J stroke. Note that this keeps the ball between the player and the net. (2 minutes)
4. Players practice again. Have the players focus on modifying the rebound angle with a J stroke. Their goal is to keep the ball between them and the net. (8 minutes)
5. Have the players review the four keys of digging: Demonstrate the emerging skills of collapsing, rolling, sprawling, and diving. (3 minutes)

Teaching Progression for the Collapse

1. Demonstrate the collapse. Have an assistant toss the ball 1-1/2 meters to either side of the demonstrator. Use the collapse with the J stroke to play the ball. Next, have a spiker or tosser hit the ball 1-1/2 meters to either side. Again use the collapse with the J stroke to retrieve the ball. Have players focus on staying low and avoiding hitting the knees, elbows, or head on the floor. (3 minutes)
2. Have players practice the collapse dig, first from a toss, then from a spike. (6 to 8 minutes)
3. Have the players review staying low and avoiding the corners of the body. Demonstrate the collapse dig again. Have the players focus on the J stroke and on playing the ball in front of the body between the knees. Highlight

the idea of recovering quickly to the feet after the dig. (2 minutes)
4. Have your players practice the collapse dig, focusing on playing the ball between the knees and recovering to their feet. (6 to 8 minutes)
5. Players return and review the key points of the collapse dig. (3 minutes)

Teaching Progression for the Extension Roll

1. Demonstrate the roll by playing balls tossed to each side, to the front, and to the back, 3 meters from your starting point. Have players focus on staying low throughout the movement. Note that the hand is held like a maestro holds a baton. (2 to 3 minutes)
2. Have players practice the roll in all directions. Stress that they should attempt the roll only as fast as they can control their movement. Do not use a ball, but rather have them visualize the retrieval and extend their "maestro" hands to the imagined point of contact. (8 minutes)
3. The players return and review the points of staying low and proper hand position. Demonstrate the roll again. Have the players focus on avoiding the corners of the body. (2 minutes)
4. Players practice again without a tossed ball. Have them focus on performing a "quiet" roll; that is, one that lacks the noisy crunching of the corners of the body hitting the floor. (6 to 8 minutes)
5. Players return. Have players review the points of avoiding the corners of the body. Demonstrate the roll again. Have the players focus on playing the ball and recovery. Make sure to practice the roll in all directions and to show the importance of being able to use the hand on the side where the ball is being played. (2 minutes)
6. Have the players roll, retrieving the tossed ball and focusing on contact with the maestro hand. Their objective is to hit the ball high into the air

and between them and the net. (6 to 8 minutes)

7. Players return. Have them review the key points of both the dig and the extension roll. (3 minutes)

Teaching Progression for the Sprawl

1. Demonstrate the sprawl, first without a ball and then with one. Have players focus on staying low in the ready position and on the movement pattern. Emphasize the sprawl's function. (2 minutes)

2. Have players practice the sprawl without a ball. (1 minute)

3. Players return. Have players review the key of staying low. Demonstrate the sprawl, retrieving a tossed ball. Have the players focus on the mechanics of the two types of contact: the "pancake" and the two-forearm contact. (2 minutes)

4. Have players practice the sprawl with both techniques of contact. (6 to 8 minutes)

5. Players return. Have them review the keys of sprawling, including staying low, avoiding the corners of the body, and playing the ball. (3 minutes)

Teaching Progression for the Dive

1. Demonstrate the dive without the ball. Have the players focus on staying low and avoiding the corners of the body—specifically the chin. Note that the technique is a *dive and slide*, not a *dive and catch*. (3 minutes)

2. Have the players try the dive through the following sequence. Allow 10 minutes for this activity:

   - Players start on both knees. Each player should locate a spot on the floor in front of him- or herself. The player extends for the selected spot, arching the back and keeping the heels up, with knees bent and chin up. The player slides, slightly.
   - The player kneels on one knee. Identifying a spot on the floor further out, the player rocks over the

"up" knee, touches the abdomen to the upper leg, and dives. As the hands reach the spot, both heels come up, and the back is arched. The player then slides, first contacting the floor with the hands, then with the diaphragm.

   - The player assumes a defensive ready position. He or she identifies a spot on the floor. *Staying low*, the player dives for the spot and slides through.
   - From a defensive ready position, the player takes steps to all points of the compass and dives off a sprint as fast as can be controlled.

3. Players return. Have them review the keys of staying low and avoiding the corners of the body. Demonstrate diving and retrieving a tossed ball. Have the players focus on playing the ball and recovering. Use both one- and two-hand techniques. Point out the importance of getting the ball high between the player and the net. (2 minutes)

4. Have players follow the sequence described in Step 2, but this time include a ball. Have them focus on playing the ball with one and two hands and getting the ball high. (10 minutes)

5. Players return. Have them review the key points of diving. (2 minutes)

6. Go to drills.

Tactical Applications

Individual tactical applications are limited by the team defensive system, which assigns specific areas of coverage. The player can adjust and move within his or her assigned area. The adjustments are triggered by the situation as it unfolds—the location of the opponent's set, the spiker's known abilities and habits, and the position and formation of the block.

At the risk of being redundant, successful floor defense is based on an attitude of tenacious determination. The level of intensity observed in a team's floor defense defines the team's personality.

Drills and Activities for Defensive Skills

Incorporate defensive drills with other skills. It is important to model floor defense as the part of the game that creates the opportunity to score.

As in the other volleyball skill categories, defensive skills can be divided into mechanics work and tactical applications. Floor defense skills have the potential to cause injury because the players make contact with the floor in their all-out effort to control the ball. Often, a player's enthusiasm to retrieve the ball overrides his or her physical ability to do so. You must carefully assess your athletes' physical ability to play defense before demanding maximum pursuit. That is why most defensive drills are coach-centered. The coach can control the tempo and range of the activity. Be demanding, but be careful.

(7.1) Juggling

Purpose.   To become familiar with contact; to control the ball with a "maestro's baton hand" on the ball

Classification.   Player-centered

Category.   Teaching

Equipment.   One ball per player, or one ball per two players

Personnel.   One or more players and a coach

Description.   Players alternate one-handed contacts above the head and below the waist, using both hands. Contact should be on the palm side of the hand; the hand is held like a maestro holds a baton. This exercise can be done many ways: individually or in pairs; alternating hands; alternating overhead and below-the-waist contact in a predesigned sequence; or the ball can be thrown into the net by one player, and the partner must retrieve the ball and get it in the air for a hitter. Use your imagination. The drill begins with a toss either into the net or within a short distance of a player.

Measurement.   Use specified time blocks, total number of contacts, or a competition to see which player can go the longest without an error.

(7.2) Pepper

Purpose.   To practice control of defensive skills

Classification.   Player-centered

Category.   Rapid-fire

Equipment.   One ball per two players

Personnel.   At least two players

Directions.   Two players face each other 3 to 4 meters apart. One player tosses to him- or herself and hits the ball at the partner's head. The partner, in a defensive ready position, takes the ball overhead, sets the ball to him- or herself, and hits back to the first player.

Measurement.   Play continues for as long as the two players maintain control. All balls should be handled overhead.

Variations.

Control Pepper.   Two players face each other 3 to 5 meters apart. Action begins with Player A setting the ball to Player B. B hits the ball back to A, who has assumed a defensive posture. Using whichever defensive technique is required, A digs back to B. B then sets back to A, who spikes back to B. Play continues for as long as the players can control it.

Repeat Pepper.   This variation is similar to Control Pepper, except one player continues to hit at the other. If possible, the spiking player directly hits the controlled dig from the defender. However, if the ball is not hittable, the spiker works with the other player until control is gained. After either a specified number of attempts or a preset time block, the players change roles.

(7.3) Coach On a Box

Purpose.   To duplicate defensive situations

Classification.   Coach-centered

Category.   Teaching/Crisis/Flow-of-play

Equipment.   Full-court setup; a container of balls; a sturdy box or table

Personnel.   Any number of players, preferably in groups of three, and one coach

Description. Many drills can be run from this setup. Basically, the coach stands on a box on one side of the net. Players are put in defensive positions (including blockers, if desired, as shown in Figure 7-11). The coach hits or throws a ball at the defensive players, duplicating situations he or she wants practiced. Groups change once the defensive group attains a specified goal.

Measurement. Use a specified number of successful repetitions to measure goal attainment.

Fig. 7-11

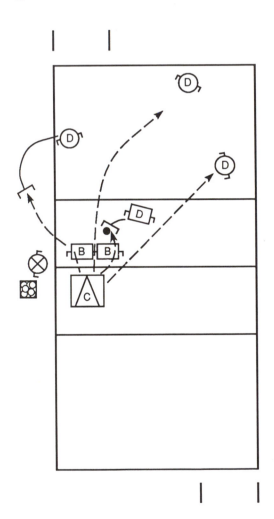

(7.4) VIs

Purpose. To teach relentless pursuit of the ball; to develop a feeling of responsibility to teammates

Classification. Coach-centered

Category. Crisis

Equipment. A container of balls and a regular net setup

Personnel. Groups of three players and one coach. At least two groups of three are desirable.

Description. A group of three players line up at the middle of the back line. The first player in line is on his or her stomach (see Figure 7-12). The coach bounces the ball to the left. The player gets up and plays the ball with the required technique. Immediately, the coach bounces a ball to the right for the next player, who also begins on his or her stomach. After playing the ball, each player returns to the end of the line and repeats until the required number of playable balls are completed. The second group of three shags balls and returns them to the coach.

Measurement. The drill is complete when a group attains a specified number of successful repetitions. If a player does not go for a ball, the group's score goes back to zero. A playable ball is defined as one that is up and on the defenders' side of the court.

Organizational tip. If you have 12 players and two courts, number the groups 1 through 4. Group 1 does the drill. Group 2 shags the balls and hands them to the coach. Groups 3 and 4 serve receive on the other court. Groups rotate after the group doing VIs completes the task.

(7.5) Compensation

Purpose. To develop floor balance, defensive recovery, and transition movements

Classification. Coach-initiated

Category. Crisis

Equipment. Full-court setup with a container of balls and a sturdy box or table

Personnel. 3, 6, 9, or 12 players and one coach

Description. The coach can be either on a box or on the floor. Three players in defensive positions are on one side of the net. The coach begins by hitting a ball at one of the defenders (see Figure 7-13). The group of three then contact it and attack to the other court. As soon as the ball is down, the coach tosses in another ball (preferably to an exposed area). When the group attains the

Fig. 7-12

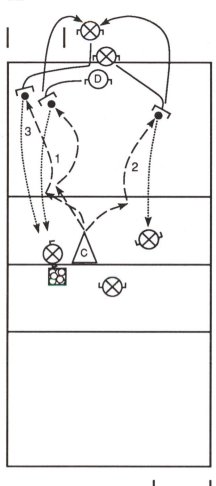

Fig. 7-13

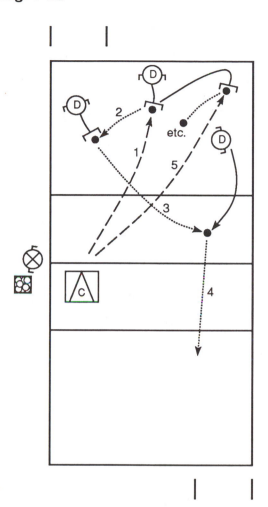

measurement goal, a new group of three begins the drill.

For variety, put a full team on the other side of the court from the triad "compensating." The full team can block and dig, but may attack only from the back row.

Measurement. A specified successful number of transition attacks must be accomplished to complete the drill.

(7.6) King/Queen of the Court

Purpose. To reinforce defensive technique; to reward defensive transition control under competitive conditions

Classification. Coach-initiated

Category. Crisis

Equipment. Full-court setup with a container of balls

Personnel. A minimum of six players in groups of three and one coach

Description. A group of three players on one side of the net take defensive positions. Three lines of players are at the opposite end line (see Figure 7-14). The coach hits a ball at one of the three players at the front of the lines. They dig and control and play three-on-three or *triples* against the other side. The group that wins the point go to (or stay on) the side with one group. The group digging the coach's hit gets three chances to continue the first contact. If a player does not go for any ball, the group of three return to the end of the line. The losing team of any series shags the ball.

Measurement. This drill is timed.

(7.7) Pursuit

Purpose. To develop transition movements

Classification. Coach-initiated

Category. Crisis/Flow-of-play

Fig. 7-14

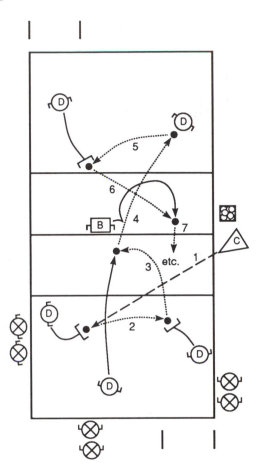

Fig. 7-15

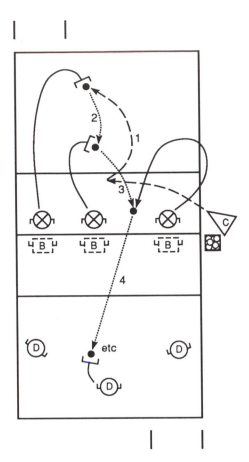

Equipment. Full-court setup and a container of balls

Personnel. One coach; groups of three players

Description. Three players begin at the net (or in the back row). The coach slaps the ball. The players jump (if at net) and the coach bounces the ball away from the players. The players pursue, control the ball, and attack back (see Figure 7-15). To make it more difficult, put another team on the other side for pursuers to play against. Groups change when the defending group completes the measurement goal.

Measurement. A specified number of successful repetitions must be attained to complete this drill.

Variation.

Piles. Players "pile up" at a designated spot. The coach bounces the ball. Players scramble out of the pile, pursue, and play the rally (see Figure 7-16).

(7.8) Deep-Court Exchange

Purpose. To develop defensive and transitional control using many repetitions

Classification. Coach-initiated

Category. Flow-of-play

Equipment. Full-court setup with a container of balls

Personnel. A minimum of 12 players and two coaches

Description. Two groups of three players set up at the end lines of each half court. One group on each court moves out onto the floor. The coach begins the action by hitting the ball at one group. That group controls and attacks from deep court (behind the 3-meter line) to the other side. As soon as the ball crosses the net, the attacking team

Fig. 7-16

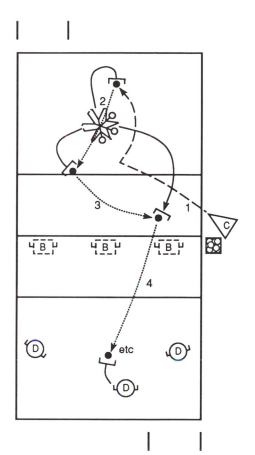

Description. Set up the court as illustrated in Figure 7-17. The coach designates what shot attackers are to hit (e.g., line, sharp cross-court, etc.) and then serves to a passer who sets the offense. The blocker takes the zone away from the hitter, channeling the hit to the back-row defender. The drill incorporates passing, setting, and hitting with the block. If a team cannot effectively control passing or setting, the coach can toss the ball for the attack. The tempo is fast; the coach serves again as soon as the ball is dug by the defender. The players rotate after each player successfully completes the defensive task.

Measurement. A specified number of successful digs constitutes completion of the drill.

Fig. 7-17

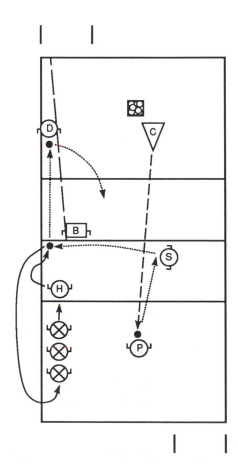

exchanges with the other group on their side. The play continues to its natural conclusion. As soon as the ball is dead, the coach on the side of the termination duplicates the terminating play until the player successfully makes the play. The drill continues nonstop as the coaches immediately duplicate any termination.

Measurement. Continue this drill for a specified period of time.

(7.9) Flinch Drill

Purpose. To teach defensive players to take channeled shots (set up by the block)

Classification. Coach-initiated

Category. Crisis/Rapid-fire

Equipment. Full-court setup with a container of balls

Personnel. At least five players and one coach

Part II: Basic Tactics

This section consists of two chapters that familiarize you with how volleyball has developed, technically and tactically, through the years, and how to design your own playing systems to blend your players' skills and athletic abilities to result in a successful team.

To develop an effective program, today's wise coach must study the evolution of the game. Studying how experienced coaches have adjusted and adapted to various conditions and situations will stimulate you to analyze your own situation. Perhaps one day you will create a new tactic or playing system that other coaches will analyze. You should consider yourself a part of volleyball's evolution. But first, you must understand basic tactical concepts and how they were established.

Chapter 8: The Evolution of Volleyball

Competition is fertile ground for the development of new ideas. As soon as volleyball became a competitive sport, people began to experiment with new ways to win. When new offenses were devised, new defenses were created to counter them. When one program involved bigger athletes who had the ability to jump higher, other programs followed suit. When some programs used technological advances to train athletes, other programs did likewise. The goal to be the best continues to motivate competitors to seek new ways to lead them to the "promised land" of victory.

A Chronological Glance

Despite its modern sophistication, volleyball has never lost its value as a lifetime sport. The original concept remains intact but has been modified to fit today's standards. The following is a chronological look at the evolution of volleyball. Obviously, all historical movements cannot be detailed here. My intention is to provide a look at the important changes in volleyball and their impact in the United States.

1895—Holyoke, Massachusetts

William G. Morgan, physical education director of the Holyoke YMCA invented *mintonette*. That game was designed as a light recreational activity to provide a less vigorous alternative to basketball. Mintonette was played over a badminton net strung at a height of 6 feet, 6 inches. Using the bladder out of a basketball for the ball, the game was played in innings like baseball. The object was to put the ball on the opponent's floor while preventing the opponent from doing the same thing to you. There was no limit to the number of players on a side nor any restrictions on the number of contacts.

Later in the year, Springfield College professor Alfred T. Halstead, who had a better feel for mass marketing, counseled young Morgan to change the name of the game to *volleyball*. He reasoned that in the world of athletics, a game entitled mintonette would get little attention. Besides, the name didn't really describe the game.

1897–1900

The Spaulding Company developed the first official volleyball during this period. A basketball was too heavy for the sport and the bladder too light.

In addition, the first set of official rules was established. These rules raised the net to 7 feet and required the use of the official Spaulding ball. At this time, the YMCA was the main promoter of volleyball.

1912–1913

The first rules revision creating the general structure for the game as it is today was undertaken. Ball handling was standardized and the rotation of players was specified. At this time the net was raised to 7 feet, 6 inches, and an official volleyball game was defined as one team accumulating 21 points.

In 1913 the YMCA introduced volleyball through its facilities worldwide. During the same year, volleyball was included in the Far East Games in Manila.

1916–1920

The American Expeditionary Force brought volleyball to Europe and passed out 16,000 official Spaulding volleyballs. The net was raised to 8 feet and games were reduced to 15 points. Two out of three games constituted a match.

1922–1925

The first United States national championship was held at the Pittsburgh, Pennsylvania, YMCA in 1922. The Brooklyn, New York, YMCA was crowned the champion. In 1924, the first scholastic program was developed by C. Lawrence Walsh and Harry Batchelor of Pittsburgh. Also during during these years, the rules were modified to restrict contacts to three on a side and to specify that the ball had to be contacted above the waist. Court dimensions were also modified to create a 35-foot-by-60-foot playing area.

1928

The United States Volleyball Association (USVBA) was founded at the Yale Club in New York City for the purposes of representing the sport both nationally and internationally and conducting an annual men's open national championship. The first reported collegiate team was formed at Oregon State College as plans for a volleyball conference were developed. Women and girls had yet to become involved in the sport.

1940–1945

U.S. troops played volleyball recreationally throughout Europe. Europeans observed the sport and recognized the competitive potential of an activity that required little equipment and space, yet accommodated a high concentration of people.

1946–1948

The first real technical and tactical systems emerged. Many teams used a 3-3 system in which each spiker had his own setter. The one-foot takeoff dominated the spiker approach, and blocking was virtually nonexistent. In 1947, the Fédération Internationale de Volleyball (FIVB) was founded to organize international competition and develop standardized volleyball rules worldwide.

1949

The first men's world championship was held in Prague, Czechoslovakia. The Soviet men beat the Czechs after four games. After 54 years, women got their first chance to play competitive volleyball! The first USVBA women's open national championship was held in Los Angeles, California. The Eagles from Houston, Texas, emerged victorious.

The 1950s

Tactically, big spikers hitting high, outside sets dominated the style of play. The 4-2 was emerging. Setters were usually short, quick, skillful ball handlers who could not hit or block very well. Blocking was static, with little lateral movement. This was consistent with the nature of spiker approaches, which were straight and predictable. The one-foot takeoff was criticized as being biomechanically restrictive of the arm swing in the air. As a result, the two-foot takeoff was developed for spikers to allow for greater shot selection.

In 1952, the first women's world championship was held in Moscow. The Soviets won the championship. The U.S. women's team did not attend those games.

1960–1964

Hirofum Diamatsu and his Nishibo Spinning Mills Club team introduced an attitude and related techniques that changed volleyball forever. Using an adaptation of the judo shoulder roll, the women on the team were coached to go after any ball aggressively. The team's success was obvious. The Nishibo team, competing as the Japanese national team, was undefeated between 1960 and 1964 and dominated the first Olympic volleyball competition held in Tokyo in 1964. In that same year, volleyball also became a part of the World University Games docket.

1969

The first collegiate-sponsored national championship, organized by the National Association for Intercollegiate Athletics (NAIA), was held for men. The USVBA had previously held a collegiate division championship as a part of its open national championship. The first women's collegiate championship was also held, sponsored by the Division of Girls and Women in Sports (DGWS).

1970–1976

The National Collegiate Athletic Association (NCAA) began its national championship for men using the "final four" concept in 1970. In 1975, the FIVB developed a formalized "mini-volleyball" guideline, designed to introduce volleyball to players between the ages of 9 and 12. The USVBA also created the first full-time training program for the women's national team in Pasadena, Texas, in 1975. The USA men's team established a full-time training center in Dayton, Ohio in 1976.

Other changes occurred in 1975. Title IX, a federal statute that required public schools to provide equal opportunities for males and females in sports was passed and volleyball became a prominent high school varsity sport for women. Full-time coaching positions opened up in colleges. Together, high school and collegiate programs provided the broad base for sport in the United States, unlike in other countries where sport clubs dominated the athletic scene. With more money and attention, volleyball for girls and women rapidly expanded as the opportunities grew.

The Association for Intercollegiate Athletics for Women (AIAW), with the backing of Title IX, developed women's sport opportunities in high schools and colleges. College scholarships and full-time coaches were made available for the first time in 1975.

1980

The U.S. boycotted the Moscow Olympic Games, dashing the hopes of the prominent USA women's team. The USA men's team did not qualify for competition.

1981

The NCAA recognized the growth in girls' and women's sports and held its first "final four" national volleyball championship for women. The AIAW was absorbed by the NCAA, calling for recruiting policies, leagues, and divisions to fall in line with men's regulations.

The USA men's national team moved its full-time training center to San Diego, California, from Dayton, Ohio. The team was ranked 19th in the world.

1981–1984

The USA men's team, under head coach Doug Beal and assistant coaches Bill Neville and Tony Crabb and along with significant input from former national coaches Carl McGown and Jim Coleman, revamped the traditional playing style. The team won America's first gold medal in volleyball at the 1984 Olympics.

The USA women's team, based in Orange County under the leadership of head coach Arie Selinger, remained one of the top three teams in the world since 1980. With their Oriental-style training regimen and big, talented athletes, they took the silver medal at the 1984 Olympics.

1985

The USA women's and men's teams consolidated their organizations in San Diego. Marv Dunphy was named head coach of the men's team and Terry Liskevych was tabbed head coach of the women. The men's team retained six players from the 1984 team. However, all of the 1984 women had retired, and Liskevych had to start from scratch.

1986-1988

The USA men completed the FIVB triple crown by winning the 1985 World Cup in Japan and the 1986 World Championship in Paris in addition to their 1984 Olympic victory. The men continued their success by taking the gold medal at the 1988 Olympics. The USA women qualified for the 1988 Seoul Olympic Games by defeating Canada in the North American Conference zone championships in Havana, Cuba.

Profiles in Progress

The philosophies of coaches and teams become golden after a team wins a world title. Other teams want to study how they accomplished their success. What follows are the stories surrounding many key developments in the sport of volleyball.

Hirofum Diamatsu

Using a training philosophy that was culturally permissible in Japan, Diamatsu held practices for his Japanese women's team a minimum of 8 hours a day, 7 days a week, for 51 weeks of the year in the early 1960s. This regimen was based on his belief that women need more discipline and training than men. His philosophy, "Make possible what seems impossible," was captivating. The mystique of the Oriental combination of politeness and discipline has lured many countries to adopt this style of training.

Matsudaira

In 1961 Matsudaira, coach of the Japanese men's team, took his squad to Europe to play. The smaller Japanese got squashed in every game of a 22-match schedule. At that time, Matsudaira decided to develop Japanese volleyball through sound marketing, innovative tactics, and precise technical training. He formulated a plan to win a medal in the 1972 Munich Olympics.

His first step was to promote "Mama's Volleyball"—nationwide recreational leagues for mothers. He reasoned that mothers then could teach their children about the sport,

providing future players and a great deal of support. Matsudaira developed specific ways to teach volleyball skills. Eventually, training became an integral part of the Japanese culture.

Tactically, Matsudaira developed what in the early days critics called "Matsudaira's Circus." It was the first combination attack offense based around one setter. This was the first recognized 5-1 system, a system most teams still use today. In this system the setter specialized in setting the multi-faceted attack, which included fakes, quick sets, back sets, and crossing patterns.

Matsudaira believed quite accurately that Japan's only chance to beat the burly Eastern Europeans was to outtrain and outwit them. Whereas European teams relied on sheer brute power hitting and one-dimensional high-ball sets, the Japanese relied on a team attack concept that required deft, quick movements. Japanese women and men, despite being rivals in their own country, pushed each other to world prominence through the 1960s and early 1970s. They changed the traditional recreational approach to volleyball to a more scientific and analytical one.

Technical and Tactical Education

In the 1970s, the sophisticated, methodical approach of the Japanese teams and their related international success and popularity spurred the traditionally powerful European countries to rethink their approach to the game. As perspectives have changed, men's volleyball has contributed significantly to the evolution of sophisticated tactics, whereas women's volleyball has led the field in developing sophisticated technique.

The East German men's team, under the leadership of Horst Baacke, streamlined the high-percentage, low-error, high-ball attack. His philosophy was to be conservative and not to gamble. His teams played the ball to the best hitter as accurately as possible with no fakes: They preferred fundamentally sound volleyball. They rose to second place in the world in 1972, losing the Olympic gold medal to the scrambling, gambling Japanese.

Poland, under Hubert Wagner, designed a primarily right-side deceptive attack using an audible system called by the right-side or play-set hitter. It was built around the quick attack. The play-set hitter called his route based on the opposing blocker's movements. At the same time, the Soviets developed a disciplined blocking scheme to counter the emerging quick, multiple attacks. Blending the big athletes of the Eastern bloc with the multifaceted Asian playing systems brought the well-heeled, broad-based programs of Poland and the Soviet Union back to world dominance.

The Cubans leapt onto the international stage with the highest-jumping athletes in the world. Schooled by the methodical, stoic East Germans, the Cubans used a static, high-ball attack. The rather staid East German playing style did not fit the flamboyant Latin culture. It inhibited the Cubans' awesome physical talent.

The women's game was dominated by the Oriental school of thought. Many nations imitated Japan's techniques and style. The Soviets, by the nature of their rigorous athletic programs, still fielded great teams, but mere imitations can never capture the glory of the original. The Oriental systems continued to dominate and mystify.

The USA Men's Team

In 1981 the USA men's team staff under the direction of Doug Beal determined that if the United States wanted to become a world volleyball power, they would have to develop a unique American style of play. The staff studied American characteristics and personality traits based on the philosophy that copying the success of others lead only to finishing second to the original. Based on the resulting principles, specializations were formulated.

Tactically, the swing offense emerged from the flair offense, developed in the late 1970s in Canada. The swing offense was based on attacking inside out, in contrast to traditional outside-in approaches. The tactical purpose of the blocking scheme was to stop the big Eastern European and Canadian hitters and to adjust to the quick Latin American attackers. A blend of specialized technique and tactics, based on simple, functional principles that harnessed the cultural idiosyncrasies of Americans, and a sophisticated scouting system led the USA team to a gold medal in the 1984 Los Angeles Olympic Games. Future Levels of the Coaching Accreditation Program detail these more complex offensive systems.

No system works without great players. Even though men's volleyball in this country is still relatively small in terms of numbers of participants, the athletes who made up the USA national team from 1981 to 1988 were outstanding.

It is important for you to understand why and how the USA's rapid ascent fits into the evolution of volleyball and use that understanding in developing your own program. Every internationally successful team has developed a unique technical, tactical, or administrative wrinkle, or a combination of these. The United States emerged as a world volleyball power when it established a full-time training center and developed an uniquely American style of play. Every coach at every level from junior high school to international teams must study the community's traditions, attitudes, economic level, and any other influential factors and design a program that harnesses the strengths of the community the team represents.

Volleyball Today

The USVBA has grown from a purely volunteer organization to, by 1989, a nonprofit corporation employing 10 full-time professional staff and many full-time support staff. The mission of the USVBA has also expanded from organizing solely a men's national championship to organizing an open national championship providing competition for men and women in all age groups. Nationals are also held for coeducational teams. The USVBA, as the national governing body (NGB), is the United States Olympic Committee's representative in the FIVB and represents the country internationally.

Age-group volleyball has expanded since 1980 into the largest USVBA competitive membership group. The sophistication of the Junior Olympic and youth volleyball clubs nationwide is largely responsible for the high quality of play found at higher levels.

Research on coaching education is now a USVBA priority. The full-time national team programs remain the USVBA's flagships and serve as the role models for and the ultimate goals of aspiring players and coaches. But education is the key to keeping our coaches prepared to meet the challenges of competition at *all* levels.

Some Perspective

Volleyball is growing quickly in the United States and in the world. Television exposure and the availability of air travel to transport teams around the world for competition add to the potential of this fascinating sport. Still, there is a place for William Morgan's original concept. Old badminton nets are still strung between trees or poles. Twenty friends gather on one side of the net and face fifteen on the other. They bat, scoop, head, and kick whatever object is used as a ball. There is light exercise and a rollicking good time to be had by all. Old mintonette, whatever it was, has turned out to be a pretty good game.

Chapter 9: Developing Playing Systems

The greatest challenge of coaching a team sport is melding the individual players into an effective team. The ultimate objective is one cohesive unit that can orchestrate its collective talents in a tactical foray against an opponent. Individual sports such as gymnastics or track and field rely on precise repetitive technique as the vanguard of success. In contrast, volleyball success relies on a team's ability to adjust and react to spontaneous situations as they occur.

A coach must therefore develop systems of play that harness the combined skills of the individuals. The classic coaching dilemma is whether to adapt the system to the players or the players to the system. This chapter is designed to give insight into this perpetual question.

Principles and Considerations

- Attempt tactically only what the players can execute technically.
- Develop systems that are appropriate to the competitive level of play.
- Expose the team's strengths and camouflage the weaknesses. Every team has strengths and weaknesses. You must evaluate your team. Develop playing systems that best display their strengths and camouflage the weaknesses.
- Volleyball is fun to play. The systems of play should reflect the joy of the game. Always keep the reasons we play volleyball in focus.
- The systems of play should be easy to practice. The amount of time required to learn the system should fit into the season schedule and into the allotted training time.
- Each playing system should be accompanied by a consistent communication system. The most efficient elements of communication are one-syllable words in easily heard tones. For example, a player should always call for the ball when playing it, using only words like "Ball!" or "Mine!" "Go!" can mean "set quick or fast." "Hut," "quick," "rip," and "red" are examples of audibles for different types of sets. Players should also be able to communicate with their hands, using different combinations and numbers of fingers to indicate particular plays.
- The playing systems should incorporate tactical flexibility. You should be able to adjust to opponents and unfolding game or match situations.

Playing systems are dynamic and come from the minds of creative coaches. Brand-new systems seldom spring into existence; rather, they evolve, influenced by bits and pieces from many varied sources.

By providing some basic concepts, I hope that coaches reading these pages will furrow their brows in thought and say to themselves, "How can I apply this to my team? What if I take a little bit of this and a little bit of that? It's not written here, but what if we tried . . . ?" And the evolution continues. . . .

Offensive Systems

You must consider how much specialization you want to encourage when choosing a system. Young players should be able to sample all playing positions in volleyball. Such a philosophy makes sense educationally. Then, as each player develops and discovers a particular niche in the game, specialization begins to be advantageous. The argument has been made that specialization at a young age allows a player to focus on what he or she *can* do and not to worry about what he or she cannot. Another advantage is being able to put young players in positions where they will experience the most success. For example, short players may be very good back-row defenders but may be limited trying to spike and block. The disadvantages include young players being stereotyped into positions, possibly locking them into certain roles for the remainder of their careers. You must consider the options and develop a philosophy relative to specialization.

The only "right" approach to this issue is to develop a sound coaching philosophy that addresses each player's best interests. The volleyball experience should be a positive force in every player's life; it is the coach's responsibility to direct it.

This chapter covers the offensive systems: the elements of serve receive patterns, attack routes off serve receive, setter placement and usage, transition attack, and coverage positions. Two basic offensive systems are also presented—6-6 and 4-2. The 6-6 is the most elementary system, whereas the 4-2 is the basic system for developing specialization.

Deciding Which System to Use

You must consider your team's specific individual strengths and weaknesses when determining which offensive system you will use. Be sure to consider your player's skills in setting, hitting, serve reception, serving order, player chemistry, floor defense, and blocking. These are the key elements of the game for which you must plan. Determine those elements your team can control and those that either cannot be controlled or are a low priority. Select your playing system to maximize your team's abilities. Consider each of the following issues and explore the answers to the questions presented as you develop your team's offensive playing system.

Setting

Setting is an *intermediate contact*. Without consistent, controlled setting, there can be few terminal contacts from the attack. Setters must make split-second choices, often while chasing down a less-than-accurate pass, and have to execute precisely. Setting is a most difficult skill that requires outstanding athletic ability. Because of the importance of setting, you should begin developing your offense around the setters and their level of ability.

Hitting

The actual spiking of the ball is a *terminal attack*. It reeks of glory. Strong attack can be a momentum changer. In serve receive situations, strong hitting yields side-outs and prevents the opponent from scoring. It also leads directly to points if the opponent does not convert to the attack effectively. What role will hitting play in your offensive scheme?

Serve Receive

A team can have the best setter in the world of volleyball. Their spikers can be fearsome. The team can make the gym and the opponent shudder during pregame warm-ups—the pounding seems life-threatening. Yet, when the game begins, that team may not be able to receive the serve. The players pass the ball all over the gym. As a result, the great setter becomes an average sprinter; the huge attackers become spectators. Without good serve receive, no offensive system can be put into action. Plan accordingly.

Serving Order

Especially in programs for young players, the serve can be the deadliest weapon. No lead is big enough if the opponent possesses a player who can unleash a potent serve. You must decide how effective your team's serving game is and whether good servers are preferable to good hitters or setters. If you are fortunate, your players will be able to combine the skills. At that point, you must consider the order in which the players serve and weigh that against the other responsibilities they must fulfill.

Chemistry

The perfect team on paper, in terms of balanced responsibilities, can be shattered on the court if the athletes playing next to each other cannot get along. All the refined skills in the world cannot make up for teammates who do not communicate. How well do your athletes play with each other?

Floor Defense

Most team systems are built around the offense. Yet in volleyball, defense scores. Should you choose to put good defenders on the floor at the expense of big hitters? How important are ball handlers who never let a ball touch the floor without relentless pursuit? How valuable are players whose efforts can shut down the opponent's attack? You must consider your answers to these questions when deciding whether to put the hardest-hitting players on the floor.

Blocking

At beginning levels, blocking plays a relatively minor role in the total effort. There is little need to form a block because strong attacks are generally inconsistent. Yet every team has at least one good attacker who

needs to be stopped at the net. Do the blocking trade-offs favor your team or the opponent? Knowing when to block is perhaps most important. The system should be designed to accommodate the whos, wheres, and whens of blocking.

The 6-6 Offensive System

The first number in any offensive system refers to how many players are attackers. The second number indicates players who are setters. Because only six players are on the floor at one time, it is obvious that the coach cannot simply add the two numbers (6 + 6) and field a legal team.

A 6-6 offense often appears to be a complicated system, but in reality it is the simplest. It means that everybody hits and everybody sets. There are no special assignments and players do not switch positions. This system is designed to introduce the game to beginners. The playing concepts are the same as in the more specialized systems. However, the 6-6 emphasizes the most important offensive principle: Make sure the spiker can always get a good swing at the ball.

The 6-6 requires little player movement as each athlete plays each position in the rotation in turn. For example, when a player is in the left front position, he or she hits and blocks left front. When a player is the middle front, he or she sets and blocks in the middle position. Therefore, balanced individuals skills are accentuated.

The 4-2

The basic 4-2 is the introduction to specialization. In fact, the basic 4-2 has spawned the most intricate playing systems employed today. The many variations of the 4-2 are limited only by your creativity.

The 4-2 recipe requires the following personnel:

- Two setters—each will set three times during his or her front-row rotational position. These players need to be quick, have stable personalities, and be good ball handlers and leaders. Ideally, your setters should be left-handed, so it's easier for them to jump and hit a tight pass.

- Two left-side hitters—each will line up to hit from the left side twice and right side once. Ideally, the hitters should be right-handed, tall, and capable of jumping high. They should possess good individual attack skills and have several shots, strong arms, and the ability to block.
- Two right-side hitters—each will hit twice on the right and once on the left. These players can be right- or left-handed. They need quickness and good movement skills. They should be able to block the middle.
- Two defensive specialists—these players substitute when the big front-row players reach the back row. These defensive roles are important. The players need to be quick and tenacious, have good defensive skills, be good servers, and be skilled serve receivers.

Players must start in their proper rotational order, but may change position as soon as the ball is put into play. Figure 9-1 illustrates the basic 4-2 rotational order.

I strongly suggest that you put your *best athletes* in the setter positions. The reason is simple: The setter touches the ball at least once in every sequence of three contacts. If a team does not have setters who can get the ball up in front of big, strapping hitters, the attack exists only as a concept. Setters control the game because of their continual contact. Without the control, your big hitters will be able to display their talents primarily during the pregame warm-up.

Balance the Rotational Order

The setters in the 4-2 should be opposite each other, as should the left-side hitters and right-side hitters. The left-side hitters should precede the setters, with the right-side hitters following, so that they each hit twice on their respective strong sides off the serve reception.

Serve Receive Patterns

A serve receive pattern is an integral part of an offensive system. There are as many serve receive patterns as there are variations of the 4-2 offensive scheme. The design principles and the basic five-player *W serve receive formation* are presented here. Theoretically, each of the six rotations could use a different serve receive pattern.

The traditional philosophy of serve receiving is to cover the court with as many receivers as possible. All receivers need to be able to see and face the server. There should be no open spaces on the floor for the server to attack. Hence, the balanced W serve receive was developed (see Figure 9-2). Players

Fig. 9-1

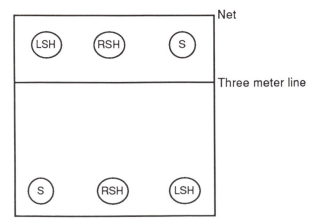

S: Setter —plays right or middle front
LSH: Left side hitter—hits and blocks from left front
RSH: Right side hitter—hits and blocks from right front
    or blocks middle front

Fig. 9-2

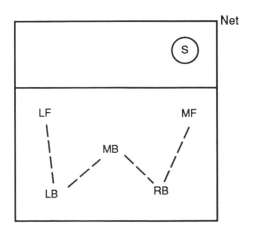

simply adjust to the server in their respective positions, keeping the server in sight and making distance adjustments based on the particular server's tendencies.

The W pattern can be easily applied to virtually any offensive system. It is perfectly suited, physically and philosophically, to the 6-6 and allows for easy switching in the 4-2. It also allows for easy transition into spike coverage.

The court is covered. No player needs to move very far to receive the ball. On paper, it is virtually impenetrable. However, there are some disadvantages. The more serve receivers there are on the court, the more targets to which the server can serve. Seldom does a team have five or six equally competent receivers. If there is a chink in the armor somewhere, the clever server can find it.

In advanced offensive schemes, the W pattern does not lend itself to running certain prescribed attack routes. Therefore, a second school of thought has emerged: Expose the best receivers; hide the weakest ones. In this scheme, hitters are placed in optimal attack-route positions without consideration for serve receive.

Two-, three-, and four-player serve receive patterns have been designed. Just as coaches identify setters, attackers with specific responsibilities, and defensive specialists, serve receive specialists can also be selected. Players who are good receivers enjoy the duty. Lesser-skilled passers like to avoid it. Relieve the less-skilled receivers of their serve receive responsibilities so they can focus on their primary roles.

This philosophy makes sense. But it too has disadvantages—mainly the glaringly open court into which the server can penetrate with the serve. Serve receive errors in two-, three-, or four-player patterns are often terminal because the passer must move great distances. In contrast, the W pattern allows even players who are not great passers to get the ball up because they don't have to move great distances first.

I recommend that young teams use the W serve receive pattern. As the offense be-

comes more specialized, serve receive patterns can follow suit. Please contrast the specialized serve receive patterns illustrated in Figure 9-3 with the W serve receive pattern in Figure 9-2.

Fig. 9-3

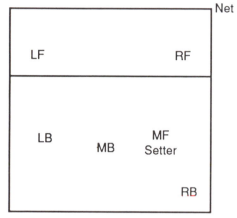

Three player receive pattern

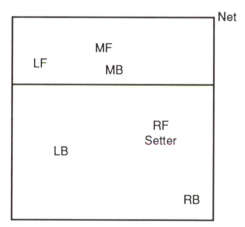

Two player receive pattern

Many advanced teams combine various serve receive patterns, using different ones in each rotation. Specialized serve receive patterns are covered in Level II of the Coaching Accreditation Program.

Spiker Coverage

It is important to develop a disciplined spiker coverage system. The coverage is mechanical in that the players cover the court in the same way on each option. The covering players must outwardly exude confidence in their spiker, but intellectually assume the hitter will be blocked. With such an attitude, the players will be ready to react and keep the ball in play. The posture of the players is similar to a defensive stance: low, stopped, leaning toward the attack, arms outspread, and eyes on the spiker hitting the ball (see Figure 9-4 for diagrams of coverage patterns).

To be effective, coverage should be close in, with three players within 3 meters of the hitter. At least one back-row player must be deep to cover a blocked ball that goes long. Most balls are blocked down. Therefore, the concentration of coverage should be immediately behind the block and low to the floor.

Attacker Routes

The routes the spikers take to where the attack originates must be built into the serve receive pattern and defensive scheme. The W receive pattern provides the simplest attack route (see Figure 9-5).

Whereas the serve receive pattern puts the attackers in a good starting position, tran-

sition attack routes must evolve out of a spontaneous defensive reaction. The routes are wholly dependent upon where the attackers are positioned in the defensive scheme and where you want them to attack. The examples diagrammed in Figure 9-6 are based on the simplest concept of left-side hitters spiking left and right-side players hitting right but blocking middle.

There are many possibilities for attack routes in transition. It is important to re-create the most frequently recurring situations and practice the most effective attack routes.

Defensive Systems

Defense is built on a simple principle: Put players in positions where the opponent will most likely attack. This is certainly easier said than done. The two systems presented here dovetail nicely with the two offensive systems previously described. They are,

Fig. 9-4

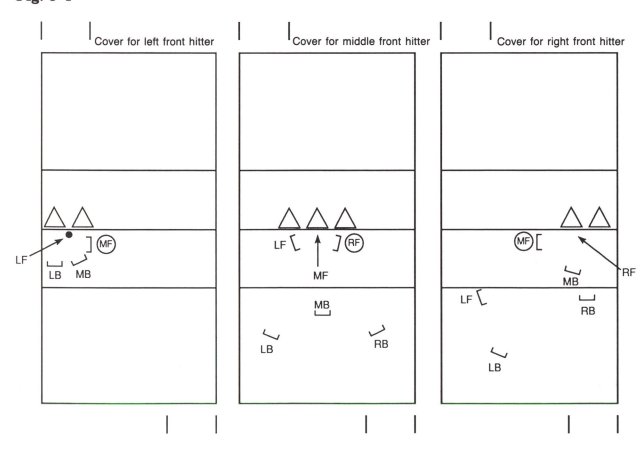

Fig. 9-5

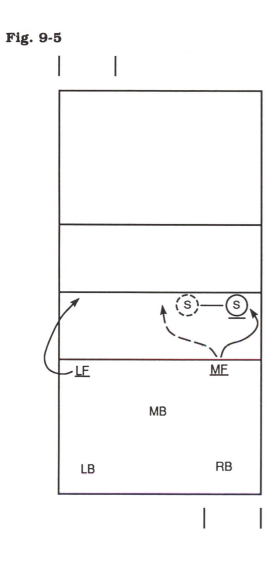

Fig. 9-6

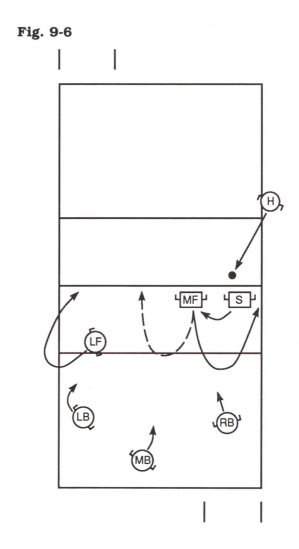

however, only general descriptions and must be adjusted to fit the needs of each unfolding competitive situation.

General Principles

- Establish floor positions that allow floor defenders to play the ball in front of them, toward teammates. (This is referred to as *on help*.)
- Establish floor positions to reduce the digging area for each defender.
- All floor defenders should be stopped and leaning toward the attacker as the ball is being hit.
- The block should be used only if the players are capable of executing one or more of the three blocking functions (see chapter 6).

Areas of Responsibility

Please note that when I refer to "left back," "middle front," and other positions, these do not necessarily mean rotational order positions. The players can switch within their own lines, in the front and back rows, after the ball is served. The positions are the relative defensive areas in each system. Many teams employ specific systems in each rotation to take advantage of their players, match up against the primary attack schemes of the opponents, or both.

Players must clearly understand their areas of digging responsibility lest there be collisions between aggressive athletes. The examples cited are just that: examples. You must adjust these examples to cover the abilities of your players.

Table 9.1   Advantages and Disadvantages of the One-Blocker System

Advantages	Disadvantages
One blocker is effective against any team that tips and hits the ball off-speed or seldom attacks with hard shots.	The one-block system is of little use against a good serve-receiving, hard-hitting team.
It is easier to make the transition to offense.	Despite more defenders on the court, each player has more space to cover because the attacker has more options.
It takes pressure off most players to have to block.	
It allows small, good ball-handling front-row players to get into defensive positions to best utilize their strengths.	The required coordination of movements, responsibilities, and positions can become confusing for players in a long rally.

One-Blocker System

Perhaps the most effective and simplest defense against a one-dimensional offense is a one-blocker system. It is also practical for a team that has only one or two really effective blockers (see Table 9.1).

Figure 9-7 diagrams player positions in a one-blocker system against an opponent's left-side attack. The single blocker takes the cross-court hitting angle and the left-front player takes the cross-court digging angle at the 3-meter line. The left back takes the deep cross-court digging angle, and the middle back plays just to the left of the blocker. The right back takes a position deep on the line, and the right-front player covers a tip shot. The defensive positions against the right-side attack would be the reverse of the positions diagrammed in Figure 9-7.

Against the middle attacker, a single blocker blocks straight on. The left-front player takes a short angle and the left-back player takes a deep angle. The right-front player covers a possible tip and the right-back defender takes a deep digging angle. The middle back lines up with the attacker's approach angle (see Figure 9-8). Remember, approximately 80% of the time an attacker hits in the line of his or her approach.

Two Blockers With Middle Back Deep

In this defense, tips and soft shots are covered by the front-row player not involved in the block, or by any back-row player who sees the play and releases.

Fig. 9-7

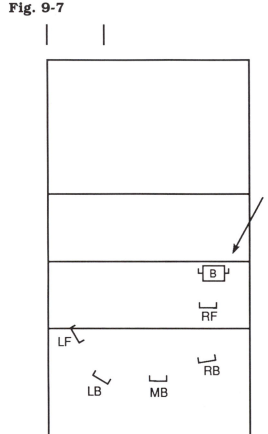

This playing system is illustrated in Figure 9-9. In an attack from the opponent's left side, the defensive left-front player straddles the 3-meter line and plays balls only to his or her front and right. The left-back defender

Fig. 9-8

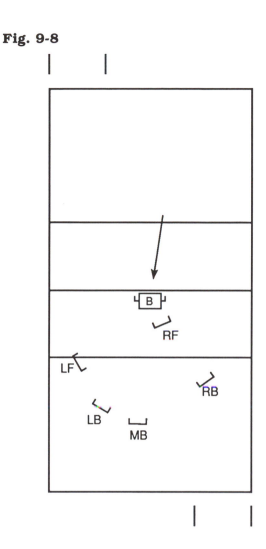

Fig. 9-9

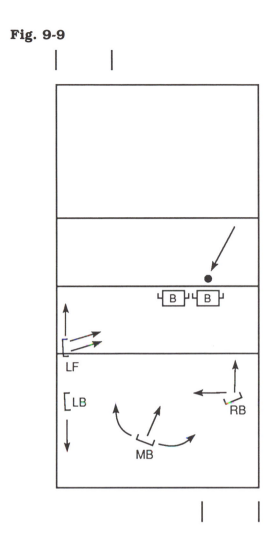

begins 4-1/2 meters off the net and plays to the corner. The middle-back defender plays balls in front, cuts off the deep angle to the left, and plays the corner to the right. The right back takes balls in front of and to the left of his or her starting position.

An attack from the right side would be exactly the opposite (see Figure 9-10). The left-back defender starts approximately on the backcourt side of the 3-meter line, covering tips forward and to the right. The middle-back player plays balls in front, cuts off the deep angle to the right, and plays the corner to the left. The right back plays to the cross-court corner. The right-front player backs down the line 4-1/2 meters and plays forward and to his or her left.

As with any playing system, this align-

ment has advantages and disadvantages. The values and concerns of the defense are detailed in Table 9.2.

The two blockers in this system must block with discipline and cannot fade beyond a position fronting the hitter. They must develop a tight block around which the back row must be able to build. The block has back-row responsibility, needing to "shade out" an area. This block shadow allows the back-row players to establish defensive positions around the block (see Figure 9-11). The area behind the block to the back line should be difficult to reach with a hard-hit ball.

The middle-back defender must be quick to move laterally and able to read the situation well. The wing diggers must be stopped

Fig. 9-10   **Fig. 9-11**

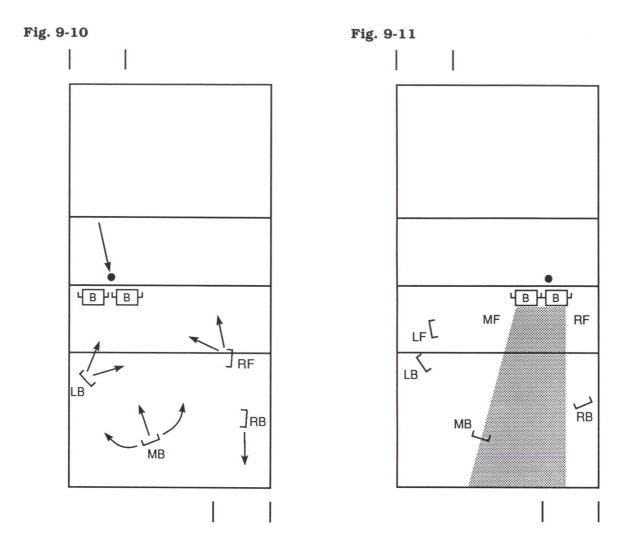

Table 9.2   Advantages and Disadvantages of Two Blockers With Middle Back Deep

Advantages	Disadvantages
This system is good against a consistent-passing, strong-hitting team.	It is susceptible to tips and off-speed shots.
It is a good system for quick, aggressive blockers and mobile back-row defenders.	Big, slow defensive teams have difficulty with the required mobility and quickness.
	It can be difficult to make the transition to offense because of the distance from defensive to offensive positions.

and on help. The line digger's outside foot should be on the line, with the inside foot slightly back.

In the two-blocker defense shown in Figure 9-11, the middle- and right-front players block. The left front drops to the 3-meter line and takes the cross-court shot angle and the cross-court tip. The left back lines up on the

ball to the left of the middle blocker. The middle back lines up in the high seam (between blockers), 1 meter inside the back line. The right back lines up on the line 3-1/2 meters from the back line. The blockers and the right back are responsible for short tips.

Defending against a left front attack would

be just the opposite of the formation described. The left- and middle-front players form a block fronting the cross-court angle. The left back comes up the line in an on-help position, where he or she can see the ball. The right back does the same as the left back, but on the right side. Both should start within ½ meter of the sideline. The middle back lines up in the high seam starting within a meter of the back line (see Figure 9-12).

Fig. 9-12

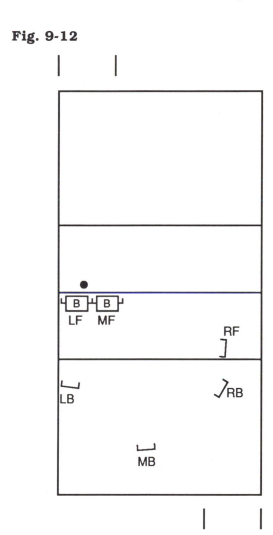

Two Blockers, Back-Row Player Up

In this system, one of the back-row players comes up behind the block to cover a tip or soft shot. With an attack from the opponent's left, the defensive left-front player starts 4 meters from the net down the line. He or she covers shots to the left and right. This player should not need to go toward the

opponent's hitter. The left-back defender has the responsibility of covering the middle back deep to the cross-court corner. This player digs balls in front and to the right. The right back defender starts 2 meters up from the back line. He or she digs to the left and front. The middle back defender follows the middle blocker and gets all the tips he or she can reach (see Figure 9-13). Defensive positions against the opponent's right-side attack are the opposite (see Figure 9-14).

The left-back defender takes the short angle. The right-back defender moves to the left corner starting point and digs forward and right. The right-front defender digs down the line away from the net. The middle back player gets every tip he or she can reach.

Advantages and disadvantages of the system are outlined in Table 9.3.

Fig. 9-13

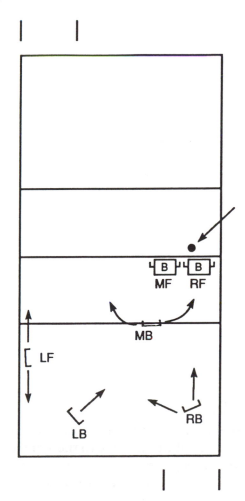

Table 9.3   Advantages and Disadvantages of the Two Blockers, Back-Row Player Up System

Advantages	Disadvantages
The system is strong against a tip- or an off-speed attack–oriented offense because a defender is placed in the area most often attacked.	If the block does not form against a powerful hitter, the middle-up back-row defender risks taking a hard face shot.
Transition from defense to offense is easy if the back-row-up player is the setter.	The deep middle back is vulnerable.
The system is solid against a hard-hitting, high-ball-setting team because the defense has time to get into position.	If the block is disrupted, the back-row defenders have great difficulty deciding where to play.

Fig. 9-14

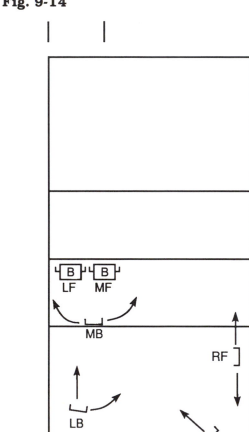

Free Ball

A free ball is one the opponent sends over the net with either a forearm pass or a standing, nondeceptive overhead pass. It is the easiest ball-control play in volleyball. As soon as players recognize that the opponent will not attack, they should yell "free." The setter then releases from his or her defensive position and goes to his or her setting position. The blockers get back off the net, first determining whether they will have to make a pass, and then moving to their attack approach positions. The back-row players release into essentially serve receive positions. The movements of players in a 4-2 system are diagrammed in Figure 9-15.

The following principles should guide your players in handling a free ball situation.

- The best ball handlers should field the ball.
- The setter should be in setting position *before* a teammate touches the ball.
- If two players are confused as to whose ball it is, the one *furthest* from the target should make the play.
- The ball should be played overhead for quicker tempo and better control.
- The attackers should first see if they should pass the ball before going into their attack routes.

Down Ball

A down ball is one that is hit overhand out of the opponent's court, from either a standing position, off balance, or deep. It is usually not worth blocking because its velocity is equivalent to that of a serve. The blockers yell "down." The setter does not have time to release to the target area. The blockers do not have time to get back. The back-row defenders hold their relative positions but

Fig. 9-15

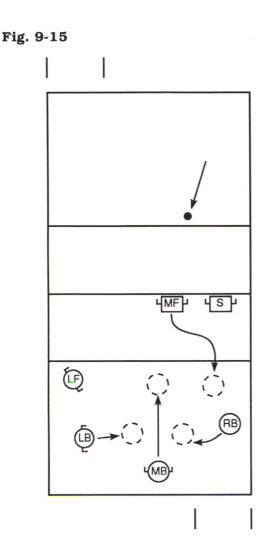

Fig. 9-16

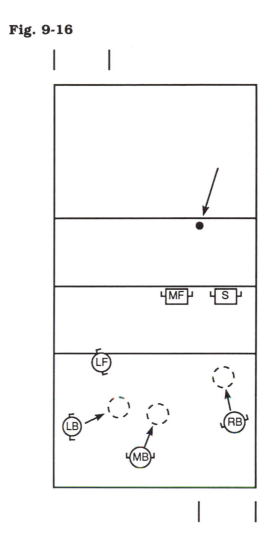

take a full step toward the attacker. In a back-row player–up defense, the close defender does not take a step but stays put, looking for a half-speed shot or a tip. The movements of the players reacting to a down ball are shown in Figure 9-16.

The difference between coverages for a free ball and for a down ball is that in a free ball situation, the blockers, the setters, or both have time to move to attack positions *before* the ball crosses the net. During a down ball, they move *after* the ball crosses the net. Otherwise, the principles for free ball situations govern the down ball as well.

Communication

A team can coordinate its systems only if there is clear, concise communication be-

tween its members. The downfall of many young teams stems from the players neglecting to verbalize their intentions. Players must practice the verbal game along with the physical one. The words used should be one-syllable and guttural, if possible. If players scream phrases at the top of their lungs, the result will be indistinguishable noise, especially in gyms with terrible acoustics and rabid fans. Guttural utterances are easy to emit and easy to pick out from the constant din.

To insure the smooth functioning of the designed playing systems, coaches must teach their players how to communicate their intentions on every play. Consider these concepts:

- Players should call "mine" or "ball" every time they are going to touch the ball. ("I have"; "I got"; or "This here ball is my baby!" are not functional.)

- Setters must verbally communicate their positions and intentions at all times.
- Key cue words describing sets, directions, and confirmation should be consciously presented as part of the system and used repeatedly. "Mine," "out," "in," "here," "high," "deep," "wait," "tip," "down," and "free" are examples.
- The words of communication should describe what a player is intending to do (e.g., "Mine!"), not what others should do (e.g., "Yours!").

Summary

Developing playing systems to fit your personnel is one of your greatest challenges. It is a creative opportunity for a teacher to become a true coach. The system will reflect your team's effectiveness. You may have taught your players the technical skills of volleyball extremely well, but if your playing systems are not consistent with their skill level, all your good teaching can be for naught.

The Volleyball
Planning Guide

Now that you know how to teach volleyball skills and some basic offensive and defensive playing strategies, you are probably eager to begin the season. But unless you know how the learning process works; how to plan your season, practices, and drills; and how to develop your program for future success, your enthusiasm can end in frustration. Take time to study this Volleyball Planning Guide. You'll find practices more beneficial for your players—and for you.

Do you know how to organize your presentation of the skills and strategies of volleyball? What do you teach first? How much emphasis do you place on certain skills? On physical conditioning? On strategy?

These questions and many more are answered in this section of *Coaching Volleyball Successfully*. Chapter 10 takes you through the important information you need to know in teaching and coaching volleyball effectively. That information is the springboard into chapter 11 and a discussion of season planning (including a sample season plan for junior high and high school programs, along with eight sample practice plans).

Designing practices and drills is the paramount concern for coaches at all levels. Chapter 12 examines this difficult topic and makes organizing practices and drills easy. Finally, chapter 13 pulls together a tremendous amount of helpful information to guide you in your efforts to build a volleyball program. Try some of the suggestions, and watch your program grow!

Four appendices and a glossary round out *Coaching Volleyball Successfully*. Appendix A provides blank outlines you may reproduce and use to plan your own season and each practice. Numerous helpful checklists are included in Appendix B. Appendix C brings you up to date on current match protocol (complete with diagrams and home match checklists). Finally, Appendix D addresses the issue of the rules of volleyball. Information on how to receive updated rules is included.

Chapter 10: Teaching and Coaching the Game of Volleyball

Understanding the Learning Process

Before you can teach effectively, you must understand how people learn. Learning physical skills is a process with measurable progressions and goals that change as skill level improves. The learning process must involve both the learner and the teacher. Your role is to ensure that proper techniques are presented and that your players enjoy their association with the sport. That requires motivation—on your part and on theirs.

Both coach and athlete must have an understanding of why they are involved in the activity. That means that you must know why you are teaching the skills you have selected and investigate the expectations and goals of your athletes. When these variables are clearly understood and accepted, learning can take place.

The three stages of learning are beginning, intermediate, and advanced. The descriptions of these stages presented here are somewhat simplified; however, the essential material is covered. For a more in-depth dis-

cussion of the phases of learning, see the *Coaches Guide to Teaching Sport Skills* (Christina & Corcos, 1988).

Mental or Beginning Stage

The goal of the beginning stage of learning is to develop an understanding of the concepts, principles, and mechanics involved in the skill. The principles of execution should be established. Drills aimed at developing this level of understanding emphasize mechanics rather than the integration of the skill into playing situations.

Keep in mind three important guidelines concerning the material you present during this phase of learning:

- Explain the reasons why a skill is executed.
- Present as few principles as possible without compromising the message.
- Movements and postures that the athlete will do naturally do not need to be discussed.

This phase of the learning process should be the shortest of the three. You'll want to move on to game-related skills as soon as possible.

Practice or Intermediate Stage

During this stage, the focus is on learning to perform the skills. Coaches spend most of their skill-teaching time in this phase, especially if they work with young or beginning volleyball players. Because players will begin to refine a motor program (similar to a computer program) for performing a skill, the learning environment should parallel the competitive environment as closely as possible.

Automatic or Advanced Stage

This final stage of learning assumes that skills have been established in set, game-related motor patterns. The player can at this phase focus on tactical applications. The subtleties of tempo control and ongoing competitive adjustments can be addressed. Although skill refinement is a goal of this phase, refinement is accomplished through a focus on playing the game.

Developing a Teaching Plan

To meet the needs of your players in each of the phases of learning, you will need to develop a teaching plan. Each individual coach and teacher is different. Each has his or her own strengths and weaknesses. You need to be yourself. But you also need to think through several important issues as you develop your teaching plan:

- Assessing fitness and skill level
- Developing a seasonal plan
- Planning practices
- Selecting drills
- Selecting an appropriate teaching style

Assessing the Fitness and Skill Level of Your Athletes

Certainly one of the most important ingredients in successful coaching is the ability to adapt your teaching methods and expectations to the appropriate level. Determine how to adjust your methods by learning about your athletes through fitness testing, observation, and conversation. You can learn more about fitness appraisal in the ACEP *Sport Physiology Course* (Jefferies, 1986; Sharkey, 1986). Understanding the age group with which you are working, their motivations, and their volleyball experience is vital to your success.

Developing a Seasonal Plan

Based on your understanding of your players' fitness and skill levels, you need to determine the order in which you will teach the skills. I suggest that you present the skills in the same sequence as they occur in a game. The exception to this sequence is that at beginning levels, blocking should be taught only after all the other skills have been presented. When blocking is presented, the coverage should be brief. The reasons for this exception are that blocking is the most difficult skill to teach and to learn, is the least frequent action, and provides the fewest opportunities for unambiguous positive feedback.

In addition to determining the order in which you will present skills, you must consider the level of skill you are trying to develop. Remember, perfection is not important in the early stages of teaching volleyball. As an athlete progresses through his or her career, skill level will improve to keep up with the requirements of the current level of competition.

In preparing your seasonal plan, you should make the following decisions about the skills you will ask your players to perform:

- Which skills will be important
- What priority each skill deserves
- What order the skills will be presented in
- How much time will be allotted to each skill
- Which days each skill will be practiced

Anticipate the possibility of adjusting your plan as the season progresses. The purpose of the plan is to give direction to your day-to-day planning. A sample plan is included in chapter 11 of this manual.

Planning Practices

The relatively small amount of on-court practice time available to most volleyball teams is a sobering reality that tempers the ideals of many a coach. When you developed your seasonal plan, you considered the skills you needed to teach, the amount of time available to teach them, and the importance of each skill. Now you must plan particular practice activities.

As you begin to plan practices, have an objective in mind for each session. Be sure that you allow time for each of the following activities:

- Warming up
- Reviewing previously taught skills
- Teaching and practicing new skills
- Practicing under competitive conditions
- Cooling down

Designing practices is discussed more fully in chapter 12. You'll find sample practice plans in chapter 11 and a practice planning form in Appendix A. Feel free to make use of these planning tools.

To coach effectively you must assess your teaching environment. How many balls are there? How many courts are available? Are the net supports freestanding or do they require support cables? Are the ball containers on wheels? Do you have adequate assistance? Your answers to these questions will influence how you plan your practices.

Evaluate your teaching environment against the checklist found in Appendix B (pages 178-180). Change the elements you can, adapt to those you cannot change, and capitalize on the elements that are satisfactory, but as an educator and a concerned coach, demand safe, effective learning conditions.

Selecting Drills

Selecting drills is also an important part of planning practices. Once you have decided your objective for a practice, you must determine what you wish to accomplish in each drill. Chapter 12 focuses on practice and drill design. The drill design questions on page 160 may be helpful in your decision-making process.

Selecting an Appropriate Teaching Style

Develop a teaching formula that is comfortable and consistent for you and for your athletes. A coach must be systematic but not inflexible. Plans on paper are modified by personality quirks, individual moods, the dynamic situations the team experiences, and the chemistry of the group. A coach must have a standard formula but also be sensitive to the unique aspects of each player, team, and situation. The wise coach is always searching out better methods of adjusting his or her coaching technique to provide better experiences for the athletes.

Related to selecting the appropriate style is the issue of evaluating the style and strategy that you select. To help players improve, coaches continually evaluate the team's progress in a variety of ways. Coaching effectiveness should also be evaluated. The relative improvement a player makes is only one indirect method of evaluating the coach's effectiveness as a teacher. Coaches should also evaluate their communication (verbal and nonverbal), time management, drill selection, enthusiasm, ability to coach physical skills, and other related coaching activities. Through evaluation coaches can learn what they need to do to become more efficient and effective. Evaluation can take the form of player questionnaires given periodically, videotaping and analyzing a practice, or bringing in a trusted colleague to observe and comment on your organization and coaching behaviors.

General Principles of Teaching Volleyball Skills

There are many principles of teaching, and each school of thought about teaching modifies the concepts. However, the list of principles here is accepted universally. You'll find these guidelines very practical as you plan your teaching strategies:

- Keep any presentation simple by using carefully chosen words.

- Use as few words as possible. Be sure to use consistent, memorable, and meaningful cues.
- Demonstrate the skill frequently. Visual instruction often has more impact than verbal instruction.
- Describe the desired end result and encourage athletes to explore ways of achieving that result.
- Provide cues, hints, and technical information as needed.
- Communicate clearly why a skill is being taught and why it should be performed in a prescribed manner.
- Answer a question with a question. This process involves players in the learning process by encouraging exploration.
- Make all learning activities compatible with the skill level of the players.
- Keep activities challenging and fun.
- Use drills that replicate the way a skill will be used in competition.

Teaching Concerns

As you present new skills to your players, you must address a few additional concerns.

Speed of Execution

Each player should perform skills at the fastest speed possible without sacrificing correct execution. Speed will increase naturally as the player's confidence in his or her ability to make correct movements increases. It is important, however, to note that volleyball skills require maximum speed at ball contact. But maximum speed for any skill is the speed at which movement can be controlled. Balance and body control are essential elements that cannot be ignored.

Perfection of Movements

Players should strive to perfect their movements, postures, and ball-contact skills during the beginning phase of learning. After all, at this stage the foundation for future learning is laid. Avoid the temptation of

thinking that you can fix problems later. It is much more difficult to correct errors after they have become habits.

Effort

Encourage your players to exert maximum effort at all times, during practices as well as games. If athletes do not work hard in practice, they will not develop the teamwork and personal skills that game situations require. Remember, you play the way you practice!

Imagery

Using imagery skills will also help your players learn skills more effectively. Visualizing a complete skill before performing it will give your players an opportunity to review the correct performance, cue up their motor program, and see a clear image of what they are trying to accomplish. You can learn more about imagery in both the ACEP *Sport Psychology Course* (Bump, 1989; Martens, 1987) and the ACEP *Teaching Sport Skills Course* (Carlton & Carlton, 1989; Christina & Corcos, 1988).

Become a Student of the Game

Volleyball is a multifaceted game. In addition to understanding the rules, the successful coach must understand the elements of the sport and how to teach skills. Take time before your season to prepare a seasonal plan. Then prepare a plan for each practice. A practice conducted without a plan is like a cake prepared without a recipe: It falls flat.

Planning is only part of being an effective coach or teacher. You need to make use of the teaching principles outlined in this chapter. Review them periodically as you work to coach volleyball effectively.

Teaching and Coaching the Game

Before you are able to analyze systems, theories, tactics, and coaching methods and their application to volleyball, you must understand the nature of the game itself. Volleyball has many unique characteristics with which you must become familiar to successfully adapt particular strategies and tactics for use in your own coaching environment.

Volleyball is characterized by the following elements. It

- is a rebound sport,
- uses intermediate contacts,
- has a congested playing area,
- offers little direct positive feedback,
- is a game of transition,
- has an imbalance of offense and defense,
- is a noncontact sport,
- has no time constraints,
- is player-dominated,
- requires similar skills of all players, and
- uses unique skills and playing zones.

As a coach, it is important that you understand each of these elements and learn to consider them in your planning and coaching activities.

A Rebound Sport

The fact that volleyball is categorized as a rebound sport means that players never sustain possession of the ball; rather, the ball is contacted briefly and directed to another player. The only exception to this is, of course, the serve.

In most other sports, athletes can compensate for poor body position at the time of possession by moving into a more advantageous position. Because your players cannot catch the ball and then move to a better position from which to release it, you must constantly train your athletes to position themselves correctly prior to contacting the ball.

Intermediate Contacts

Common volleyball strategy encourages the use of three contacts per team possession on each side of the net. Because most contacts, then, are not terminal hits, controlling the rebound of the ball is important. The need for control highlights the necessity of moving into position for an intermediate hit prior to contacting the ball.

In addition to good ball control, cooperation among team members is essential. For this reason, the interaction of players and the development of teamwork should be dominant themes in coaching volleyball.

A Congested Playing Area

Volleyball is unique in that a high concentration of people play in a small area. The congested playing area makes it vital to organize the positioning of players and their movements. Balanced coverage of all parts of the court is an important goal of the successful coach.

In achieving balanced coverage, be sure to consider the relationships between players positioned next to each other. Team dynamics become prime coaching concerns, partly because of the congested playing area.

Little Positive Feedback

Because playing volleyball itself offers few opportunities for immediate positive feedback, some difficulties are created in the learning process. One of the key elements of effective teaching is providing timely positive feedback to learners. Help your athletes identify correct execution by continually reinforcing desirable behaviors. For example, if the player directs the ball where you want it to go in a passing drill, reinforce the behavior with a positive comment.

It is more difficult to find inherent positive rewards in defensive skills. Giving unambiguous positive feedback to your players' attempts at blocking and back-row recovery skills requires a great deal of creativity. "Nice try" can get old. Start the learning process on a more positive note. Concentrate on serving, passing, and offensive skills, where unambiguous positive feedback can be found more easily, in the early phases of teaching athletes to play volleyball.

A Game of Transition

The roles of offense and defense can be confusing. Volleyball does have offensive and defensive skills, but they are not as separate as they may appear to be in other sports. The ball does not stop between the time your team takes an offensive role and when it must play defense. And, unlike any other sport, your team may switch frequently between offense and defense without a point being scored or a violation being called.

There are four ways to score a point in volleyball: a service ace, a stuff block, a controlled defensive play resulting in an attack (known as "transition"), and an unforced error.

A serve has been described as both an offensive and a defensive skill. It is offensive because the server directs the velocity and trajectory of the ball. It is defensive in that the serve is intended to at the least disrupt the opponent's offense and at the most cancel it. A stuff block is clearly a defensive play. A controlled dig is also defensive and leads to a point through the team offense. The controlled dig can be likened to an interception returned for a touchdown in football.

The opponent's unforced errors can be credited to a stalwart defense that intimidates the foe into attempting shots not usually found in their attack scheme. The opponent's unforced errors obviously cannot be practiced. However, your team's overall discipline and consistency is reflected in your opponent's errors.

It has often been said that the best offense is a good defense. This is particularly true in volleyball. Traditionally aggressive offenses are sometimes handicapped by unforced errors that result in lost points. Conversely, the conservative defense, which simply waits for the opponent to make mistakes, is not likely to produce success. To be successful, teams must strive to be aggressive defensively to create opportunities to score points.

As a coach you must understand the nature of this game of transition. To be successful, your team must be able to shift gears fluidly. In addition, you must learn to integrate offensive and defensive concepts into training sessions and tactical discussions early in the development of your athletes.

Imbalance of Offense and Defense

Probably more than in any other team sport in the world, the offense has a tremendous advantage in volleyball. The offense achieves success (by scoring a point or a side-out) over 70% of the time at the top level of play for men and over 60% of the time in women's competition. This imbalance has increased in recent years in spite of the changes made by the FIVB rules commission to try to narrow the gap.

For example, moving the antennae closer together so they are only 9 meters apart and not counting a touch on the block as one of the three legal contacts were new rules designed to give the defense more opportunity to control the attack, therefore making the attack area smaller. (High school rules in 1988 still had the antennae a ball width outside the vertical sideline markers.)

Noncontact Sport

Volleyball is a team game with a physical barrier that prevents most direct one-on-one contact. The players are in control of their own games, and in many respects they control their own success and failure, regardless of the skill level or actions of their opposition. Coaches must train their players to reach a level of ability that allows success regardless of the strength of the opponent.

The nature of volleyball as a noncontact sport also influences the type of player that chooses to participate. Volleyball players tend to deal with frustration and aggression in very different ways than do athletes in team sports where physical contact can release frustration and moderate the highs and lows of performance. In volleyball, athletes play within themselves and compete against self-imposed standards perhaps more than they compete against opponents.

Lack of Time Constraints

The rules of volleyball present no time limit. Teams compete until one team scores 15 points and has at least a 2-point advantage over the opponent. As a consequence, the last point must be scored by the victorious team. A team cannot run out the clock as in football or, on a limited basis, basketball. In softball and baseball, the "clock" is represented by innings.

Because no time limit can stop play, there is constant pressure to score points. Coaches must teach their players to create opportunities to score, to win the game rather than wait for an opponent to lose.

Some tournaments utilize an 8-minute stop-time clock to stay on schedule. (The clock runs only when the ball is in play.) A game ends either in the normal fashion (15 points, a team must win by 2) or at the end of the 8-minute, stop-time period. In timed games, a team still must win by 2 points.

A Player-Dominated Game

Volleyball is more player-dominated, as opposed to coach-dominated. Communication between the coach and athletes is restricted. As a result, the coach must prepare the team well before they walk into the arena for competition. Players must learn to adapt to the situations they face independent of the coach's comments. Over the years, the traditional restriction of coach involvement has been relaxed. Still, with the continual rebounding of the ball, the actions of the players dominate the outcome of the game.

Players Must Be Able to Play Many Roles

The rules of volleyball require that players rotate to each of six positions. Thus, volleyball is dominated by the theory that all players must become equally adept in all phases of the game. The rules tend to direct coaching thought away from specialization and toward the *universal player theory*. Having a team in which all six starting players are equal in all respects has been the goal of coaches for years. Unfortunately, however, this goal has retarded the development of some of the top teams in the game.

To guide the training of players, the coach must understand the rotation concept, the limitations of specialization, and the rules

of the game. Each player must become familiar with playing in all portions of the court and must be equally comfortable in the front or the back row. As young players learn to play volleyball, the rotation concept is perhaps the most dominant rule with which they must become familiar.

The rotation rule also dictates the activities coaches must include in practice. Many coaches believe that because the universal player is the ideal, they must take time to train all players in all skills. This task becomes virtually impossible in most real-world situations. There are simply not enough hours in the day to train all of the athletes equally well. To be successful, the coach must overcome the constraints imposed and work within the rotation rule to build limited specialization.

Unique Skills and Playing Zones

Running, shuffling, sidestepping, diving, rolling, and various combinations of these skills comprise the movement skills used in volleyball. The coach must focus specifically on developing these skills during practice time. During the course of playing volleyball, the athletes will need to make each of these skills second nature.

Further, the underhand pass is unique to volleyball. In most sports, the ball is contacted with the feet, the hands, or an implement of some sort. Because contact is made with the forearms, special eye-arm coordination is required.

Finally, in volleyball there are two unique zones of play. Most sports are played at a level between the top of the head and the knees, in something we call the *middle zone*. Volleyball, however, involves two additional zones. Many balls are played very close to the floor in the *low zone*. For that reason, coaches must teach players to become comfortable diving, rolling, and using flying recovery techniques, all of which are standard skills.

The other zone utilized in volleyball is the *high zone*, which spans from the top of the athlete's reach to a point 3.5 or more meters above the floor. Because much of the game is played in this high zone, and because jumping skills are called upon more frequently in volleyball than in any other sport, coaches must devote training time to the skill of jumping. You can review each of the three zones in Figure 1-1 on page 8.

Summary

Volleyball is unique in many respects. You must continually examine its various components as you decide on a teaching method. Familiarize yourself with how skills are applied during the tactics of actual play. Learn to understand the emotions your players feel as they face each dynamic situation in volleyball. Design your training activities to duplicate these situations so that your athletes can practice appropriate physical and emotional responses.

Chapter 11: Season Planning

No matter how long or short it may be, there is a specific volleyball season for your team. It can be 6 weeks, 6 months, or an entire year. Whatever the season, one of the coach's first tasks is to plan it, to make the time spent efficient and effective. That means preparing a seasonal plan that considers physical conditioning, individual skill development, playing systems development, tactics training, competition, team cohesiveness training, and problem solving.

The "Season" at a Glance

The "season" is commonly viewed as the competitive portion of a total volleyball program. In this text, season planning really focuses on the total volleyball program, with specific emphasis on the playing season with its technical, tactical, and physical development requirements organized into logical time blocks.

A total volleyball program includes the following phases: preseason, competitive season, league playoffs, championship competition, and postseason. Physical conditioning and skill development are, of course, part of each phase but are described here as specific points of emphasis (and are termed phases).

Preseason

Every program has a preseason. It may last a month, 2 weeks, or only 3 days. This phase includes initial assessment, team development, and competition that does not count toward league standing. At this stage, competition is used for team evaluations.

Competitive Season

This phase should be the highlight of the program, and it includes league play. Emphasis should be placed on play. Correct technical skills at practice, and let your players play during matches. It is through observing their play, however, that you note what technical and tactical adjustments need to be made during practice. Practices during the competitive season should be designed specifically to improve play during the season.

League Playoffs and Championship Competition

This phase must be treated like a separate season. The emphasis is still on play. Give your attention at this point to reinforcing the techniques, tactics, and emotions that got the team into position to play for a championship. It is important to focus on the opportunity and keep the experience in perspective.

There is a great story about John Robinson and his ability to keep perspective when he coached the University of Southern California football Trojans. They were playing Notre Dame at the Los Angeles Coliseum in one of football's most heated and traditional rivalries. Notre Dame led by 4 points with

5 seconds left. The Trojans had the ball on the Fighting Irish 15-yard line. The sellout crowd of 90,000 fans were in a frenzy. John Robinson called his quarterback to the sidelines for his last time-out. The national television commentators up in the booth speculated about what tricky play Coach Robinson might have for the final, desperate effort. End around? Double pass? Quarterback draw?

With his arm over his quarterback's shoulder, John Robinson said, "Take a look around you, son. Feel it. Smell it. Hear it. It is not often a person gets the opportunity to be in this situation. Take a moment and soak it in. Enjoy this moment. Call whatever play you feel good about and do your best."

Of course, teams can't guarantee their being in the playoffs. For most teams, competition ends with the regular season. If this is the case for your team, move directly into the postseason.

Postseason

This phase involves both active rest and evaluation of players and coaches. Active rest is any vigorous but relaxing activity in something other than volleyball. It is important that even the most dedicated player take a break from volleyball, yet not compromise his or her physical condition.

This is also the time to reflect on the season and evaluate the performances of players and coaches.

Physical Conditioning

This phase includes strength development and jump training. At the high school level, a physical conditioning program should be general and should develop and reinforce lifelong physical fitness habits. Your specific training program may be limited by facilities, equipment, and time available. However, these potential limitations should not be excuses to avoid physical conditioning. Physical conditioning is an ongoing process. Areas that need attention for volleyball players include strength and power training through a well-planned, well-supervised weight training program; jump training to increase vertical jumping ability through

power, endurance, and technique practice; and aerobic activity to solidify a general fitness level. Jump and weight (resistance) training for the volleyball athlete is covered in the Level II volleyball text for the Coaches Accreditation Program (CAP).

If you are unsure of how to design efficient and effective physical conditioning programs, consult with people in your community who have verifiable expertise, and read some of the excellent books written on the subject. Several are listed here for your reference.

Physical Conditioning References

Corbin, C.B., & Lindsey, R. (1984). *The ultimate fitness book*. Champaign, IL: Leisure Press.

Fleck, S.J., & Kraemer, W.J. (1987). *Designing resistance training programs*. Champaign, IL: Human Kinetics.

Jefferies, S.C. (1986). *Sport physiology study guide*. Champaign, IL: Human Kinetics.

Radcliffe, J.C., & Farentinos, R.C. (1985). *Plyometrics*. Champaign, IL: Human Kinetics.

Riley, D.P. (1982). *Strength training by the experts*. Champaign, IL: Leisure Press.

Sharkey, B.J. (1984). *Physiology of fitness*. Champaign, IL: Human Kinetics.

Sharkey, B.J. (1986). *Coaches guide to sport physiology*. Champaign, IL: Human Kinetics.

These books may be purchased by calling 1-800-342-5457 (in Illinois, 1-800-334-3665).

Skills Development

This phase includes continued physical conditioning with an emphasis on developing skills. Give particular attention to precise technical execution of the basics and introducing new wrinkles with more advanced tactical implications.

The skills development phase should run from approximately mid-February to the end of April if your program plays the traditional fall season. The amount of time spent depends on several factors, including athletes' involvement with other scholastic sports or their participation in Junior Olympic club teams, facility and coach availability, and, in some cases, state governing body regulations.

Many junior high and high school volleyball players play two seasons: scholastic volleyball with their school teams and junior club volleyball in the USVBA's Junior Olympic program. Collegiate players can play up to three competitive seasons: collegiate competition in the fall, USVBA Open in the spring, and international play in the summer.

Developing a Plan

The coach must first determine the total time available for training. This is often restricted by scholastic federation policy. A 15-week block that includes preseason, competitive season, and playoff phases is used here as a generic example. The coach's primary focus must be on these three phases. However, taking scholastic restrictions into account, the coach must look at an *annual* plan.

Annual Plan

In junior high and high school, many athletes are multisport participants. Therefore, training involvement is sport-specific, restricted to the in-season sport. Some volleyball players, however, want to focus exclusively on volleyball. Encourage them to play USVBA club volleyball and assist them in developing an annual training program. College and international coaches can develop true annual training programs because their players are a captive audience, focusing exclusively on volleyball.

Principles for Planning Use of Time

If you are coaching a team with a 15-week season, the total training time you have available is approximately 188 hours:

$$\left.\begin{array}{l} \text{15 weeks} \times \\ \text{5 days a week} \times \\ \text{2-1/2 hours a day} \end{array}\right| = \begin{array}{l} \text{12-1/2 hours a week} \\ \times \text{ 15 weeks} \\ \text{187-1/2 hours total} \\ \text{training time} \end{array}$$

This formula is actually based on an average. During the preseason, many teams train for more than 2-1/2 hours a day. Some train 6 days a week for the first 3 weeks. It depends on state restrictions and your own philosophy.

A coaching staff and a team never get one minute back. Time passes into history forever, whether it was used effectively or not. Those who use their training time most effectively and efficiently have the best chance for a successful competitive season.

You must first assess your team's level of physical conditioning, competence, experience, and motivation and then prioritize their training needs based on that assessment. After you list the elements to be covered, you must identify the percentages of time you will spend on each skill or strategy. Remember, the percentage of time you allocate at this point is never etched in stone. You must be able to adjust your plan as situations develop and specific needs emerge. The plan is just a guideline. Without it, however, you will allow time to be wasted and important ingredients to be ignored or forgotten.

Physical Conditioning and Warm-Up

The elements to have in your plan include warm-up, physical conditioning, skills development, development of playing systems, team-building activities, game plan instruction, and team information sessions. Before you develop a season plan, you need to evaluate the role that warm-up and physical conditioning will play in your scheme.

What some people consider a warm-up is viewed as physical conditioning by others. That distinction is wholly dependent upon an individual's physical condition relative to volleyball. It is extremely important that you assess each player's physical condition and adjust training accordingly.

Warm-ups should consist of sport-specific movements and take as little time as possible. If floor time is limited due to tight facility scheduling, your team should warm up in a hallway, classroom, annex, or any other safe location before they take the floor. Floor time should be used for developing specific volleyball skills and strategies as much as possible. The goals of a warm-up include

- raising the body temperature for activity (getting the blood moving),
- elevating the heart rate,
- loosening up the joints, and
- establishing a focused mind-set on practice.

At the end of the warm-up, each player should be mentally and physically ready to train. The players should be perspiring lightly and breathing heavily, but not panting. (In humid climates, however, there is no such thing as "perspiring lightly." Just sitting in a rocking chair, idling along, causes profuse sweating and panting. Adjust your standards accordingly.) Remember, players should not be exhausted prior to training.

Warm-ups should take between 10 and 20 minutes. Jogging, serving, light ball handling, calisthenics, flexibility exercises, volleyball-related footwork, and short court one-on-one games are some examples of good warm-up activities.

Physical conditioning should also be volleyball-specific. Thus training is generally an isolated part of practice that occurs *after* the general practice. Exhausted players are not efficient at executing skills correctly. But tired players can build endurance.

You should be aware that a residual physical conditioning effect occurs as a result of a training session. Players will be in better physical condition after they practice. However, to *increase strength* and to develop power, athletes must make specific concentrated effort.

Four-Week Training Schedule

This particular model, which includes 2 weeks of preseason and 2 weeks of competition, is applicable for high school junior varsity and varsity teams. Junior high and junior club programs need to adjust the model to their own levels, facilities, and time constraints.

This model represents a total of 75 hours

of practice time, broken down in the following manner:

Preseason (2 weeks)—2 sessions
a day at 2-1/2 hours each   = 50 hours
(school begins)

Early season (2 weeks)—1 session
a day at 2-1/2 hours   = 25 hours

Total = 75 hours

It is important to note that the time block for a practice session represents the average time span of a competitive match, including warm-up, protocol, and postmatch activities. The overall goal of the plan is to develop the team to be able to compete effectively in the league.

A sample plan is located on pages 132-134. The following key will help you interpret the material:

T10 — Specific teaching time for skill, drill, or other activity

* — Skill is included in another activity

P20 — Practice time to be devoted to a skill

For example:

Activity	Time	Meaning
Emergency skills	T15	Emergency skills are taught specifically for 15 minutes.
Floor Defense	P20	The team practices floor defense for 20 minutes.
Digging	*	Digging is included in other practice activities.

The specialization column indicates the time during which players work on their specialties. As a result, activities in each column take the full time allotments. It is also important to decide the percentage of time you are willing to devote to each activity. In this model, there are a total of 4,500 training minutes. The coach has decided to focus on floor defense, ball handling, and attack. Serving takes less time to learn and is incorporated into virtually every drill involving serve receive.

Also, remember in reading the 4-week plan that the first 2 weeks are made up of two 2-1/2-hour sessions (3000 minutes). If you are not in a position to schedule two sessions a day, either attempt to extend your preseason or modify this schedule to meet your needs. Warm-up and cool-down time must be divided in half to reflect two sessions. Specific focus on floor defense, ball handling, and attack account for 31% of practice time in the first week. This individual attention decreases throughout the season as more focus is placed on team drills.

Weeks 3 and 4 are made up of one 2-1/2-hour session each day. The focus shifts to team drills but reviews critical individual skills. Approximately 34% of practice involves competitive and combination drills. This rises to 60% by mid-season.

The plan on pages 132-134 is a model of an important process. Adjust it to fit the needs and limitations of your own program. A blank planning form is included in Appendix A.

Sample Four-Week Seasonal Plan

The following plan, designed for a high school junior varsity or varsity program, includes a 2-week preseason and the first 2 weeks of the competitive season. The plans presented here call for double practices during the first 2 weeks. If this is not possible in your program, feel free to modify the program as necessary. Time allocations for each component may also be varied to meet your needs.

The seasonal plan grid shown on pages 132-134 illustrates the content of 4 weeks of training and is a guide for allotting specific time to each training activity. Use it as a reference to insure that you give adequate attention to each area. Specific practice plans based on the particular personnel and conditions for each year must be modified, but should be based on these practice plan outlines.

Instructional Goals

- To help players develop the skills and strategies necessary to successfully compete at their level
- To test the athletes' physical condition and work on improving endurance and strength
- To help players develop team behavior standards, goals, and roles

Player Behavioral Objectives

- Players will develop a program philosophy, team behavior standards, goals, and roles.
- Players will test their physical condition and work on improving endurance and strength.
- Players will demonstrate the desired level of competence in the following skills:

  (a) Serving: Players will put 15 balls in a row in the court, serve position 5 and 1, within 2 meters of the sideline and end line 50% of the time.

  (b) Forearm pass: Players will demonstrate the ability to pass the serve with correct footwork and will be able to control free and down balls.

  (c) Overhead pass: Players will be able to pass a free ball forward with accuracy and will be able to front set a high ball.

  (d) Attack: Players will be able to hit with power and control the deep line and cross court.

  (e) Blocking: Players will understand the concept of fronting the hitter and will be able to employ the two-step move correctly.

  (f) Floor defense: Players will be able to dig a straight-on shot using a J stroke, will be able to collapse dig, will be able to roll at least to his or her strong side, and will be able to dive and slide.

- The team will engage in team-building activities including problem solving and fun group projects.
- Players will engage in many competitive drills to get comfortable in competitive situations.

- Players will learn how to practice efficiently and effectively.
- Players will learn how to communicate within the systems of play through the use of one-syllable words.
- Players will learn the 5-1 offensive system and basic patterns.
- The setters will be trained specifically in their duties within the system.
- Players who are deemed capable will learn the quick set.
- Two defensive systems will be taught.
- Individual players' roles within the systems will be learned.
- Players will learn basic tactical concepts of the systems so they will understand basic game plans.

Sample Practices

The following eight practice formats are presented on pages 135-151 to demonstrate the use of the practice outline form found in Appendix A (p. 176). Two practice sessions from each of the 4 weeks presented in the season plan are illustrated. These examples show you how a practice looks on paper. You must develop your own style of practice design to fit your personal philosophy. The elements of practice and drill design are presented in chapter 12, "Practice and Drill Design."

Special Considerations for Planning the Competitive Phase

For the purpose of illustration, we will consider a season in which there are 10 weeks of league competition. The schedule calls for two matches a week, on Tuesdays and Thursdays. The competition phase can be subdivided into three segments; early season (the first 3 weeks of competition), mid-season (the middle 4 weeks), and the stretch run (the final 3 weeks).

Early Season

Training time: 3 weeks, 3 days per week, 2-1/2 hours per day totals 22-1/2 hours of training

The early part of any competitive season is extremely important in laying the groundwork for future competition. You must organize practices that allow your athletes to experience success and give them the opportunity to develop more refined skills.

In addition, you must be sure all your players maintain their level of physical conditioning without expending too much time. It is easy to get caught up in the competitive whirlwind and forget the basics.

Practices at this juncture should be devoted to finalizing your playing units, smoothing out the wrinkles in your offensive and defensive systems, emphasizing tactical applications of skills, and developing skills (particularly in beginning level teams). At the same time, you should be studying your competition and determining what adjustments you will need to make to be successful. That task demands that you observe your own team to identify its personality.

Throughout this segment of your season, you will design practices based on the emerging needs of your team. Customize them based on the early competitive results. Obviously, the team's successes and failures will play a major role in the adjustments you need to make. So too will the roles you assign each player. Be sure to clarify those roles as early in the season as possible.

Mid-Season

Training time: 4 weeks, 3 days per week, 2-1/2 hours per day totals 30 hours of training

Practices at this stage should reflect the continual smoothing of the team's ability to function technically, tactically, emotionally, and psychologically. Your team should be a cohesive unit by the middle of the season, especially if it is playing well. Fine-tuning and tactical considerations are the primary focus of practices during the mid-season. Stay with things that are working.

The middle of the season sees the true personalities of the players emerge. Early on, players put their best behavioral feet forward. After all, they want playing time or a starting position. By mid-season, reality sets in: Playing roles are established and a pecking order becomes ingrained. Dreams and goals are either clarified or misted over.

Coaches must be sensitive to the ebb and flow of the group's dynamic interpersonal relationships. Every task-oriented group faces at least one crisis during its life span. (A volleyball team's "life" is the season. Each year's team is different, so a new "life" begins every year.) The crisis and how it is handled is usually the key to the group's success or failure. One thing is certain: Crisis does not go away. It cannot be ignored. Crisis provides the opportunity for teammates to communicate their feelings and opinions. In doing so, they discover they are not alone in their thoughts. The players can learn to face each other and themselves honestly. Mutual respect is gained. Friendship is not necessarily a result, but the team's bond, based on mutual respect and common goals, is tightened.

If your team is struggling, it may need a face-lift during the mid-season. Try involving more young players or employing a new system. Focus on further individual skill development.

The team that is winning everything at mid-season may have a tendency to sweep problems under the net and avoid them because the winning feels good. Nobody wants to jeopardize a good thing. Often, pressure builds and competition becomes more intense as the successful team heads into the stretch run.

If a team has not had to face adversity in the early and mid-season, the stress in the final weeks of the season and in postseason play can be devastating. Consider creating controlled adversity in some late mid-season practices, forcing players to deal with stress. It may seem like a gamble, but the dividends will pay off in the stretch run.

When a winning streak is broken in any sport, the classic cliché crosses the coach's lips: "The loss will do us good. It will force our team to work harder, to focus on the fundamentals, to clean out the complacency." Or something like that. These comments are borne of the early and mid-season winning streak. Be aware of it.

The Stretch Run

Training time: 3 weeks, 3 days per week, 2-1/2 hours per day totals 22-1/2 hours of training

You and the team know your status heading into the final 3 weeks: The team either is on a roll and a sure bet to make the playoffs, is knotted with several others for a playoff berth, or is out of the running. Each situation requires different action.

The Team on a Roll

Practices for a team on the move should carry an upbeat tempo—relaxed, yet intense. Drills, exercises, and activities that have been successful throughout the year should be continued and the winning routines perpetuated. If the previous competition has been boringly easy, then the competitive challenges must come from within the team. Add a new offensive or defensive option. Create competitive intersquad games. Devote some time to working on more advanced tactics.

The Team in a Knot With Others

A team fighting for a playoff bid must focus on exposing its strengths and camouflaging its weaknesses. Strong tactical work on each opponent is crucial to your success. You must spend time analyzing and coaching for specific matchups. Practices for teams in this situation are a mix of focused tactical work and high-intensity individual work to boost the confidence and toughness of both the team and the individual team members.

The Team That Is Out of the Running

If your team realizes it is out of the playoff picture, the temptation is to coast. When preseason dreams and goals are dashed, motivation is often low. As a competitor, you too can feel disappointed. In these times the true educator and motivator in you must rise like a phoenix. Adjust the long-range goals you have set. Develop short-term, measurable, reachable goals. Give young players a chance to play. Honor older players who have not had much court time during their careers. Introduce new wrinkles. Above all, never let the discipline fall. Do not lower your behavior standards. Use the disappointment as a resolve for harder work next year.

Preseason Training Intensity in Late Season

A study conducted in the Soviet Union several years ago analyzed the physical condition of club team athletes at the end of the preseason, at mid-season, and at the beginning of the playoffs. The results of the study indicated that all players were in the best shape at the end of the preseason. By mid-season, the regular players were in better shape than the bench warmers but still in worse condition than they were at the end of the preseason. Further, the researchers discovered that the players were in the worst physical condition at the beginning of the playoffs, with a difference still present between regulars and substitutes.

The reason for this phenomenon seems obvious: As a season progresses, more time is devoted to tactics and less to physical training. The deterioration of the conditioning level is faster for substitutes than for regulars because substitutes get less playing time.

The Soviets found, however, that if a team added a solid week of preseason physical conditioning intensity 2 to 3 weeks before the playoffs, it could regain its preseason condition level. This assumes the team has done some consistent maintenance work during the early and mid-season. Think of the advantage a highly conditioned team would have!

Additional Concerns

Be aware that the mid-season is often the time when fatigue-related injuries occur. Coaches must be alert and sensitive to this possibility and plan activities accordingly. Work to prevent injuries when possible, and care for them effectively when they do occur.

In addition, realize that it is difficult to sustain high levels of intensity for every match. Identify key matches to emphasize throughout the season, and increase training levels prior to those matches. Plan carefully. You want a fresh, energized team moving into the playoffs.

Special Considerations for the Playoffs

Your team made it! Dark horse? Cinderella? Favorite? First time? Always make it? Finished strong? Limped it? Front runner? However a team qualifies, under whatever conditions, competing in championship playoffs is an exciting, fun time. You and your players must keep the experience in perspective. It is not a matter of life or death; it is an honor for an elite few. This time should be savored . . . enjoyed . . . shared.

In preparing for the playoffs, practices should be intense. Spend time reviewing the systems that got your team where it is. Always remember, though, that practices should be enjoyable but disciplined.

Expectations heavily influence the practice environment. You must adjust to the ambiance, yet control the atmosphere surrounding the team. If the mood is tense and serious, you loosen it up; if the team is inappropriately cocky, you must tighten the reins; if outside influences are destructive, you must close training to outside observers.

Playoff participation is the ultimate in competition. Naturally, the stress is high. The wise coach takes advantage of the opportunity to teach young players about pursuing goals relentlessly—win or lose.

Special Considerations for Postseason and Beyond

No athletic person ever stops exercising unless injury prohibits it. Still, it is productive to get away from a particular sport after a long training and playing season. That is the purpose of active rest. Many junior high and high school athletes move on to other sports—this is a good break. Full-time volleyball players should also take a few weeks' break to participate in recreational activities, maintain their general conditioning, and rejuvenate the mind.

The serious, one-sport athlete *should* train year-round. However, if the annual cycle begins at too young an age, burnout can occur. As a result, many good players drift into other activities before they can become great players. You must temper enthusiastic dreams, goals, and impatience. Encourage young players to play a variety of sports. They need to learn how to compete, how to play. When an athlete is ready to train year-round, then you must provide sound advice and a plan for development.

Summary

A functional season plan is perhaps the most important ingredient in developing a successful program. Take time to create one that fits your philosophy, teaching environment, and style. In the appendix you will find some additional tools to assist you with your planning. The Program Development and Starting a Season checklists (Appendix B, pp. 178-180) were designed by Pam Parks, a CAP/ACEP instructor and a highly successful high school and college coach. Appendix C (pp. 182-184) provides a match protocol format with the playing court and marching diagrams. Together with the checklist for home matches, these forms provide samples of how to present a volleyball match that will be pleasing to spectators and players. Use these tools or develop others that you can use from year to year and that require only small additions or adjustments from time to time. It will make your role as coach much easier.

4-Week Instructional Schedule for Volleyball

Goal: To help players learn and practice the individual and team skills needed to play a regulation game after 4 weeks.

T(10): Teach and practice the skill initially for 10 min.   *: These skills are practiced during the drills.

P(10): Review and practice the skill for 10 min.

Week 1

	Day 1		Day 2		Day 3		Day 4		Day 5	
	Session 1	Session 2	Session 3	Session 4	Session 5	Session 6	Session 7	Session 8	Session 9	Session 10
Warm-up	T15	P15	P15	P15	P10	P10	P12	P10	P12	P10
Cool-down	T5	P5	P5	P5	P5	P5	P5	P5	P5	P5
Physical conditioning		T20		P15		P20		P20		P25
Serving										
Technique	T20	P10	P10	*	*	*	P10	*	*	*
Tactics		T10		P15	*	*	*	P10	*	*
Forearm pass										
Technique	T20		P15	*	*	*	P10	*	P10	*
Serve receive	*	T10		*	P30	*	*	P15	*	P10
Overhead pass										
Technique		T20	P10	P8	P10	*	P10	*	P15	*
Setting					T20	*	*	P10	*	P10
Attack										
Technique	T20			*	*	*	P10	P10	*	P10
Individual tactics		*	*	*	*	*	*	*	*	*
Combinations			T15					T20		P10
Blocking										
Technique			T10	*	P10	*	*	*	P10	*
Tactics				T10	P10	*	*	*	*	*
Floor defense										
Digging	T20	*	P10	P10	P25	P15	P23	P20	P10	*
Emergency skills		T20	P10	*	*	*	*	*	*	P10
Specialization			T20	P12	*	P30	*	*	*	*
Combined skill/ competitive team drills				T30		P40	P40		P28	
Systems										
Side out offense									T20	*
Transition offense									T10	P10
Defense										T20
Team procedures	T20	T10								

4-Week Instructional Schedule for Volleyball (Continued)

Goal: To help players learn and practice the individual and team skills needed to play a regulation game after 4 weeks.

T(10): Teach and practice the skill initially for 10 min.   *: These skills are practiced during the drills.
P(10): Review and practice the skill for 10 min.

	Week 2									
	Day 6		Day 7		Day 8		Day 9		Day 10	
	Session 11	Session 12	Session 13	Session 14	Session 15	Session 16	Session 17	Session 18	Session 19	Session 20
Warm-up	P10	P10	P10	P10	P10	P10	P10	P10	P10	P10
Cool-down	P5	P5	P5	P5	P5	P5	P5	P5	P5	P5
Physical conditioning		P25		P20		P20	P20	P15		P15
Serving										
Technique	P5	*	*	P5	P5	*	*	P5	P5	*
Tactics	*	P5	*	P5	*	P10	P5	*	*	P5
Forearm pass										
Technique	P5	*	P15	*	P10	*	P5	P5	*	*
Serve receive	P10	*	*	P10	*	P10	P10	*	P10	*
Overhead pass										
Technique	P5	*	P5	*	P10	*	P5	P5	P5	P5
Setting	P10	P15	P10	P15	*	P10		*	*	*
Attack										
Technique	P5	P5	P5	*	P10	P10	*	P5	P5	P5
Individual tactics	P10	*	P10	*	*	*	P10	*	*	*
Combinations		P25		*	*	*	*	P5	P5	P5
Blocking										
Technique	P5	*	*	P10	P5	*	*	P5	*	P5
Tactics	P10	*	*	*	P10	*	*	*	*	*
Floor defense										
Digging	P10	P10	P10	*	P20	P8	P10	P10	P10	P10
Emergency skills	P10	*	P10	*	*	P7	P10	*	*	*
Specialization	*	*	*	P25	P35	*	P20	*	*	*
Combined skill/ competitive team drills		P20	P40	P15		P30	P10	P50	P10	
Systems										
Side out offense	P10								P25	*
Transition offense	P10		*	*				*	*	P30
Defense	*	*	*	*				*	P30	P25
Team procedures										

(Cont.)

4-Week Instructional Schedule for Volleyball (Continued)

Goal: To help players learn and practice the individual and team skills needed to play a regulation game after 4 weeks.

T(10): Teach and practice the skill initially for 10 min. *: These skills are practiced during the drills.
P(10): Review and practice the skill for 10 min.

| | Week 3 | | | | | Week 4 | | | | | Total | % |
| | Day 11 | Day 12 | Day 13 | Day 14 | Day 15 | Day 16 | Day 17 | Day 18 | Day 19 | Day 20 | | |
	Session 21	Session 22	Session 23	Session 24	Session 25	Session 26	Session 27	Session 28	Session 29	Session 30	min	time
Warm-up	P10	P10	P10	P10	P10	P10	P10	P10	P10	P10	324	9
Cool-down	P5	P5	P5	P5	P5	P5	P5	P5	P5	P5	150	4
Physical conditioning	P15	P15	P15	P20		P15	P15	P15	P10		335	9
Serving												
Technique	P5	P5	P5	P5	P10	P5	P5	P5	*	P5	125	3
Tactics	*	*	*	*	*	P5	P5	*	P5	*	80	2
Forearm pass												
Technique	P10	P5	*	P5	P5	*	P10	P5	*	*	135	4
Serve receive	*	*	P20	P10	*	P15	P10	*	P10	P5	185	5
Overhead pass												
Technique	P5	P5	P5	P5	P5	*	P5	P5	*	P5	153	4
Setting	*	*	*	*	*	P10	P5	*	P5	*	120	3
Attack												
Technique	P10	P5	P10	P5	P5	P10	*	P5	P10	P5	165	5
Individual tactics	*	*	*	*	*	*	P10	*	P10	*	65	2
Combinations	*	P10	*	P5	P5	*	*	P5	*	P5	95	3
Blocking												
Technique	*	P10	*	*	*	P10	*	P5	P5	*	90	3
Tactics	*	*	*	*	*	*	*	*	*	*	40	1
Floor defense												
Digging	P10	P10	P10	P5	*	P15	P10	P10	P10	P5	316	9
Emergency skills	*	*	P10	*	*	*	P5	*	*	P5	97	3
Specialization	*	*	*	*	P10	P20	P15	*	*	P15	202	6
Combined skill/ competitive team drills	P50	P40	P30	P50	P65	*	P10	P50	P40	P55	703	20
Systems												
Side out offense	*		*	*	*			*	*	*	55	2
Transition offense	*	*	*	*	*			*	*	*	60	2
Defense	*		*	*	*			*	*	*	75	2
Team procedures	*			*	*					*	30	1

Practice Plan #1

Total time: 120 minutes

Instructional goal:
To introduce players to the basic skills and strategies of volleyball

Equipment: Volleyballs

Activities:
Serving
—Progression (pp. 11, 14)
Forearm Passing
—Progression (pp. 26-27)
Attacking
—Progression (pp. 50-51)
Floor Defense
—Progression (pp. 81-82)

Component/time	Activity/drill	Organization	Coaching points
Introduction and warm-up 15 min	Introduce yourself and the coaching staff; jog (4 min); stretch (6 min).	Begin in a group. Players should jog at their own pace. Then bring the group together for stretching.	Make a point to speak with each player. Try to learn all team members' names. Be sure players do not bounce while stretching.
Teach 20 min (35 min)	Teach the serving technique.	Bring the group together for explanation and demonstration. Spread out on available courts for experimentation.	Players can learn either the underhand or the overhead serve. Be sure all players take their time, concentrate, face the target, and toss the ball.
Teach 20 min (55 min)	Teach the forearm pass.	Follow the procedure just described.	Focus on getting into position before the ball arrives, contacting the ball on the forearms, and controlling the direction of the ball.
Teach 20 min (75 min)	Teach the spiking action.	Follow the same procedure.	Concentrate on the run-jump-hit rhythm.
Teach 20 min (95 min)	Teach floor defense techniques.	Follow the same procedure.	Remind players to stay low, avoid the corners of the body, play the ball, and recover quickly.
Teach 20 min (115 min)	Go over team rules, policies, and procedures. Review volleyball rules involving each of the skills presented.	Meet in a group. It may be valuable to walk through some situations to review the rules.	Ask for questions and clarify any confusion.
Cool-down 5 min (120 min)	Light stretching	Continue in the group.	Encourage players to stretch at the end of each bout of physical activity. Set up the time and location of the next practice.

Practice Plan #5

Total time: 120 minutes

Instructional goal:
To improve passing skills and communication for teamwork

Equipment: Volleyballs, basketball hoops, container for balls, and a sturdy box or table

Drills:
Forearm Passing
    —3.5 Butterfly Serve Receive
Overhead Passing
    —4.1 Two Targets
    —4.6 The Setting Game
Blocking
    —6.1 Ball Over the Head
    —6.3 Blocking Pin to Pin
Floor Defense
    —7.2 Control Pepper
    —7.5 Compensation

Component/time	Activity/drill	Organization	Coaching points
Warm-up 10 min	Jog and stretch	Individual work	Encourage players.
Practice 30 min (40 min)	Butterfly Serve Receive drill		Stress moving into position early and directing the ball to the target player. This process will get your team into a controlled offense. Remind players to call the ball prior to playing it.
Practice 10 min (50 min)	Two Targets drill	Work in groups of three.	Ask each passer to accurately pass 10 balls before rotating positions. Stress balanced body position and being in position early.
Teach 20 min (70 min)	The Setting Game drill	This drill is played with a basketball hoop. Use as many stations as are available to you. Players should work in pairs.	Remind players that the key to successful setting is accuracy.
	Go over the principles of setting.	Present the principles in a group. Then break into groups made up of a setter, a passer, and a hitter to practice the principles.	Remind players as they practice that they must set the ball high between the attacker and the net, set the ball inside, and select the easiest option.

Component/time	Activity/drill	Organization	Coaching points
Practice 10 min (80 min)	Ball Over the Head drill		Stress lining up with the hitter. Keep players rotating quickly.
Practice 10 min (90 min)	Blocking Pin to Pin drill		Focus on middle blockers moving into position quickly. Insist that outside blockers front the hitter.
Practice 25 min (115 min)	Control Pepper drill	Players work in groups of two or three.	Players try to keep the ball in play for as long as possible. Any defensive skill may be used in this drill.
	Compensation drill	Work in groups of three or six. 	Stress the importance of keeping a balance on the floor. Be aware of your players' tendency to creep toward the ball. Insist that players call the ball before playing it.

(Cont.)

Practice Plan 5 (Continued)

Component/time	Activity/drill	Organization	Coaching points
Cool-down 5 min (120 min)	Players stretch on an individual basis.	Bring the group together.	Review the practice. Be sure to point out good performances and encourage athletes to continue working hard. Announce the time and place of the next practice.

Practice Plan #12

Total time: 120 minutes

Instructional goal:
To integrate offensive skills into sequential combinations

Equipment: Volleyballs, tape, container for balls

Drills:
Serving
—2.4 Horse I
Overhead Passing
—4.5 Six-Player Rotation
Attack
—5.1 Pairs Bounce/Self-Hit
—5.9 Three-Player Rotation
Floor Defense
—7.4 VIs

Component/time	Activity/drill	Organization	Coaching points
Warm-up 10 min	Players jog and stretch.	This warm-up should be led by one or two players.	Make sure that all major muscle groups are warmed.
Practice 5 min (15 min)	Horse I drill	The targets for this drill must be laid out before practice. Players work in pairs.	Emphasize repeating the same serving motion each time.
Practice 15 min (30 min)	Six-Player Rotation drill	Players work in two teams of six per court. Have an equal number of balls in use at each court. When all balls at any one station are used up, those players begin jogging around the perimeter.	Encourage players to work cooperatively to keep the balls in play. Stress proper mechanics.
Practice 5 min (35 min)	Pairs Bounce/Self-Hit drill	Players work in pairs. Multiple groups of pairs may work at one net.	Emphasize using the approach. Discourage standing at the net. Each partner should have at least five spikes in this time period.

Component/time	Activity/drill	Organization	Coaching points
Practice 25 min (60 min)	Three-Player Rotation drill	Groups of three face other groups of three. 	Focus on the need for accuracy in all three positions. Allow each group to play 20 balls during this time period. Those who use their allotment before the end of the drill put away the equipment today.
Practice 10 min (70 min)	VIs drill	Divide the team into groups of three. Place half of the groups on the court if you have enough courts. If not, you can perform this drill outside of a court. Players left over shag balls and return them to the coach.	Reward hustle and determination. Remind players to avoid the corners of the body.
Practice 20 min (90 min)	Work on combined skill activities.	Arrange players on the court. Assign them a wave as illustrated. Players play one point and then "wave through." 	Try out different combinations of players in this drill. Require players to call all balls. Insist that no ball fall to the ground without someone making an attempt to play it.

(Cont.)

Practice Plan 12 (Continued)

Component/time	Activity/drill	Organization	Coaching points
Practice 25 min (115 min)	Perform physical fitness activities.	Set up a circuit of eight fitness activities. Include jumping, jogging, stretching, and weight stations. Players begin at different stations and work for 2 minutes at each. Players run one lap of the court between stations.	Players will be getting tired. Be sure you offer encouragement to each group. Monitor each station to be sure that exercises are being performed correctly.
Cool-down 5 min (120 min)	Players walk and stretch.	After players have walked for at least 3 minutes, bring them together to stretch.	Review the practice with players. Invite their comments. Announce the time and place of the next practice.

Practice Plan #19

Total time: 120 minutes

Instructional goal:
To review offensive and defensive systems and their basic skills

Equipment: Volleyballs and a container for balls

Drills:
Forearm Passing
  —3.7 Three-Point Game
Overhead Passing
  —4.1 Two Targets
Attack
  —5.2 Rhythm Hitting
  —5.3 Setter Initiates
Floor Defense
  —7.2 Repeat Pepper
  —7.6 King/Queen of the Court

Component/time	Activity/drill	Organization	Coaching points
Warm-up 10 min	Players jog and stretch individually.	Players spread out on the court.	As players are warmed up, move them into practicing individual skills.
Practice 5 min (15 min)	Players serve to each other.	Players divide themselves evenly on both sides of the available courts and serve to each other.	Walk behind each serving line to observe each server. Make comments only when you have isolated a problem or when praise is warranted.

Component/time	Activity/drill	Organization	Coaching points
Practice 10 min (25 min)	Three-Point Game drill	Divide players into groups of at least three on the available courts. Two groups may use each court.	Observe play and remind players to keep their wrists together and face the ball. Players should also be reminded not to "swing" at the ball.

Component/time	Activity/drill	Organization	Coaching points
Practice 5 min (30 min)	Two Targets drill	Divide the team into groups of three with two balls at each group. Alternate passers after 1-1/2 minutes.	Stress getting into position early, contacting the ball close to the forehead, and keeping the body balanced.
Practice 5 min (35 min)	Rhythm Hitting drill	Players form two lines: a hitting line and a handing line. Toss the ball to hitters one meter back from the net. Players shag their own balls and move into the handing line. From the handing line, players move to the hitting line.	Toss the ball as consistently as possible, one meter from the net. Consider only flaws in technique during this drill. Encourage players to keep their position away from the net to protect the approach lane.
Practice 5 min (40 min)	Setter Initiates drill	Divide the team into groups with setters. Two groups may work on each available court.	Watch for your hitters' tendency to follow the pass into the net. Remind players to move into attack position after passing the ball.
Practice 10 min (50 min)	Repeat Pepper drill	Divide the team into pairs. Pairs spread out on the floor. Players each try to keep the ball off the floor for 2 minutes; then switch positions. Repeat this pattern one more time.	Emphasize moving to the ball and sacrificing to make a play on the ball. Remind players to return to the defensive ready position as quickly as possible.

(Cont.)

Practice Plan 19 (Continued)

Component/time	Activity/drill	Organization	Coaching points
Practice 10 min (60 min)	King/Queen of the Court drill	Divide the team into groups of three. Put at least two groups of three on each available court.	Remind players to continue play to a dead ball. Reward good offensive play in transition.

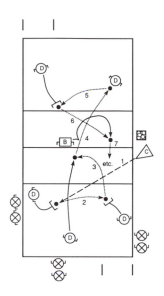

Practice 25 min (85 min)	Review team side out offensive systems.	Walk through any plays you wish to run. Practice combinations and those plays.	Answer any player questions. Encourage thought and innovation.
Practice 30 min (115 min)	Review team defensive roles and positions.	Simulate opponent offensive play by holding a ball at the angle at which it will cross the net. Check player positioning. Then toss the ball into play and play to an attack.	Work with an assistant to move the defense around in their reactions to ball position. Answer queries about position or role. Point out lapses in coverage and repeat the missed coverage situation.
Cool-down 5 min (120 min)	Players stretch individually.	Players remain in a large group.	Discuss the practice. Make any generalized group comments. Announce the time and place of the next practice.

Practice Plan #22

Instructional goal:
To review major skills and combine them into a game structure

Equipment: Volleyballs, a sturdy box or table, and a container for balls

Drills:
Forearm Passing
 —3.3 Same-Side Triads
Overhead Passing
 —4.2 Free-Ball Passing
Attack
 —5.4 Setter Chase
Floor Defense
 —7.3 Coach On a Box

Component/time	Activity/drill	Organization	Coaching points
Warm-up 10 min	Players do individual jogging, stretching, and skill work.	Players space themselves in the gym.	Circulate and assist players as necessary.
Practice 5 min (15 min)	Players practice serving.	Divide players on both sides of the net. Players on one side of the net start with the balls and serve. Those on the opposite side receive the serve and hit the ball in the air to themselves. Then, they serve.	Focus attention on the mechanics of a good serve. Players merely going through the motions will not help the team. Encourage receivers to control the ball to themselves.
Practice 5 min (20 min)	Same-Side Triads drill	Divide the team into groups of at least three. Station each triad on a court (or court segment).	Rotate player positions after 1-1/2 minutes. Stress moving into position rather than reaching outside of the body line. Control is the goal.
Practice 5 min (25 min)	Free-Ball Passing drill	Work in groups of six.	Stress body position and legal hits.
Practice 5 min (30 min)	Continue the Free-Ball Passing drill.	Add the variation of having the target player set the ball to a target spiker who hits.	Assist hitters in improving their timing and approach angle.

(Cont.)

Practice Plan 22 (Continued)

Component/time	Activity/drill	Organization	Coaching points
Practice 10 min (40 min)	Setter Chase drill	Form two spiking lines on each side of the same court.	Assign a setter to the target position. Alternate setters at this position. Bounce the next ball as soon as the hitter contacts the ball to keep this drill moving.
Practice 10 min (50 min)	Continue the Setter Chase drill.	Add blockers to the drill.	Remind players to front the hitter and to jump vertically rather than move horizontally. Alert players whenever they contact the net or the center line.
Practice 10 min (60 min)	Coach On a Box drill	Work in groups of six. Players should rotate after each successful defensive play.	Vary the situations you set up. Use the situations you expect to see from opponents. As players improve, require a specific play from the defense. Be sure players are aligned in positions they will be playing in actual competition.

Component/time	Activity/drill	Organization	Coaching points
Practice 40 min (100 min)	Scrimmage	Play a game complete with typical substitutions.	Officiate this game as closely as possible to the way your competition is officiated. You may make comments for the first 15 minutes of the scrimmage. Then just officiate and allow players to focus on their play. Note any comments you want to make at the end of practice.
Practice 15 min (115 min)	Complete a jump training session.	Set up a circuit of jump training activities. Include skipping, lateral bounds, side hops, quick leaps, and single-leg stride jumps.	Be sure to encourage players throughout this segment of practice.
Cool-down 5 min (120 min)	Players stretch all major muscle groups.	Form a large group.	Make the constructive comments you collected during the scrimmage. Announce the time and place of the next practice.

Practice Plan #25

Total time: 120 minutes

Instructional goal:
To work on serving trajectory and work into integrated-skill games

Equipment: Volleyballs, elastic, tape, and a container for balls

Drills:
Serving
—2.3 Hula Hoop/Elastic
Forearm Passing
—3.2 Points of the Compass
Overhead Passing
—4.3 Three-Meter Game
Attack
—5.5 Horse II
—5.6 Deep-Court Hitting
—5.9 Three-Player Rotation

Component/time	Activity/drill	Organization	Coaching points
Warm-up 10 min	Alternate jogging, sliding, and hopping around the court area. Then have players stretch before allowing individual skill warm-up.	All players work in a group for the movement sequence. Stretching and skill warm-up are on an individual basis.	Watch for and correct any movement errors or incorrect stretching or skill practices.
Practice 10 min (20 min)	Hula Hoop/Elastic drill	Divide the team equally on the available courts. String elastic between the antennae (at the top) prior to practice.	Assist players in adjusting their service trajectory as necessary to make the ball pass between the net and the elastic.

(Cont.)

Practice Plan 25 (Continued)

Component/time	Activity/drill	Organization	Coaching points
Practice 5 min (25 min)	Points of the Compass drill	Players work in pairs. Align groups on the court so the tosser is at the net and the passer is facing the net.	Remind players of the footwork patterns needed to move in all directions. Stress keeping the wrists together and getting into position behind the ball.
Practice 5 min (30 min)	Three-Meter Game drill	Divide the team into groups of three, which will play against each other on the available courts.	Stress moving into position to pass the ball, getting the hands up early, and using the extend-and-pray follow-through.
Practice 5 min (35 min)	Deep-Court Hitting drill	Divide the team equally on all available courts. Form two player lines at each court. One line hands the ball to the coach, the other hits.	Focus on attaining controlled body position and timing. Offer corrective suggestions as necessary. Remind players of the run-jump-hit sequence.
Practice 5 min (40 min)	Three-Player Rotation drill	Work in groups of three, facing another group of three on a divided court.	Ask players to focus on transition and teamwork as well as the accuracy of their individual skills.

Component/time	Activity/drill	Organization	Coaching points
Practice 10 min (50 min)	Hitters play Horse II drill. Setters work on setting for particular plays.	Hitters pair off on one court; setters work on the other.	Encourage hitters to assist each other if they notice technique errors. Comment on any errors or excellent performances you notice. Encourage setters to help each other in learning to perform certain setting sequences that will be used in game play. Comment as necessary.
Practice 65 min (115 min)	Scrimmage	Set up as if this were an actual game.	Officiate and offer comments as a coach. Ask setters to use the plays they have just practiced. Ask hitters to plan where they want to hit before they hit. Call time-outs to have long discussions with players. Reserve the last 10 minutes to discuss team game play with the group. Ask for comments from the team.
Cool-down 5 min (120 min)	Players stretch all major muscle groups.	Continue activity in the large group setting.	Talk with any players you believe need an extra lift after practice today. Announce the time and place of the next practice.

Practice Plan #28

Total time: 120 minutes

Instructional goal:
To improve accuracy in serving and attacking, to practice transitions, and to integrate individual skills into a team play concept

Equipment: Volleyballs; tape; chairs; hula hoops; weighted, inflatable clowns or other suitable targets; and a container for balls

Drills:
Serving
   —2.2 Target Progression
Overhead Passing
   —4.4 Two Contact/Narrow Court Game
Attack
   —5.7 Target Practice
   —5.9 Three-Player Rotation
Blocking
   —6.3 Blocking Pin to Pin
   —6.4 Block Transition Hit
Floor Defense
   —7.2 Repeat Pepper
   —7.8 Deep-Court Exchange

Component/time	Activity/drill	Organization	Coaching points
Warm-up 10 min	Players practice blocking along the net, back sliding the sideline, sliding the back line, and jogging the opposite sideline, and repeat the process. Then perform partner stretching activities.	Players jog at their own pace and do stretching activities in a large group.	Remind players to apply pressure during stretches until they feel resistance.
Practice 5 min (15 min)	Target Progression drill	Use six players as targets. They must receive the ball and hit a playable ball.	Alternate attention between serving technique and forearm pass technique. Make any corrections necessary.
Practice 5 min (20 min)	Continue the Target Progression drill.	Switch the side of the court that is serving.	Continue alternating focus. Make any corrections required.
Practice 5 min (25 min)	Two Contact/Narrow Court Game drill	Divide the available courts into narrow courts. Align players in the following manner: 	Taping of some lines will have to be done prior to practice. During the drill, do not let sloppy footwork or the failure to get into position early go without comment.

Component/time	Activity/drill	Organization	Coaching points
Practice 5 min (30 min)	Target Practice drill	Divide the team into equal lines on the available courts. Assign a setter to each group. Start the ball with the setter, who tosses to the hitter, who passes the ball back to the setter to initiate play. Place hula hoops on the court in areas you would like to see attackers hit in a game situation.	Assist players in learning their angle of approach. If players are unable to hit a particular target, provide assistance in discussing the appropriate movement pattern.
Practice 5 min (35 min)	Three-Player Rotation drill	Divide the team into groups of six, three on each side of a court.	Look for and praise good attack movement and balance. Remind players of the need to call for the ball and react as a unit.
Practice 5 min (40 min)	Blocking Pin to Pin drill	Work in groups of 10 or 12 on available courts.	Focus on the movement of the blockers. Remind players that they need to front the hitter and keep multiple blockers close together. Be aware of the position of the offside blocker. Comment when necessary on positioning of all blockers.
Practice 10 min (50 min)	Repeat Pepper drill	Divide into pairs and spread the team out over the court area. Players switch roles in this drill every 2 minutes.	Encourage hustle in this drill. The key to effective floor defense is desire. Praise players who try for everything. They will assist your team effort immeasurably.
Practice 15 min (65 min)	Block Transition Hit drill	Divide the team into groups of eight. Place four players on each side of the net. Continue play on each point until a dead ball. Then immediately put another ball in play.	Concentrate on the ability of your players to transition between defense and offense and back. Be aware of floor movement. Make any individual or group comments as necessary.

(Cont.)

Practice Plan 28 (Continued)

Component/time	Activity/drill	Organization	Coaching points
Practice 10 min (75 min)	Deep-Court Exchange drill	Divide the team into groups of three. Assign groups to the ends of all available courts. Move one group of three onto the floor from each end of the court for each cycle.	Again, focus on team movement for transition. Positioning, coverage, and communication are key concerns.
Practice 25 min (100 min)	Scrimmage	Divide the team into groups of six to compete against each other on available courts. Use substitutions if necessary.	Try not to interrupt play with too many comments. Allow your team to get into the flow of play. Be sure to allow yourself about 5 minutes of the time allotment to make comments at the end of the scrimmage session.
Practice 15 min (115 min)	Weight training	Place players at a weight training station. Players work at their own assigned resistance. Each should perform three sets of five repetitions at each of the stations.	Be on the lookout for incorrect technique, which can cause serious injury. Encourage players throughout this segment of practice.
Cool-down 5 min (120 min)	Use partner stretches to restretch the muscles.	Players work in a one-court area.	Comment on the practice. Answer any player questions. Announce the time and place of the next practice.

Practice Plan #30

Total time: 120 minutes

Instructional goal:
To review skills and simulate a game situation

Equipment: Volleyballs, a sturdy box or table, and a container for balls

Drills:
Floor Defense
—7.3 Coach On a Box

Component/time	Activity/drill	Organization	Coaching points
Warm-up 10 min	Complete a team warm-up and stretching sequence prepared by team members and approved by the coaching staff.	The team should work in a large group.	Be available to the players, but allow them to work without your direction. Comment only if safety is a concern.
Practice 15 min (25 min)	Setters practice the sets required for the plays the team will use. Hitters form spiking lines and practice a variety of down-the-line and cross-court shots.	Setters work on one court, hitters work on the other. Have a coach toss the ball for hitters.	Offer encouragement and constructive comments to all players during this period. Stress technique!

Component/time	Activity/drill	Organization	Coaching points
Practice 5 min (30 min)	Relay race	Set up a relay race that requires players to dig, dive, and collapse. Have players repeat any skills that were performed incorrectly or halfheartedly.	Be sure players use the appropriate footwork. Encourage really going for the ball.
Practice 5 min (35 min)	Coach On a Box drill	Work in groups of six playing against another group of six. Create the situation you want to simulate by the way you toss the ball into play.	Watch for positioning, defensive movement, and correct digging technique. Comment as necessary.
Practice 5 min (40 min)	Set up spiking lines as in the pregame spiking warm-up.	Divide the team into two lines. Have each hitter toss his or her ball to the setter who sets the ball for the attack. Players shag their own balls and move into the next line.	Observe attack technique. Offer praise and positive corrections. Remember, this is a pregame drill!
Practice 10 min (50 min)	Practice a variety of plays.	Have players form three lines simulating front-line players. Toss the ball to the center player, who passes to the setter, who sets to any one of the hitters. Players rotate from left to right after contacting the ball. Start hitters on their preferred side. Alternate setters as needed.	Observe the activity. Offer encouragement and positive error-correction information.
Practice 10 min (60 min)	Practice both serving and serve receiving.	Divide the team on both sides of the net. One team serves to the other. Receivers play the ball to a staff member stationed at the center front. That person gives the ball to a player on the receiving side to serve. Roles reverse after six serves.	Watch the performance of your team. Make any suggestions that can be easily incorporated. Save major changes for a more appropriate time.
Practice 55 min (115 min)	Run a simulated game.	Run through the exact pregame routine your team will follow for home matches. Assign a staff member to officiate or secure the services of an official.	Coach this scrimmage as you would a game. Use your typical substitutions and time-out strategies.
Cool-down 5 min (120 min)	Have players stretch all major muscle groups.	Bring all players together in a limited area.	Ask for reactions to the scrimmage. Review any procedural concerns. Announce the time and place of the next practice or game.

Chapter 12: Practice and Drills Design

The standard cliché for coaches is that the success of any team in a contest is built in the practice gym. Many an athlete protests, saying, "I'm a game player, not a practice player." The coach responds with the time-tested adage, "You play the game like you practice." The coach, of course, is correct. Clearly, quality practice leads to quality games.

Most coaches feel they do not have adequate time, space, or facilities to practice. Yet, there is a danger in investing too much time on things one cannot control, like limited space, inconvenient time slots, league or association restrictions on length of practice or seasons, meager funding, and so on. Coaches as well as players must focus on what they *can* control. Of course, a coach must continue pursuing improvement in the training conditions. But concern over what's wrong with a situation should never overshadow the positive elements of what a coach is trying to create.

Practice

The word "practice" can cover every element of a team's development. Practice is not just an organization of drills. It is an ongoing opportunity to develop attitude, desirable behavior patterns, commitment, positive cumulative effect, physical conditioning, and techniques and tactics. These elements are intertwined. Blended together, these ingredients make up the final product that we commonly call a "team." Let's look at the recipe for a practice.

Attitude

The team attitude begins with you, the coach. It is a great advantage for any coach to be able to look into a mirror and see the same person others see. It isn't as easy as it sounds. We all have difficulty seeing the person others see—we are biased about ourselves. Either we are too self-critical or not critical enough. Adolph Rupp, the late "baron" of Kentucky basketball, once said, "We're never as good as we think we are nor as bad as we think we are."

The coach initiates how a team is going to feel about itself and view particular situations. If you blame the officials, a low budget, or pitiful facilities for your lack of success, then the team will also. If you are enthusiastic, believe in yourself, see an opportunity for growth even in the most dire situation, then your team will also.

Look in the mirror. Do you see the person others see? Because you are the person who will have the most significant influence,

153

positive or negative, over the team, you are your own best tool in dealing with your players. Get to know yourself and what you can do. Good practices, good matches, and a good program depend upon the attitude you project daily.

Behavior Patterns

Practice is the forum for developing the behavior patterns you want your team to follow. All functions of practice should *have a design*. The disciplines and routines of practice should be consistent. If specific behavior patterns are implanted in practice, they will carry over to traveling habits and, of course, to match behavior. The coach's behavior is the vanguard of team behavior. The coaching staff should do the following:

- Always start practice on time—every time! (That means the coach should be at practice early to insure everything is ready.)
- Always be dressed in clean, neat, coaching apparel.
- Always be well-groomed.
- Always have practice outlined—preferably in a journal or notebook.

In return, ask your players to do the following:

- Always be ready to start practice on time—every time.
- Set up the practice gym.
- Always fold up personal equipment (sweats, towels, etc.) and store them neatly in a designated area.
- Prepare mentally for each practice, focusing on areas they need to concentrate on.
- Be in neat, clean practice gear representing the organization for which they play.

The practice area should be neat, clean, and well-organized. It should represent the attitudes and positive behavior of a team by its preparedness. *It is the place where the players become the team*; it should reflect the team's personality and the behaviors that make up that personality.

Commitment

A commitment by you and your players to the standards of the program, tempered by discipline and cooperation, insure desirable behavior patterns. The behavior patterns— that is, the lifestyle—of the team are molded in the practice gym. On a daily basis the routines of preparation as well as actual training activities must be consistent in terms of expectations. Demand behaviors of yourself and your players that reflect a winning attitude and pride in everything the team does.

Positive Cumulative Effect

The foundation for any coaching philosophy should be the cumulative effect. How a coach treats any individual situation does not stand alone as witness to his or her total makeup. One bad practice does not cast a permanent pall over a team. No one knows the exact time when a person becomes a good player, a good guitarist, a good architect, or a good anything. A person gets to his or her destination in life by stringing together a long series of experiences. This is especially obvious in goal-oriented activities such as competitive sports.

There is a natural cumulative effect. The team and what it represents is an accumulation of its experiences. As coaches, we want the series of experiences to be productive and positive to result in a quality program.

Everything that you, your players, and your staff do contributes to the cumulative effect, either positively or negatively. If a coach is pretentious, inconsistent, and undisciplined, the accumulation of negative experiences will be reflected in the team's lack of pride, poor self-image, and lackluster performance. On the other hand, if a coach requires high standards in behaviors of the players, the team will reflect the accumulation of good experiences.

The cumulative effect can easily be identified in practice. A team should never waste a day, an hour, even a minute. If a team can maximize every opportunity available to them, the result will be a highly successful program.

Physical Conditioning

It is a well-known fact that a human being who is in great physical condition performs all human functions better than one who isn't. However, a coach needs to be aware of principles of physical conditioning relative to volleyball (or whatever activity may be involved).

Physiological research shows the following:

- A participant must be well-conditioned to obtain the benefits of a warm-up.

- Warm-up and physical conditioning should be *specific* to the activity to be performed.

- Warm-up should last at least 10 minutes (to allow muscle temperature to stabilize) but no longer than 20 minutes (or glycogen stores will begin to deplete).

Without question the volleyball athlete must be in superior physical condition, prepared for explosive, aerobic function as well as for the prolonged jumping required during a 3-hour match. Physical conditioning should be planned and should be specific to the demands volleyball puts on the body. Remember, though, if specific physical conditioning takes place before technical skills practice begins, or if the warm-up is too intense or too long, the quality of skill development can suffer. Do not confuse warm-up with physical conditioning, nor physical conditioning with skill development.

There will be residual physical conditioning benefits from a physically difficult skills practice. You must be careful to balance the focus on skills development and physical training without obliterating the player's ability to perform effectively.

It is of critical importance to be very sport-specific in every aspect of athletic training. There is virtually no transfer of skills from one activity to another. For example, an individual who trains for long-distance swimming cannot step out of the water and run a marathon without feeling serious pain. Even though the cardiovascular system is in great shape, the muscle usage and body rhythm of the two activities are completely different.

We must repeatedly train the muscles to perform the same movements and velocities that the skill activity requires. This concept of specificity shatters many schools of thought, like the use of lead-up games and drills that are not game-related. Sometimes warm-ups are designed based on tradition and convenience rather than on efficiency and effectiveness.

For example, are traditional spiking warm-up lines the most effective way to warm up for spiking practice? How often in a match does an attacker start from outside the court, toss a perfect ball to the setter, and then approach and hit?

Research has shown that the most efficient way to train a skill is to practice that skill as specifically as possible in the exact activity in which it will be used. Therefore, it is more efficient and effective to simulate real movements as soon as the skill is learned. A spiking warm-up would be better if the spiker started at the net or at serve receive position and moved to the approach position. Also, the ball should be passed in a realistic manner so setters and spikers can practice realistic patterns every time.

Techniques and Tactics

Practice is the time to develop and hone the skills and playing systems for your team. The basic teaching of skills is described in Part I, chapters 1 to 7. Basic system development is described in chapter 9.

Designing a Practice

You must be familiar with some basic definitions of words related to practice and drills before you design your training program.

Movements:	The body mechanics required to execute a physical skill.
Skill:	A series of gross movements, fine movements, and postures necessary to perform a required physical task effectively.

Repetition: One successful execution of a skill.

Set: A series of a required number of repetitions.

Drill: A measured series of sets, closely monitored by a coach or coaches, designed to blend individual skills into an orchestration of team skills to gain a desired, unified effect.

Practice: A block of time scheduled to include a series of drills organized in a logical progression based on predetermined performance goals.

Season: A block of time on the calendar scheduled to include competitions and practices designed for mutual influence.

Practice Ingredients Checklist

Carefully examine the following checklist of the ingredients in a good practice. Note any items your program may lack. Then prioritize the missing ingredients. Decide which you can control and change and which you either can't control or deem unimportant. Add any items that may not be listed that you feel will enhance your practice regimen.

Purposes of Practice

☐ To prepare the team for every situation that will occur in competition
☐ To mold a group of individuals into a team
☐ To provide experiences in which the individual and the team can discover their maximum human resources

Required Coaching Skills

☐ A sound knowledge of the game's movements and skills
☐ A well-developed list of principles and keys for teaching techniques
☐ A sound knowledge of the tactical application of technical skills
☐ A sound knowledge of physical conditioning and training principles

☐ Creativity
☐ Organizational skills
☐ Communication skills
☐ Ability to duplicate the serve either by throwing or serving
☐ Ability to duplicate spiking with control either by throwing or spiking
☐ Ability to toss underhand or overhand with control to duplicate sets and free balls
☐ Ability to control the tempo of a drill when required

Ideal Facilities and Equipment

☐ Minimum of two balls for every player
☐ One net and court per six players
☐ No more than 30 feet beyond sidelines or end lines and no less than 20 feet to walls
☐ Floor-inserted standards with no support cables
☐ Nets with unbreakable antennae
☐ A basket or cart on wheels to contain at least 24 balls
☐ Ability to set up a center court
☐ Ceiling of 25 to 40 feet in height
☐ Good lighting
☐ A safe training environment—a minimum of stored equipment, no sharp wall attachments or protruding floor attachments
☐ Good training equipment (jumping, physical, technical)

Player and Staff Responsibilities

☐ Players taught how to practice (rules, communication, specific practice skills)
☐ All players' belongings neatly stored
☐ All team members wear appropriate practice or coaching uniforms

Players' Practice Skills

To make practice function at the most efficient level, the players must correctly execute basic practice techniques:

☐ *Handling a ball:* Any ball handed to the coach running a drill must be put on his or her hip. (If the coach is left-handed, the ball is put on his or her left hip; if right-handed, his or her right hip.)
☐ *Bouncing a ball:* In any drill that requires one player to bounce a ball to another, the player bounces the ball one time so that it ends up at about the receiver's waist.
☐ *Shagging:* Players must be positioned to protect teammates who are working. Shagging is not a rest period!

☐ *Tossing:* If a drill requires the ball to be tossed, the player tosses with two hands, underhand.

☐ *Communication:* All specific communication phrases or words will be used in practice.

☐ *Effort:* A player should go as hard as possible for as long as he or she can.

Rules

☐ No sitting down in practice unless announced by the coaches.

☐ Practice always starts on time.

☐ Any overt display of displeasure or frustration will not be tolerated. The player will be removed from activity or dismissed from practice. The team cannot afford losses of emotional control during competition or practice.

☐ Any taping or therapy will be done prior to practice. A trainer will be available 30 minutes prior to the start of practice.

☐ Players (and staff) will wear *only* team practice uniforms.

☐ Mentally prepare for each practice by reviewing what will be gained from each experience. Begin practice by mentally preparing for practice!

☐ Except for the first and last line-up, the last player into a called line-up will do 10 dives, rolls, push-ups, or the like.

☐ Except on a water or rest break called by the coaches, players jog and run everywhere during practice.

☐ Players shag their own balls. A player never asks another pair or group to shag his or her ball.

☐ When shagging balls in a drill, never allow a ball to roll through the drill, particularly a spiking drill.

☐ If a player must leave practice for any reason, he or she must notify the coach.

☐ Every time a player touches a ball in practice, he or she calls it by saying ''ball'' or ''mine.''

☐ In any drill, if a player does not go for a ball, that player will start that drill over. There is *never* a reason for not going for a ball.

☐ When teammates are in any fatiguing drill, the others must be encouraging.

☐ If a player must miss a practice or be late, he or she must notify the coach in advance.

☐ On a weekly basis, groups of four players will be assigned to set up the courts. The courts must be up 15 minutes prior to the start of practice.

☐ Players must report injuries or sickness to the coaching staff immediately upon detection.

General Phases of Practice

A good practice is made up of a logical sequence of activities that is based on and leads to the preset goals. Consider the following phases when designing a practice:

1. *Warm-up*—Involves raising body temperature, increasing flexibility, improving cardiovascular conditioning (through jumping, sprints), and performing specific, game-related movements.

2. *Foundation work*—Includes an individual fundamentals progression, using two or more players focusing on one or two skills.

3. *Combination work*—Composed of drills using several skills in specific game-related applications.

4. *Team work*—Involves full team drills applying techniques and skills.

5. *Stress work*—Includes crisis or frenzy drills for individuals or the whole team to develop successful execution under stress.

6. *Physical conditioning*—Composed of jump training and specific strength training activities.

7. *Cool-down*

Themes, Tempos, and Logical Progressions

When designing a practice, you must keep in mind the tone required for the maximum positive cumulative effect. Each practice should have a theme that keeps the players focused on the session's goals. For example, you can have a fundamental practice for skill refinement, a tactical practice where all activities are geared to develop strategic plays, or a ''heart'' practice designed to make the team perform under stress. The theme sets the focus for each session.

Each drill has a certain tempo. Based on the theme, the tempo for each activity is consciously established. If a drill is designed for teaching a new skill, the tempo may be slow and methodical, quiet and analytical. An intense, stress-producing defensive drill may be high-tempo, almost frenzied. You control the tempo with your voice inflections and body language, the speed at which repetitions are performed, and the way you measure success.

Each practice needs a logical progression of activities to be effective. For example, individual skills worked on early in practice should be the same ones emphasized in team drills later in the session. You must also consider the ebb and flow of physical intensity throughout training. It should match the attitude and physical condition level of your athletes. Ideally, the pattern of intensity changes in a practice and should follow that found in an actual competitive match.

Residual Benefits

Besides its value in teaching a group of people to perform the skills of volleyball in an organized fashion, there are residual benefits to good practice planning. A positive cumulative effect leads to a team with cohesiveness, common spirit, mental power, commitment, camaraderie, discipline, and communication skills. These elements make up the team personality. Physical conditioning, of course, is another benefit.

Even though you have meticulously planned your program and led your athletes with enthusiasm and consistency, you cannot guarantee wins. With responsible leadership, however, you can always guarantee a good *team*.

Designing Drills

Drills are an integral part of a practice. As such, they need to be carefully designed to fulfill the objectives and theme of each practice. The types of drills used dictate the tempo in a practice. You must consider the fatigue level of the players along with the realistic ebb and flow of the game situations you are trying to duplicate. Remember, you are teaching the players how to play the game. The drills should be as close as possible to game-like situations.

You must keep track of the drills that you use, why they are used, and the objectives of each. It is important to examine specific drills, such as those found in this book. The wise coach, however, learns to design his or her own drills so practices can be custom-made for his or her own team.

Because volleyball is a rebound game, the ball is seldom directed intentionally back through the exact incoming trajectory line. Therefore, controlled deflection to the desired target must be considered in every drill. In the very beginning stages of teaching ball contact, familiarizing the player with the feel of the ball is important. In fact, timed, straight-on, quality contact is in itself an initial reward for the beginner. As soon as possible, however, meaningful contacts with realistic goals must be instilled. Volleyball's rebound angles and targets must be considered when you design drills.

Types of Drills

Drills can be organized into four categories: teaching, rapid-fire, frenzy or crisis, and flow-of-play. The drills in chapters 2 to 7 are labeled according to these categories.

Teaching Drills

These drills are slow and methodical, like the ones described in chapters 2 through 7 as teaching progressions. They are not necessarily game-related but stress mechanics. Specific movement patterns are carefully scrutinized in these drills.

Rapid-Fire

These drills have a fast tempo with many contacts in a short time. They are timed and are closely supervised. Triad drills involving three players and two balls, detailed on page 161, are examples of rapid-fire drills.

Frenzy or Crisis

These drills are performed at a very fast tempo and focus on intestinal fortitude combined with skills under stressful conditions.

A certain number of total successful repetitions or successful repetitions in a row terminates the drill. Many defensive drills and team drills in preparation for competition are in this category.

Flow-of-Play

All team drills and some smaller group drills that blend two or more skills fall into this category. The tempo is based on the skill sequence involved. A number of successful repetitions in a row or a total of successful repetitions are common ways of measuring these drills.

Drill Organization

Drills are either coach-centered, player-centered, or coach-initiated. Select the organization style that best fits your needs. The drills have been categorized according to the following definitions.

Coach-Centered Drill

A coach-centered drill is one in which the tempo is controlled by the coach. The coach controls the players' range and movement by placing the ball in the position where he or she wants the player to contact it. An example of a coach-centered drill is a diamond drill (see Figure 12-2) described on pages 161-162.

Player-Centered Drill

A player-centered drill is initiated and carried out by the player(s). The Butterfly Serve Receive drill (3.5) is an example (see p. 29).

Coach-Initiated Drill

A coach-initiated drill is one in which the coach begins the action by putting the ball and players in the situation desired and letting the play continue to its natural conclusion. An example of a coach-initiated drill is Piles (7.7), a variation of the Pursuit drill, on page 86.

Drill Measurement

Volleyball is measured by the score. Goals and measurements are an integral part of the game. Therefore, as we teach the skills, we must create the mind-set of goals and measurements.

A drill can be timed, have a goal of a certain number of successful repetitions, require a certain number of successful repetitions in a row, have a certain time block with required successful repetitions, or have a goal of a number of successful repetitions along with a certain number in a row. Some coaches have other modifications. One option is a goal of successful repetitions with negative scores for unforced errors. A suggested measurement tool is listed with each drill example in chapters 2 to 7.

In team drills, scoring can be more creative. Different scoring systems in team drills make for variety and create the emotional situations that are part of volleyball. A great deal of frustration accompanies long periods of siding out, having to score the winning point without being able to run out the clock, and the quick turnaround of emotional highs and lows; you must re-create these situations in practice so your players can learn to deal with them effectively. The opportunity to come from behind in volleyball is different than in any other sport because time is not a factor in the current rules.

There are many types of scoring systems, including fast score, big and little points, handicaps, and winning points burden. Experiment with these options.

Fast Score

This type of scoring uses no side-outs. A point is scored on every play. Fast scoring puts pressure on the serving team to serve and block without making a mistake. In regulation volleyball, the serving team only loses the *ball* if the server makes an error. In the fast score format, the serving team loses a *point* in this situation, thus putting more pressure on the server.

A variation of this format is to reverse the scoring roles, allowing points to be scored only by the *receiving* team. With the value put on the serve-receiving team's successful execution, this variation puts emphasis on consistent side-out play.

Big and Little Points

The Level II *Coaching Volleyball Successfully* manual discusses this concept in more depth. Basically, this system requires one team to successfully execute two plays in a row (2 "little points") to score one "big point." It is designed to teach players the patience required to deal with the side-out element of volleyball, where consistency is required even though points may not be scored.

For example, Team A is playing Team B. Team A serves and scores. They have earned one little point. As soon as that play is completed, the coach throws an easy ball to Team B. If Team A wins that play, they score their second little point and therefore earn one big point. If Team B successfully executes, then A's first little point is nullified and they start again. Before the drill, the coach determines how many big points must be scored to win.

Handicaps

This system gives one team more points than the other before they start. This is applicable when there is an imbalance between the first and second teams. For example, the coach sets up a situation where Team B is leading 13 to 10 over Team A. They play to the natural conclusion of the game. This system can be easily adapted to a variety of circumstances and is a wonderful way to practice key situations.

Winning Points Burden

When running any drill, whether it's measured in total successful repetitions or in points, the winning points burden can be applied. Simply make the team or player score or execute successfully two little points to get the final big point or repetition. For example, if a player must kill 10 spikes before he or she is done, require that to get the final repetition he or she must put down 2 in a row.

This type of scoring teaches players to play through to the end of a game and not coast or get cautious. Remember, in volleyball you must score the final point and not wait for a clock to run out or an opponent to err.

Drill Design Questions

When you design a drill, ask yourself the following important questions. Additional questions are provided, in some instances, to assist you in determining your answer to the main issue:

- Is the drill efficient?
  - (a) What is the number of ball contacts to be made during the allotted time segment?
  - (b) Is the organizational flow balanced and easy to follow?
- Does the drill demand a quality performance?
  - (a) How is it measured?
  - (b) Are production objectives challenging?
- Does the drill keep everyone involved?
  - (a) What are the roles of the players?
  - (b) Is specific leadership required?
  - (c) Should specific communication systems be used?
- Is the drill game-related?
- What is the work-to-rest ratio?
- Is the drill interesting?
- Is success measurable?

If you come up with one or more no's in answer to these questions, reevaluate the drill. You may be able to make some modifications. If not, find an alternative drill.

Drill Considerations

- Each drill should have a nickname so explanation should be kept at a minimum. Once explained, the drill's nickname should trigger the player's roles and expectations.
- Each drill repetition should be allowed to continue to its natural conclusion—a dead ball.
- Drills should duplicate the tempo of expected game behaviors.
- Drills should usually be competitive. Competitiveness is a skill that needs to be developed.
- Drills are a place to work out problems. Create uncomfortable situations that your players must deal with. It's better to clash in practice than during a match.

- Drills should always end on a positive note, no matter how long it takes.

Some General Formats for Drills

These are some examples of drill activities that can be used in developing your own specific drills. Many of these can be found in the drill examples in chapters 2 to 7.

Individual Player Drills—
Teaching Drills, Player-Centered

These drills are used to teach individual skills, with the emphasis on correct motor patterns. The following elements characterize such drills:

- They require one ball for each player.
- They do not require an elaborate equipment setup.
- They provide ball control training.
- They are motor-pattern–related, not game-related.
- They boast many repetitions in a short time.

Pair Drills—Teaching Drills, Player-Centered

These drills have the same goals as those found in individual drills, except that two players work with each other. Their characteristics include the following:

- They use one ball for two players.
- They do not require an elaborate equipment setup.
- They are mechanics-related, not game-related.
- They have a high number of repetitions.
- They focus on ball control.
- They develop some coordination between players.

Triads—Rapid Fire, Player-Centered

These drills duplicate the angles used in playing volleyball (see Figure 12-1). Triads are the most efficient drill patterns for giving players maximum opportunities to respond in the shortest period of time. Also, the relationship between players and their required movements are game-related. The following elements characterize this type of drill:

- They use two balls and three players.
- They can be used for a variety of skills.

- They still focus on one skill.
- They require many repetitions in a short time.
- They encourage players to begin to work together.
- They can be game-related.
- They duplicate game rebound angles.

Fig. 12-1

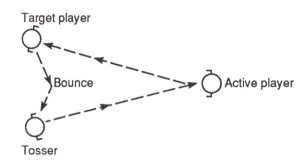

In the illustrated example, the tosser tosses the ball (underhand) to the active player so that he or she must move and adjust. The active player forearm passes the ball to the target player, who bounces the ball back to the tosser so that it hits him or her at hip level. The tosser tosses another ball as soon as the active player has passed the previous ball. This drill is timed. After several repetitions, have players rotate.

Diamond Drills—Rapid Fire, Coach-Centered

This drill format is game-related, excellent for warm-up, and can be used to create the specific player relationships required in playing a game. It has the following characteristics:

- It is a station drill.
- It involves all players.
- It has a fast tempo.
- It combines several skills.
- It is timed.
- It is game-movements–related.

An example of this type of drill is illustrated in Figure 12-2. The coach (C) bounces the ball to Player 2. Player 2 sets to Player 3 who starts at the net, backs off as the coach bounces the ball, approaches, and spikes. After Player 3 hits, he or she rotates to Position 4. The coach immediately bounces a second ball to Player 2 who sets to Player 1. Player 1 hits and rotates to Position 2. Player 2, after setting two balls, rotates to Position 3. Player 4 shags two balls, takes them to the coach, and rotates to Position 1. For variety, a block can be added. Or the coach can hit balls at Position 2, and Player 1 can set. Using the diamond pattern, the coach can recreate any player relationship situation.

Fig. 12-2

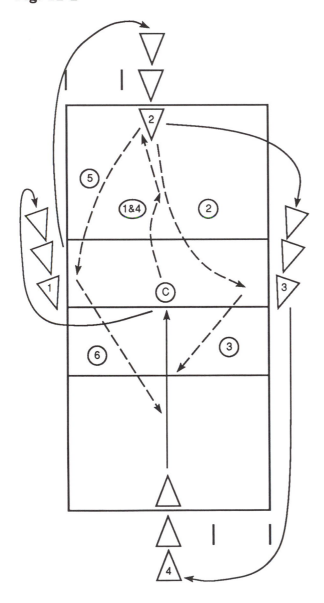

Shuttles—Rapid-Fire, Player-Centered

Shuttle drills are good warm-ups. They are also good choices when you have few balls

and many players. Typically these drills (see Figure 12-3) have the following characteristics:

- They focus on ball-handling skills.
- They utilize required movements.
- They are not game-related.
- They require three to five players for one shuttle line.

Fig. 12-3

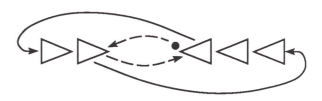

Waves of Three—Flow-of-Play, Player-Centered, and Coach-Initiated

This type of drill is an excellent way to teach team functions and blend individual skills into a team effort. In these drills, athletes work in groups of three that participate as a unit in full team drills. This drill format is characterized in the following manner:

- It uses several skills in concert.
- It focuses on game-related tactical application of skills.
- It allows work with desired combinations of players in specific tactical situations.

The wave design is illustrated in Figure 12-4. Court A players run the offensive skills the coach wants to work on. Court B players run the prescribed defensive skills. After a predetermined amount of time on successful repetitions, players "wave through." P1 goes to P2, P2 goes to P3, P3 goes to P4, and P4 goes to P1. Players are surrounded by their teammates with whom they will play in matches, and they work on four major elements of the game in one drill: offensive back row play, floor defense, defensive front row play, and defensive back row play.

The drill designs presented here are just examples. Many other designs are possible. Create your own based on the previously stated criteria. Be sure, however, that you keep this principle in mind when you are designing practices and drills: *Only* *teach tactically what your team can execute technically.*

Fig. 12-4

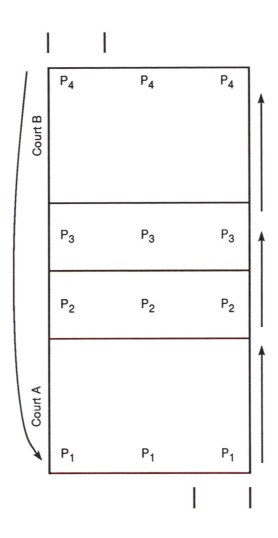

Chapter 13: Developing a Volleyball Program

Any activity for which goals are set requires preparation to meet those goals. In volleyball, this requires coordinating the tasks of a number of people, and it demands a well-thought out plan.

Coaches can easily get caught up in the day-to-day tasks of the job and lose sight of the overall purpose. Athletics can dominate the coach's life. Players need continual counseling, the press wants answers, administrators demand fiscal reports. In college athletics, recruiting is a siren of insatiable appetite. Custodians require strict regimens in facility use and game plans. Videos, practice plans, and actual practice sessions all need attention. Normal school and community involvement is expected of the coach—and junior high and high school coaches also teach. Developing a program with educational and competitive goals while meeting the expectations of an institution or organization is difficult. To meet this challenge, coaches must be very organized. They must be able to balance ideals with reality and temper short-term goal satisfaction with long-term standards.

When developing a volleyball program at any level, the following elements must be considered:

- Leadership
- Athletes
- Equipment and facilities
- Funding
- Community or institutional support
- Tradition
- Marketing

Leadership

A successful program needs highly motivated, hard-working, well-qualified leaders. A good leader must be a good delegator. He or she must be able to recognize his or her deficiencies and secure people who are experts in those areas. Usually, the leader of a volleyball program is the head coach, but this does not always have to be the case. If someone is interested in developing a volleyball program but is not qualified to coach, that person must locate a strong head coach. Likewise, an excellent volleyball coach may not be a good administrator. The responsible head coach needs to identify a strong administrator to organize the program.

The key to running a successful program is to put qualified people in positions that best suit their expertise. To be successful, your program must have direction. The leaders must identify that direction and clearly communicate the goals to all coaches and athletes. Each person involved must understand what is required to achieve the program's objectives. Identifying several types of goals will assist you in that process. They are long-range objectives, long-range goals, intermediate goals, and short-term goals.

Long-range objectives define the program. They are the projected achievements your team will strive to accomplish in the next 3 to 4 years. These objectives set the tone of every activity in which your team is involved. Of course, the objectives are subject to revision based on the progress the team makes on the more controllable, shorter-term goals.

Long-range goals are goals set for the current year. They are measurable and are specific to the personnel and conditions of any given year. These goals further define the actions of all players and coaches.

Intermediate goals help to move each individual toward accomplishing the long-range goals. These goals should encompass only a month or two and should be measurable. They are the focus of practice sessions during their specific time period.

Short-term goals lead specifically to the accomplishment of intermediate goals. These goals tend to be daily or weekly goals and must be measurable, attainable, and clearly understood. Although these goals must represent specific tasks, they must also be flexible to compensate for the changing situation. For that reason, the most effective short-term goals are daily goals. For more information on how to set goals, consult the ACEP *Sport Psychology Course* (Bump, 1989; Martens, 1987).

The importance of goals cannot be overemphasized. To ensure your success, be sure all players and staff are committed to the goals and standards of operation that you and your team have established. If there is disagreement, move quickly to settle the issue. You owe it to yourself and to your team!

The following materials illustrate the different types of objectives and goals that you can set for your team or program. These particular goals were selected after a great deal of investigation into each of the ele-

ments of a good program. You must look carefully at the athletes, equipment, funding, support, tradition, and marketing of your own program to set your sights on the future. Use these examples to guide you in your work.

Long-Range Objectives (To Be Accomplished in 3 Years)

- To qualify for the state tournament
- To establish identifiable traditions for the program that help it become an integral part of the community

Long-Range Goals (For a Specific Year)

- To secure the needed training equipment (balls, nets, antennae, jump training materials) to run an up-to-date program
- To establish standards of training and play
- To develop a sense of "team"

Intermediate Goals (For a Month-Long Period)

- To evaluate each player in accordance with his or her individual short-term goals
- To consult with staff members on policies for training, travel, and practice

Short-Term Goals (For a Day or Week at the Most)

- To consult with Ken, Jill, Laura, and Bill on their progress this far in the season
- To establish clear policies governing training absences, travel preparations, and practice decorum

Athletes

Coaches seldom lose on paper—you never plan to lose! Jack Donohue, Canada's national men's basketball coach, once said, "Wanna be a great coach? Get great athletes." (Jack was the coach at New York's Power Memorial high school during the reign of young Lew Alcindor, later known as Kareem Abdul-Jabbar.)

Coaches must convince good athletes of the prestige, value, and enjoyment of competitive volleyball. If the program is well-organized and well-promoted, provides creative and diverse opportunities, and furnishes the athletes with motivational goals, then securing good athletes is easy. The key is to show potential players that volleyball is a challenging, enjoyable, prestigious sport. The coach must be sensitive to what motivates young people in the team's community.

Great potential is developed through progressive programming that reaches down to the elementary schools. Community recreational organizations, YMCAs, Boys Clubs, and parks and recreation programs are all great environments for the development of volleyball. The United States Volleyball Association Junior Olympic programs are another option. Contact the USVBA for information on Junior Olympic programs. Don't forget the parents! Let's learn from Japan's Mama's Volleyball program. Encourage parents to play. After all, volleyball is a great lifetime sport. When parents participate, they tend to involve their children. Children who enjoy something at a young age are likely to continue as they grow older.

Equipment and Facilities

Good equipment is a must, and having quality training equipment should be a high priority. The related costs are generally one-time expenses. Although you will probably need to purchase additional balls and nets, other staples such as standards, antennae, and ball carriers usually last longer than the coach. Additional training equipment and apparel are discussed in the Level 2 manual.

Balls

Practice balls should be the same as the official game ball used in competition. (These vary with state and national associations and different leagues.) Ideally, you should strive to have two balls for every player. If your program is just starting, shoot for one ball per player.

Ball Containers

Ball containers should be used not only for secure storage, but as an integral part of practice as well. Without containers during practice, the gym can resemble the inside of a commercial popcorn popper operating at full tilt. The containers should be waist-high and on wheels. Ideally, you should be able to close the containers, but they should have lids designed so that balls can be put on top without rolling off. (The advantage of this is obvious if you have ever had to continually dip into the depths of a ball bag. Chiropractors love it when coaches use deep-dip ball bags.)

The ideal container stores up to 24 balls, can be locked, holds at least 6 balls on a waist-high closed lid, and rolls on wheels. Towel carts, plastic 30-gallon garbage cans, and grocery carts are low-cost alternatives that are functional but less than ideal.

Net Standards

Net standards are the most expensive pieces of equipment but generally represent one-time expenses. They are also the most important. Quality standards will survive the program, the gym, and most natural disasters.

Do not compromise on net standards! They should not require support wires or floor bases; rather, they should be freestanding and fit into a floor receptacle. The net crank should be on the side of the pole opposite the court and should be removable. In addition, there should be a minimal number of flanges and other potentially impaling features. Try to purchase poles that telescope and allow for various heights. Be sure the net cables can be tightened in straight lines.

Pole Pads

Most competitive associations require the use of padding around the poles. You'll find that most companies that sell standards also sell pads to fit them.

Net Antennae

Net antennae are required in competition and should always be used during practice. Use one-piece, unbreakable, attachable antennae. You'll need one pair per court.

Court Lines

Although court lines are neither pieces of equipment nor facilities, they are obviously important. They need to be accurate and, most importantly, prominent. If the competition court lines are buried beneath the spaghetti of other game boundaries, the impression is given that volleyball is not important.

Practice Nets

A program needs practice nets and at least one competition net. Nets need to be at least 32 feet long with a cable running through the top. The cable needs to be long enough to attach to one pole and reach the ratchet on the other. There is a new type of synthetic rope being used in some nets that is stronger and easier to handle than cable. You might want to investigate it. The net does not need a cable in the bottom. Here, a piece of nylon line will suffice and, in fact, is easier to secure. The net must have a white 5-centimeter border. Check your league's current volleyball rules for further details.

If you are using a steel cable, it is important to check it for burrs. As nets are continually set up and taken down, the cables coil, and individual strands break and stand ready to puncture any human appendage in the area.

A Safety Note

Safety for participants is the most important rationale for selecting equipment. Remember, the net standards should be floor inserted without support cables or protruding bases. There should be few flanges on the poles, and those required for tying off the net lines should be covered by pole pads. Further, the crank that is used to tighten the net should be on the side away from the court and covered by the pole pads. The crank handle should be removable. Finally, the official's stand should attach to one of the standards and be thoroughly padded.

Safety must always be foremost in your mind. Continually check all equipment for exposed, sharp edges or points. Tape, pad, replace or repair them immediately.

In terms of athletic facilities, Americans tend to be spoiled. Many teams and coaches feel that to keep up with the competition, they simply can't function effectively without three courts, indirect lighting, and a Jacuzzi. But some of the greatest teams in history were developed in the dankest of gyms, with dim lighting and no heat. This is not to say that quality facilities are not important. In fact, marketing volleyball effectively to a coddled public and athletic community is easier if you have squeaky-clean, spacious, well-stocked facilities. They are also nicer to train in. A limited facility, however, should never be an excuse for a pathetic program. Adapt. Adjust. Clean it. Exploit its unique charm. Make it a place of affection. If high standards of maintenance and equipment organization are acquired, even the oldest facility can be a great training venue. The program's dignity and pride can be found in the facility's upkeep and presentation. Be sure, though, that the facility is safe.

Always strive for improved facilities, yet at the same time keep existing ones as functional as possible. Ideal volleyball facilities include the following elements:

- Two practice courts with 10 feet between, and 12 feet to the nearest walls
- 30 feet to the nearest ceiling obstacle
- A featured center court with seating on the side and ends
- A videotape position behind the court, elevated 15 to 20 feet
- Indirect lighting with enough candlepower to support TV coverage
- Smooth walls of a neutral color, not white
- Two locker rooms with showers
- Easily accessed, but secured, storage room

Funding

It has been known to happen: A committee, or an administration, or an influential person has recognized the desirability of a volleyball program and has hired a coach. Yet little or no funding is set aside to handle the program's expenses. The coach, effervescent at the beginning of the assignment, quickly wilts in the financial desert. Beyond human resources, financial considerations dictate a program's limitations. People—creative, motivated people—can secure the necessary funds. It is imperative that you know the financial base available upon which you can build a program. Every new program needs a grubstake.

If your institution or organization has limited financial resources, you need to know what other options you have. Fundraisers? Gate receipts? Booster club? Sponsors? Are these options legal? The flexibility of, potential for, and restrictions on developing a fund-raising base must be clear.

Identify interested people in the community who have expertise in fund-raising and finances and are interested in young people and in volleyball. Every community has these people. They want to get involved. Find them. Educate them about the philosophy and needs of your program and allow them to use their expertise in raising funds. The ACEP *Sport Administration Course* (Leith, in press) can also supply you with some fund-raising ideas and strategies.

Community/Institutional Support

The good coach and athletic administrator must develop strong public relations skills. Competitive scholastic athletics are never played in a vacuum, nor should they be. They cost money. The money comes from boosters, school funds, gate receipts, community sponsors, and parents. People want to know how their money is spent. They want to know if they are contributing to a quality product.

The coach's responsibility is to develop the quality and share it with the supporters. The program should be fun for everyone. Most people who support athletics experience the triumphs and defeats vicariously. To insure a program's ongoing stability, the community and the represented institution must continually be cultivated. This phenomenon occurs at all levels, including junior high schools, junior clubs, high schools, and colleges.

Involve people in the show, but not in the decisions. As the coach you must maintain a balance: Share the experience, but clearly distinguish between involvement and decision making. This can be a tough task, especially if the team is losing or if an outspoken parent does not feel his or her offspring is getting enough court time. These situations test the coach's charm, communication skills, resolve, and diplomacy.

Ways to involve the community in your program include parents' appreciation days, theme nights at matches, media games, media luncheons, service club presentations, exhibitions, clinics, appearances at community functions, and awards banquets. Your only limitation is your imagination. Create. Have fun. Brainstorm ideas with players, parents, and community leaders. Make sure you screen any ideas to ensure they are appropriate and enhance rather than detract from your program.

Tradition

The complete volleyball program should be an experience that the players and the community they represent can all enjoy. Annual activities, such as a media match fund-raiser or costume night, become associated with your sport and are expected. These events are eagerly anticipated by athletes and supporters. Over time, the events become a part of a community's tradition. Tradition is important to the feelings of security and stability. Traditions are rallying points in good and bad times.

You must be aware of the importance of developing traditions. Create unique events identified with volleyball. People in any community need special activities in which they can immerse themselves. As an example, one high school holds a "Sundae Monday" event. The Monday before the league opener, an ice cream–eating contest is held. Businesses, elementary schools, and organizations enter their champions. Awards are given for style, sundae-eating costumes, quantity of ice cream consumed, and devouring speed. No one really cares who's the best, but everyone has fun setting a tone for the upcoming volleyball season.

Always keep in mind that sports are to be played and enjoyed. Some people coach. Some play. Some cheer. Some donate. All should enjoy.

Marketing

People who are dedicated to amateur sports, or what many athletic administrators refer to as "non-revenue–producing sports," often shy away from marketing. Sport marketing has become associated with big-time college and professional sports. Much of the hype and glitter is distasteful to pure sport aficionados. However, everyone who loves volleyball wants to see it recognized, enjoyed, and reported. Reality in our society dictates that to sell volleyball to a sophisticated sport media and public, we must engage in sport marketing at some level.

There are some basics you must follow if your athletes and sponsors are to receive the recognition they deserve. Whether your program is big or small, you can

- prepare news releases;
- develop an adequate media mailing list;
- prepare low-cost publications that explain your sport;
- make media phone calls;
- alert the media to interesting aspects of your sport and key competitions;
- make covering your competitions an easy, pleasant experience for the media,

who will then wish to return and do more the next time;
- introduce your top athletes to the media and get them some coverage in the papers or on radio and television; and
- be known as a good organization to work with and develop solid friends in the media that you can approach with a valid story angle.

There is no question that the best relationships and the best results in contacting the media come from a personal visit or phone call. The news release, however, is still the major vehicle used to reach the masses of media and interested parties in your sport that you cannot contact personally.

The quality of your news release dictates the use it gets, so take your time in its preparation and delivery. It's not a license to ramble . . . it's not a chance to practice self-therapy because you flunked 10th grade composition . . . it's the vehicle for telling a media contact *who, what, where, when, how,* and *why.* Make it simple to read, easy to find the major facts, and keep a reader's interest. Keep in mind that you can also turn off the reader's interest in three paragraphs. Follow these guidelines in preparing your statement:

- Hold your reader's interest. Feature current or future events as your lead story. Avoid past history!
- Keep the language simple and snappy.
- Use quotes in lay language.
- Box off and feature your major points such as time, place, date, ticket information, phone numbers, and so on.
- Print your news release on one side of the page only.
- Make sure your press contact's name, phone, and address are displayed prominently at the top of the release.
- Capsule a short headline at the top of the story telling the reader what's ahead.
- List a release date and time (if you desire).
- Check your spellings of names, dates, sites, times, and the like.
- Quote the boss, not yourself.

A Final Word

Developing a good volleyball program requires planning and the involvement of interested, enthusiastic people. A functional philosophy defined by the program's goals is the foundation upon which the program is built.

A volleyball program should be fun and rewarding for all. It will have its frustrating moments, of course. If people keep the program in perspective and remember that it is a vehicle for young people's growth, the frustrations will be minimal. It is important to remember that the total experience for everyone involved is paramount. If winning is the only measure of the program's success, it is doomed to failure. No one can guarantee winning. Yet a quality program can be guaranteed, and winning is a by-product of a good program. It is something to be appreciated and enjoyed. The total program is to be respected, valued, and honored. The good volleyball program contributes to the participants' quality of life—and that should be the prime focus.

Appendix A:
Season and Practice
Planning Outlines

Instructional Schedule for Volleyball

Goal: To help players learn and practice the individual and team skills needed to play a regulation game after 4 weeks.

T(10): Teach and practice the skill initially for 10 min.   *: These skills are practiced during the drills.
P(10): Review and practice the skill for 10 min.

Skills	Session 1	Session 2	Session 3	Session 4	Session 5	Session 6	Session 7	Session 8	Total % time
Warm-up									
Cool-down									
Physical conditioning									
Serving									
Technique									
Tactics									
Forearm pass									
Technique									
Serve receive									
Overhead pass									
Technique									
Setting									
Attack									
Technique									
Individual tactics									
Combinations									

Blocking
Technique
Tactics

Floor defense
Digging
Emergency skills

Specialization

Combined skill/
Competitive team drills

Systems
Side out offense
Transition offense
Defense
Team procedures

Practice Plan # ___

Total time: _____ minutes

Instructional goal:

Drills and activities:

Equipment:

Component/time	Activity/drill	Organization	Coaching points

Appendix B:
Checklists

Program Development Checklist

1. Goals
- [ ] a. School philosophy
- [ ] b. Coaches' goals
- [ ] c. Administrative goals

2. Promotion
- [ ] a. Newspapers—school and local (provide stats)
- [ ] b. City council—state awards or recognition
- [ ] c. Student council—recognition
- [ ] d. Summer travel, interstate, international
- [ ] e. Establish traditions: special uniforms, warm-up, special exhibitions
- [ ] f. Booster organization, parent group, PTO
- [ ] g. Make everyone feel that they are a part of the team

3. Logistical support
- [ ] a. Assistant coaches
- [ ] b. Trainers or doctors
- [ ] c. Parents
- [ ] d. Scorers
- [ ] e. Videotaper
- [ ] f. Photographer
- [ ] g. Computer person
- [ ] h. Managers
- [ ] i. Bus drivers
- [ ] j. Assistance from other sports teams
- [ ] k. Linespeople
- [ ] l. Ticket people/Program sales
- [ ] m. Scoreboard operator
- [ ] n. Announcer
- [ ] o. Concessions

4. Forms and contracts
- [ ] a. Health histories
- [ ] b. Insurance coverage
- [ ] c. Physical forms
- [ ] d. Eligibility forms
- [ ] e. Referee contracts
- [ ] f. Game contracts

5. Coordination of facilities
- [ ] a. Be organized
- [ ] b. Rapport with other coaches
- [ ] c. Rapport with athletic director

6. Administrative support
- [ ] a. Athletic director
- [ ] b. Principal
- [ ] c. Superintendent

7. Practice time
- [ ] a. What hours are available
- [ ] b. Minimum acceptable
- [ ] c. Coaches' philosophy
- [ ] d. Goals of team

8. Teams
- [ ] a. How many players per team
- [ ] b. JV and varsity only
- [ ] c. How many coaches
- [ ] d. How many courts
- [ ] e. Practice together or separately

9. Cutting players
- [ ] a. Procedure used
- [ ] b. Volleyball ability versus athletic ability
- [ ] c. Cut seniors
- [ ] d. How many on varsity, on JV

10. Equipment needed
Minimum:
- [ ] a. 24 uniforms—12 varsity, 12 JV (not accounting for size range, not necessarily new)
- [ ] b. 1 ball per two players (NOT rubber)
- [ ] c. Knee pads—optional
- [ ] d. Standards—good competitive variety
- [ ] e. 2 cables—new
- [ ] f. Antennae
- [ ] g. Scorebooks
- [ ] h. Game balls
- [ ] i. Standard pads (protective devices)
- [ ] j. Referee stand
- [ ] k. Ball bags
- [ ] l. Training kit and supplies
- [ ] m. Ice chest
- [ ] n. Towels
- [ ] o. Videotapes

11. Extra equipment
- [ ] a. Two practice courts and standards for each
- [ ] b. Practice nets and separate game nets
- [ ] c. 2 sets of antennae

- [ ] d. Team banner
- [ ] e. Team socks
- [ ] f. Team sweat suits (for warm-ups)
- [ ] g. Knee pads—higher quality
- [ ] h. 18 varsity uniforms to fit 12 players —in 2 years pass them down to JV and buy 18 more
- [ ] i. More and higher-quality volleyballs
- [ ] j. Volleyball holders (carts)
- [ ] k. Ball bags—leather
- [ ] l. Scoring devices for more than one court—tournament play
- [ ] m. Replacement parts for standards
- [ ] n. Replacement uniforms (in case of loss or theft)
- [ ] o. Practice clothing
- [ ] p. Training devices: jump standard, inner tubes, boards, bands, weight belts, corrals, volley target, hoops, etc.
- [ ] q. Coaching textbooks—manuals, etc.
- [ ] r. Financial assistance for coaches to attend clinics and workshops

Starting a Season Checklist

1. Meet with assistant coach and define roles and responsibilities

2. Define coaches' goals

3. Team tryouts
- [ ] a. Cuts?
- [ ] b. Format of tryout
- [ ] c. Net and court set up for practice

4. Varsity/JV selection
- [ ] a. Post these?
- [ ] b. Conferences?

5. Team goals
- [ ] a. Season
- [ ] b. Individual
- [ ] c. Group
- [ ] d. Measurable?

6. Equipment security and care
- [ ] a. Policies of uniform care and post-match procedures
- [ ] b. Ball counting and care at practice and matches

- [ ] c. Setup and takedown of nets and standards for matches and practice

7. Skills emphasis: All season, high priority
- [ ] a. Movements
- [ ] b. Defense
- [ ] c. Serving
- [ ] d. Serve receive

8. Skill emphasis: Progressive
- [ ] a. Overhead passing
- [ ] b. Attacking
- [ ] c. Blocking

9. Team drills
- [ ] a. Incorporate them as soon as varsity is determined
- [ ] b. Make them progressively more detailed
- [ ] c. Make them game-specific

10. Conditioning
- [ ] a. Do more early; progressively decrease to maintenance levels
- [ ] b. Consider conditioning value of drills

11. Establish team rules
- [ ] a. Conduct
- [ ] b. Dress
- [ ] c. Competition
- [ ] d. Practice
- [ ] e. Travel

12. Finalize starting lineups
- [ ] a. For first match
- [ ] b. Work this unit together
- [ ] c. Leave mind open to change during the next weeks

13. Begin organizing crew to work home matches
- [ ] a. Scorer
- [ ] b. Linespeople
- [ ] c. Stat people
- [ ] d. Announcer
- [ ] e. Ball shaggers/3-ball system
- [ ] f. Officials

14. Establish routine pregame procedure for your team

☐ a. Meet at the same time
☐ b. Meet at the same place
☐ c. Same pregame talk format
☐ d. Organized game plan presentation
☐ e. Team "fire-up" tradition

15. Pregame warm-up

☐ a. What are they going to do: Cheer? Chant?
☐ b. Work in a circle? In lines? Individual warm-up, team warm-up?
☐ c. Pepper? Team drills? Hitting lines?

Each team is different. Warm-up reflects a team's personality and general organization.

Appendix C:
Match Protocol

Match Protocol Sheet
(for 7:30 P.M. Start)

6:30 - 7:00   Court available for both teams' warm-ups. (Each team stays on own side of net. No hitting.)

7:00 - 7:10   Shared hitting (please hit the lines).

7:08   Team captains meet with officials for instructions and coin toss.

7:10   Serving team gets 5 minutes of full-court warm-up.

7:15   Receiving team gets 5 minutes of full-court warm-up.

7:20   Both teams warm up by serving.

7:22   Teams assemble for march in.

7:23   March in.

7:24   Anthem, official and team introductions.

7:30   First serve.

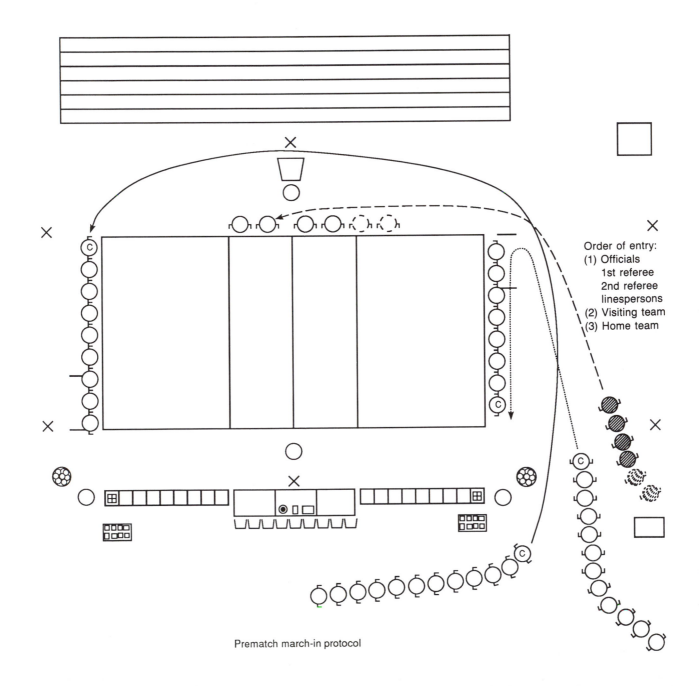

Order of entry:
(1) Officials
     1st referee
     2nd referee
     linespersons
(2) Visiting team
(3) Home team

Prematch march-in protocol

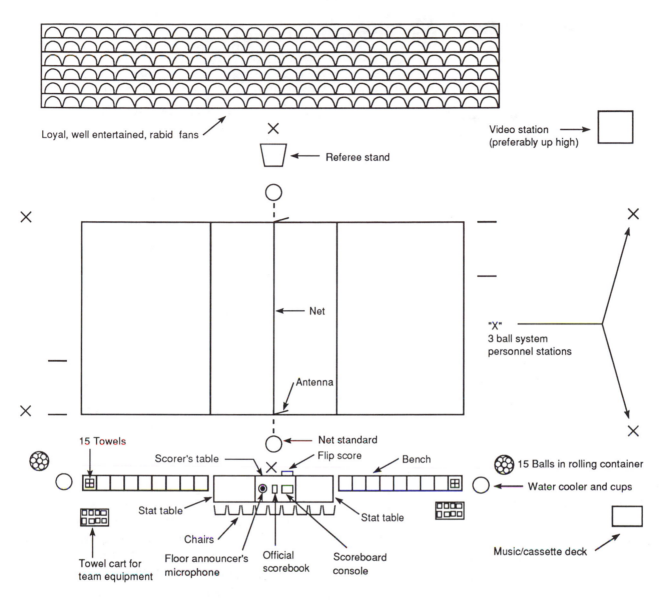

Loyal, well entertained, rabid fans

Referee stand

Video station
(preferably up high)

Net

Antenna

"X"
3 ball system
personnel stations

15 Towels

Net standard

Scorer's table

Flip score

Bench

15 Balls in rolling container

Water cooler and cups

Stat table

Stat table

Chairs

Music/cassette deck

Floor announcer's
microphone

Official
scorebook

Scoreboard
console

Towel cart for
team equipment

Match court setup

Checklist for Home Matches

1. Court setup

- [ ] a. Game net
- [ ] b. Antennae
- [ ] c. Center court standards
- [ ] d. Standards' safety pads
- [ ] e. Padded referee's stand
- [ ] f. Four court towels (for wiping up floor moisture)
- [ ] g. Two ball containers with 12 to 15 balls each for warm-up
- [ ] h. Floor dust mop

2. Scorer's table setup

- [ ] a. Score sheets and pencils
- [ ] b. Team roster
- [ ] c. Lineup cards or sheets
- [ ] d. Rule book
- [ ] e. Two programs
- [ ] f. Score clock console
- [ ] g. Three game balls
- [ ] h. Ball pump and needle
- [ ] i. Linesmen flags
- [ ] j. Flip score (for backup if scoreboard fails)
- [ ] k. Statistic sheets and pencils
- [ ] l. Microphone, program, team rosters for announcer
- [ ] m. Soft drinks in ice bucket for officials

3. Bench setup

- [ ] a. Water cooler, filled with ice water, and cups
- [ ] b. 15 towels
- [ ] c. Towel cart for team equipment storage
- [ ] d. Protocol schedule sheets

4. Video setup

- [ ] a. Secure area for video camera (home team and visitor)
- [ ] b. Extension cord
- [ ] c. Camera, tripod, recorder
- [ ] d. Blank tapes (prelabeled with match date, place)

5. Music setup (if no pep band is available)

- [ ] a. Tape deck
- [ ] b. Protected area for equipment
- [ ] c. Tapes: Warm-up music, preset tape with march-in music and anthem, school fight song

6. Personnel

- [ ] a. Two to four linespersons (in matching, appropriate attire)
- [ ] b. One official scorer
- [ ] c. One scoreboard operator
- [ ] d. One floor announcer
- [ ] e. Three to six statisticians (2 or 3 for each team)
- [ ] f. Six people for 3-ball system and warm-up shagging
- [ ] g. One person operating video (trained as to what to tape, what to say—i.e., score, server, what player blocked, spiked, etc.)
- [ ] h. One person to operate music
- [ ] i. Two officials (will be assigned under league or association guidelines)
- [ ] j. One or two people at the gate selling programs and tickets

It is a good idea to store match equipment by setup category.

Appendix D:
Sources for Rules

An attempt to publish the complete rules of volleyball in this manual would create more confusion than it would solve. In the United States several sets of rules govern volleyball. Junior and senior high schools in most states play under National Federation of State High School Associations (NFSHSA) rules. All women's junior collegiate and collegiate programs play under rules written by the National Association of Girls and Women in Sport (NAGWS). Some club divisions of the USVBA play modified international rules. Collegiate men, the national men's and women's teams, the open men's and women's club divisions, and all the rest of the countries in the world play according to the international rules of the Fédération Internationale de Volleyball. In addition, the rules are in a constant state of flux. It is important, therefore, that you know which set of rules your program will use and obtain a copy. The addresses of organizations from which you can order volleyball rules are listed here.

Junior high and high school rules can be ordered from either your state high school association or the NFSHSA at 11724 NW Plaza Circle, P.O. Box 20626, Kansas City, Missouri 64195-0626.

Collegiate women's programs can obtain rules from the NAGWS at 1900 Association Drive, Reston, Virginia 22091.

All USVBA and collegiate men's programs can obtain the appropriate set of rules from the USVBA at 3595 E. Fountain Blvd., Suite I-2, Colorado Springs, CO 80910-1740.

Tell Us What You Think

It is our commitment at ACEP to provide coaches with the most complete, accurate, and useful information available. Our authors, consultants, and editors are continuously searching for new ideas and are constantly seeking to improve our materials. Now that you have read and studied this book, it is your turn to tell us what you liked and did not like about it. *Please take a few minutes to complete the following survey and send it to ACEP, Box 5076, Champaign, IL 61825-5076.*

Book Evaluation for
Coaching Volleyball Successfully

Instructions: For each statement mark the spaces in the left-hand column that correspond to what you think of this book. We are interested in your opinions so feel free to mark more than one response to each statement.

1. The organization of this book
   ___ (a) presents material in an easy-to-understand progression
   ___ (b) is helpful
   ___ (c) is confusing

2. The material presented in this book is
   ___ (a) easy to read and understand
   ___ (b) difficult to read and understand
   ___ (c) too simple
   ___ (d) too complex

3. Figures and illustrations are
   ___ (a) helpful
   ___ (b) distracting
   ___ (c) technically correct
   ___ (d) technically incorrect
   ___ (e) confusing

4. Coaching points and teaching progressions
   ___ (a) highlight material in the book well
   ___ (b) progress from basic to advanced concepts
   ___ (c) are helpful
   ___ (d) are distracting
   ___ (e) are too repetitive

5. Drills
   ___ (a) need illustrations
   ___ (b) are helpful
   ___ (c) are confusing
   ___ (d) are too advanced for beginning players
   ___ (e) are too simple for beginning players
   ___ (f) are easy to use
   ___ (g) are difficult to use

6. Instructional schedules are
   ___ (a) helpful
   ___ (b) easy to understand
   ___ (c) difficult to understand

7. Practice plans are
   ___ (a) helpful
   ___ (b) confusing
   ___ (c) too basic
   ___ (d) too advanced
   ___ (e) easy to use
   ___ (f) difficult to use

8. Coaching aids are
   ___ (a) helpful
   ___ (b) not helpful
   ___ (c) easy to use
   ___ (d) difficult to use

Yes or No
   ___ **9. I feel more knowledgeable about coaching volleyball to beginning athletes than I did before reading this book.**
   ___ **10. I would like to attend a workshop or clinic covering the material presented in this book.**

Glossary

Active rest—Physical activities athletes participate in that are not directly related to the sport for which they train. Active rest takes place in the off-season.

Advanced stage of learning—The stage of learning at which a skill can be executed without conscious effort of learning, so the focus of learning is on the tactical application of the skill. This stage is also known as the autonomous phase.

Angle of deflection—The trajectory the ball takes after contacting a body surface.

Annual plan—An overview of a program's activities and when they occur during the calendar year.

Association of Interscholastic Athletics for Women (AIAW)—Formed in the 1970s, the AIAW organized collegiate athletics for women until 1981, when the National Collegiate Athletic Association (NCAA) began organizing women's sports in NCAA institutions.

Attack—The attempt by one team to terminate the play by hitting the ball to the floor on the opponent's side. The term refers to an individual effort or a combined team offensive pattern.

Attack angle—The direction of a spiker's approach to a set ball and the imaginary path of the spike across the net if hit in the same line as the approach angle.

Attack approach—The accelerating running movement of a spiker, usually involving three or four steps, to the point where the spiker jumps to hit the ball.

Attacker—Also "hitter" or "spiker." A player who attempts to hit a ball offensively with the purpose of terminating the play in his or her team's favor.

Back-row players—The three players in positions 1, 6, and 5 on the rotational order grid during any given rotational order. These three players are not allowed to jump from in front of the 3-meter line to attack a ball above the top of the net.

Backslide—An offensive attack approach route used by a middle-front player to spike a ball that is set low and behind the setter.

Ball container—Any container that can hold at least 12 balls. It should be on wheels and able to be locked. Most volleyball equipment companies sell containers.

Beginning stage of learning—The stage of learning at which the learner develops an understanding of the concepts of a skill and consciously practices the mechanics. This stage is also known as the conceptual phase.

Big point—Used in scoring certain drills, it represents the successful execution of one or more plays in a row. The number of consecutive plays required to score a big point is determined by the particular drill and the coach.

Block—(n) The combination of one, two, or three players jumping in front of the opposing spiker and contacting the spiked ball with the hands; (v) The action of stopping or slowing a spiked ball with the hands above the net.

Blocker(s)—The player or players responsible for blocking the opponent's attack.

Block shadow—The area behind the block in which the opposing spikers cannot hit the ball hard.

Bump—(a) Descriptive slang for forearm passing; (b) Last name of unrelenting ACEP editor.

Bunting—A descriptive but seldom-used slang term for forearm passing. Bumping is more commonly used.

Coach-centered drill—Any drill in which the coach controls a specific contact to one player.

Coaching points—Specific issues of emphasis to be made during the teaching process. Coaching points focus primarily on the tactical application of the technique.

Coach-initiated drill—Any drill in which the coach puts the ball in play for several players or the full team at a predetermined position. The ensuing play is completed by the players to its natural conclusion.

Collapse—A defensive player sits over one heel while playing a ball and rolls on his or her back. Used to play balls close to the floor and to cushion hard-hit spikes during retrieval attempts, this skill is also known as a half roll.

Competitive season—The weeks during the year in which league, regional, state, and/or national competition is scheduled.

Control block—A block attempt that deflects and slows down a spiked ball so the back-row defenders can easily play it.

Corners of the body—Toes, ankles, knees, hips, shoulders, elbows, wrists, and the head are "corners" that should be protected when a player executes any floor defensive retrieval technique.

Court lines—Any 5-centimeter-wide line required on a regulation volleyball court, including the side and end lines, center line, 3-meter lines, and serving area hash marks.

Cross-court shot—An individual attack directed at an angle from one end of the offensive team's side of the net to the opposite sideline of the defensive team's court.

Cross step/Brake step—A footwork pattern designed to allow a player to move quickly to a correct, balanced precontact position in either forearm or overhead passing.

Defensive system—A team tactical system of deploying players to positions to defend against an opponent's attack. An effective system deploys players in the areas most likely to be attacked and takes the strengths and weaknesses of the individual defenders into account.

Dig—(slang) The act of retrieving an attacked ball close to the floor.

Dive—A defensive retrieval technique in which a player extends for a ball near the floor, causing both feet to leave the floor. The player contacts the ball with one or both arms and slides on the abdomen and thighs.

Down ball—An attacked ball from the opponent that the blockers assess as not being hit hard enough or being contacted too deep in the opponent's court to require a block attempt. The blockers call "down" and wait until after the ball crosses the net to move into their own attack-approach positions.

Drill—A measured series of sets closely monitored by a coach or coaches designed to blend individual skills into an orchestration of team skills to gain a desired unified effect.

Extension roll—A defensive retrieval technique similar to a dive, except that after contacting the ball with either one or two arms, the player turns as the body contacts the floor and rolls as the momentum of the movement carries the feet over the shoulder, returning the player to his or her feet.

Fast score—A scoring system whereby a point is scored on every play instead of only by the serving team.

Fédération Internationale de Volleyball (FIVB)—This organization is the international governing body of volleyball of which the United States Volleyball Association (USVBA) is a member. The FIVB represents all of volleyball on the International Olympic Committee (IOC).

Feedback—The coach's verbal reinforcement and corrections using specific teaching keys given to players while they are performing skills.

Flair offense—An offensive system developed by the 1976 Canadian Men's Olympic Team where the right-side attacker's approach route begins with the setter in a line perpendicular to the net. The right-side attacker approaches at the same time as the middle attacker and flares left or right just as the middle attacker begins to jump. "Flair" is intentionally used as a play on the word "flare," which accurately describes the system's approach patterns.

Float serve—A serve hit so that the ball does not spin during flight.

Floor defense—Any retrieval of an attacked ball that gets by the block.

Forearm pass—One of the six basic volleyball skills. It is a ball-handling skill that a player uses to legally contact the ball at a level below the waist using the forearms as the contact surface.

Four-step approach—The most basic of the attack-approach patterns. For a right-handed hitter, the correct four-step approach is to step with right foot, then the left, then right, then left. Each time a foot touches the floor is considered a step.

4-2—A playing system that has four spikers and two setters.

Free ball—Any ball that the opponent returns easily, allowing the blockers enough time to get back into their attack-approach positions before the ball crosses the net.

Fronting the hitter—A position a blocker assumes in relationship to the attacker's approach. The blocker is in a position so that the attacker's arm swing would cut the blocker from the toe of the outside foot to the heel of the inside foot.

Front-row players—The three players in a rotational order (2, 3, and 4) who are eligible to contact a ball in front of the 3-meter line above the net, either by spiking or blocking.

Game-like environment—The conditions of any training activity that closely resemble the conditions of a competitive game. These include physical conditions such as the court, net, antennae, lighting, and playing space; organizational conditions such as the orientation of the players relative to the playing area, the trajectory of the ball, and the rebound angle requirements; and mental conditions such as stress levels, communication requirements, problem-solving requirements, and role responsibilities.

Hit—Also "spike," "attack." The specific contact in spiking to put the ball to the opponent's floor with force.

Hitter—Also "spiker," "attacker." The player who is responsible for hitting the ball.

Inside the block—A ball that has been attacked in the cross-court angle so that it passes by the block nearest the center of the court.

Intermediate contacts—The first two contacts with the ball in the sequence of three allowable contacts for the receiving team. For example, serve receiving and setting are intermediate contacts.

Intermediate goals—Goals that require attainment in order for long-range goals to be achieved. In a 4-year cycle, intermediate goals are set annually to be achieved approximately monthly.

Intermediate stage of learning—The stage of learning in which the learner's focus is on performing the skills in tactical situations. The skills have not been assimilated but still must be consciously applied. This phase is also known as the associative phase.

International rotational order grid—The six sequential court positions that correspond to the serving order—right back (server) position 1, right front position 2, middle front position 3, left front position 4, left back position 5, middle back position 6.

J stroke—A modified forearm pass technique where the thumbs are turned up and the elbows are bent, forming a "J." This technique is used to dig hard-hit balls and balls played close to the net.

Junk—Slang for off-speed shots, balls intentionally hit off the block, deflected shots that do not travel in expected paths or to anticipated locations.

Knuckler—An emergency one-hand technique used to play a ball close to the face and tight to the net. The fingers are curled at the second knuckle and the hand is cocked back. The ball is actually contacted on the heel of the hand.

Line shot—A ball hit down the opponent's line on the side of the court from which the spiker is attacking.

Little point—A single successful execution of a play in a required sequence of plays, specifically used in a drill scoring system requiring two or more successful plays executed in a row (see *Big point*).

Long-range goals—These goals are developed for each year or season. They are measurable and specific. Intermediate goals are the building blocks for long-range goals.

Long-range objectives—These are specific projected achievements 3 or 4 years ahead. These objectives define the direction of the program.

Mintonette—The original name of the game of volleyball, created by William Morgan.

Movements—The body mechanics required to execute a physical skill.

Multiple block—More than one player involved in a block attempt.

National Association of Girls and Women in Sport (NAGWS)—An affiliated member of the American Alliance for Health, Physical Education, Recreation and Dance (AAHPERD) that researches and promotes quality athletic programs for girls and women, including players' and coaches' educational clinics; provides annual updates; and prepares rules for collegiate athletics.

National Association of Intercollegiate Athletics (NAIA)—Organized in 32 regions nationwide, the NAIA administers leagues and national championships for its member collegiate institutions in 11 men's and 10 women's sports.

National Collegiate Athletic Association (NCAA)—The NCAA administers college and university athletic programs in three divisions. There are 13 men's and 9 women's national championships in Division I, 10 men's and 7 women's championships in Division II, and 13 men's and 11 women's championships in Division III.

National Governing Body (NGB)—Any national sport organization that represents its sport as a sanctioned member of the United States Olympic Committee and the International Governing Body, which in turn represents the sport on the IOC. The United States Volleyball Association is volleyball's NGB in the United States.

National Junior College Athletic Association (NJCAA)—The governing body of junior college athletics in the United States.

Net—The net must be constructed only of 10-centimeter-(4-inch)-square duck mesh. It cannot be less than 9.50 meters (32 feet) long and 1 meter (39 inches) wide throughout its full length when stretched. A double thickness of white vinyl or canvas must be sewn along the top of the net's full length. A flexible cable shall be stretched through the upper and lower edges of the net and attached to the net standards.

Net antennae—Two 6-foot, 3/8-inch-diameter poles attached to the net 9 meters (30 feet) apart, indicating the vertical extension of the sideline. In high school rules the antennae are set 8 inches outside the line on each end of the net, putting them 31 feet, 4 inches apart.

Net standards—The poles at the sides of the court to which the net is attached so that the net is stretched tight to the legal length.

Offensive system—A team tactical system that uses the players to attack the ball against an opponent in an effective manner. The system should consider players' offensive strengths and weaknesses and coordinate the individual elements so that team members can attack at their discretion.

Off-speed shots—Any ball spiked with less than maximum force but with spin.

One-blocker system—A team defensive scheme that uses only one blocker; all other players assume floor defensive positions.

On help—A player's defensive floor position and body posture that allows him or her to play an attacked ball in front of him or her and toward his or her teammates.

Opportunities to respond—The critical step in the learning process in which players contact the ball as many times as possible, attempting correct techniques and receiving meaningful feedback from the coaches.

Overhead float serve—A serving technique in which the ball is contacted above the head without any spin imparted on the ball.

Overhead pass—A ball-handling skill using both hands simultaneously to contact the ball above the head and direct it to the intended target.

Overlap—This occurs when, as the ball is being served, one player in a rotational order is beyond an imaginary line defined by an adjacent player's foot placement.

Pairs—Two players working together in a drill.

Pancake—A one-hand floor defensive technique where the hand is extended and slid along the floor palm down while the player dives or extension rolls, so that the ball bounces off the back of the hand.

Player-centered drill—A drill in which the players control all the action.

Playing system—The organized scheme a team will use offensively and defensively to play the game. The system should be designed to expose the players' strengths and hide their weaknesses.

Playoffs—The phase of a competitive season where, by virtue of their season record, teams play other teams with similar win/loss records to determine who advances to the championship round of any given level of play.

Point of contact—The place on the court or along the net at which the ball is contacted.

Postseason—The period immediately following the regularly scheduled competitive season. For teams who have won or finished high in their leagues, this period represents playoffs for advancement to championships. For teams with mediocre or losing seasons, this phase represents time to pursue other activities for awhile.

Posture—Body position while performing a skill.

Practice—A block of time scheduled to include a series of drills organized in a logical progression based on predetermined performance goals.

Precontact position—The floor location arrived at and the body posture assumed before the ball arrives.

Preseason—The phase of the program just prior to the competitive season during which team organization, technical training, physical conditioning, and player selection takes place.

Progression—A logical sequence of game-related activities used to teach an individual skill or a team playing system.

Ready position—The flexed, yet comfortable posture a player assumes before moving to the point of contact.

Rebound angle—Angle of the contact surface of the body at the moment of ball contact; commonly refers to forearm passing and hand position in blocking.

Repetition—One successful execution of a skill.

Reverse bump—A desperation ball-handling technique sometimes necessary but seldom encouraged. It occurs when a player brings the hands together up in front of the face, elbows bent. The ball is contacted in front of the face on the back of the forearms.

Rotational order—A lineup turned in by the coach to officials prior to each game describing the sequence in which the players will serve. The players must adhere to this lineup relative to court positions prior to each serve.

Scoop—(slang) Refers to the action used in the J stroke. The ball is played with the hands clasped together, the thumbs parallel and pointed up, and the elbows bent.

Season—A block of time on the calendar scheduled to include competitions and practices.

Seasonal plan—A detailed, organized, logical scheme designed to give specific direction to the teaching and coaching of a team through a predetermined period of time. The season includes the phases of preparation, competition, playoffs, and active rest.

Serve—One of the six basic skills; used to put the ball in play. It is the only skill controlled exclusively by one player.

Serve receive—The tactical skill of directing the opponent's serve to the setter so that he or she can set. Forearm passing is the most common technical skill used to serve receive.

Serving order—See *rotational order.*

Set—(a) The tactical skill in which a ball is directed to a point where a player can spike it into the opponent's court. Overhead passing is the most common technical skill used to set. (b) In international volleyball, *set* also refers to what is commonly called a game in the United States. (c) A specified number of repetitions in any training activity.

Shagging—Retrieving balls that have been played, missed, or terminated in a drill and returning them to the leader of the drill.

Short-term goals—Specific tasks to be accomplished during a relatively short period of time (usually a day or a week) that are required to meet intermediate and long-range goals.

Shot—Any directed individual attack attempt.

Side-out—Occurs when the receiving team successfully puts the ball away against the serving team, or when the serving team commits an unforced error, and the receiving team thus gains the right to serve.

Silver tip—Ursus Horribilis, or grizzly bear. The light reflecting off the bear's fur makes the ends of the hair appear silver.

6-6—A playing system in which each player assumes the responsibility of the rotational position he or she is in at any given time.

Skill—The coordinated, effective function required by a specific motor task.

Skill mechanics—The specific, coordinated body movements required to successfully complete a motor task.

Skip step—Resembles a hop. The feet are moved simultaneously from one position to

a new balanced position. Primarily used to describe a common footwork pattern in ball handling.

Spike—Also *hit* or *attack*. A ball contacted with force by a player on the offensive team who intends to terminate the ball on the opponent's floor or off the opponent's blocker.

Spike coverage—Players on the attacking team assume low ready positions around their teammate, who is spiking, and move to retrieve the ball if necessary.

Spiker—One who is spiking or is preparing to spike.

Sprawl—A floor defensive retrieval technique in which a player immediately goes to the floor on his or her front and extends with one or two hands to play the ball.

Strategy—A general plan considering all related elements that is developed to solve a problem.

Stuff—A ball that is deflected back to the attacking team's floor by the opponent's blockers.

Swing offense—An offensive system in which the attacker's approach pattern begins inside the court and goes outside. In traditional offensive schemes, attacker approaches are outside in.

Tactical application—The specific use of individual skills in carrying out the strategies in any given play.

Tactics—The playing systems and individual responses based upon the methodical evaluation of the strengths and weaknesses of one's own players, varying conditions, and the strengths and weaknesses of an opponent.

Target—The player who is intended to receive the ball in any given play. The target can be the setter who is in the correct court position, an opponent who is designated to receive a serve, or a spiker who is waiting to receive a set.

Target area—The court position where the target player should be.

Teaching keys—The words or phrases that are used to describe a correct execution of all or a portion of a skill. These verbal cues are used during the feedback phase of the teaching process.

Technique—The mechanics of a skill.

Terminal attack—A spike or tip that has been successfully executed so that it is unplayable by the defensive team.

Terminal contacts—Contacts the results of which lead directly to points or side-outs for the contacting team. Stuff blocks, spikes, and ace serves are all terminal contacts. An unforced error such as touching the net is also considered terminal.

Three-step move—The lateral three-step movement used by a blocker, usually the middle blocker, to get outside to block. Usually the blocker uses this foot pattern traveling left to right.

3-3—A playing system that has three spikers and three setters.

Tip—An attack technique that the spiker uses to place the ball gently with the tips of the fingers of one hand. The wrist is stiff. The ball cannot come to a visible rest on the fingers.

Tossing—An important but often ignored skill used by coaches and players to initiate a drill. Specifically, the two-hand overhead toss is used to duplicate the dynamics and trajectory of a serve, and the two-hand underhand toss is used for accurate placement in ball-handling drills. One-hand tosses should not be used because they are difficult to control and put an unrealistic spin on the ball.

Touch block—Another term for *control block*.

Trajectory—The curve the ball takes on its path from one player to another.

Triads—Groups of three players working together within a drill.

Two blockers, middle deep—A team defensive scheme that deploys two front-row players blocking and the middle back-row player staying within a meter of the back line.

Two blockers, middle up—A team defensive scheme that deploys two blockers and a back-row player playing at the 3-meter line behind the block to cover the tip.

Two-step move—The most common blocker foot pattern used to move laterally with speed and balance to get in front of a spiker. The move is used by all blockers to cover 1 to 3 meters with control.

Underhand serve—A serving technique in which the ball is contacted at about waist height by the serving hand.

Unforced error—An error committed by a player that is unrelated to the opponent's play. Touching the net, stepping over the center line, and serving into the net are examples of unforced errors.

United States Volleyball Association (USVBA)—The national governing body of the United States, representing volleyball on the United States Olympic Committee; also a member of the Fédération Internationale de Volleyball and responsible for developing volleyball programs from youth clubs to the national teams.

Universal player theory—A theory which states that all players should become equally adept at playing all positions and phases of a volleyball game.

W serve receive formation—A common five-player serve receive pattern with the setter either behind a player or near the net, depending on rotational order position. The five players are on the court so they have a direct line of sight to the server and are in the correct rotational order. The positions of the players would be at the points of a *W* if the letter were drawn on the floor.

Water witching—Slang for a player who follows a ball with the hands but does not move to establish good body position. The result is ball contact with poor balance.

Waves—A type of team drill that has groups of three players organized in front- and back-row combinations on both sides of the net. When the goal of the drill activity is met, the groups of three "wave" through: The front row of Court A goes under the net and becomes the front row of Court B, the Court A back row becomes the Court A front row, Court B's front row becomes that court's back row, and Court B's back row becomes Court A's back row.

Weight transfer—Refers to a player moving the body weight from the back foot to the front foot while executing a skill.

Winning point burden—A scoring system for drills in which a player must successfully execute two or more prescribed drill requirements in a row to score the final point.

Zone block—When the blockers are in good position relative to the opposing spiker, they take away a significant portion of the defensive back court in which the spiker can hit.

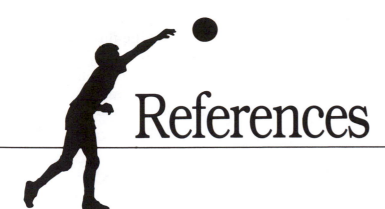

References

Bump, L.A. (1989). *Sport Psychology Study Guide*. Champaign, IL: Human Kinetics.

Carlton, M.J., & Carlton, L.G. (1989). *Teaching Sport Skills Study Guide*. Champaign, IL: Human Kinetics.

Christina, R.W., & Corcos, D.M. (1988). *Coaches Guide to Teaching Sport Skills*. Champaign, IL: Human Kinetics.

Jefferies, S.C. (1986). *Sport Physiology Study Guide*. Champaign, IL: Human Kinetics.

Leith, L.M. (in press). *Coaches Guide to Sport Administration*. Champaign, IL: Leisure Press.

Lucas, J. (1988). *Pass, set, crush* (2nd ed.). Mercer Island: Euclid Northwest Publications.

Martens, R. (1987). *Coaches Guide to Sport Psychology*. Champaign, IL: Human Kinetics.

Sharkey, B.J. (1986). *Coaches Guide to Sport Physiology*. Champaign, IL: Human Kinetics.

Index

About the Author

William J. Neville, head coach of the University of Washington women's volleyball team and former head coach of the national men's volleyball team, is one of the foremost authorities on volleyball in the United States. He has coached three Olympic volleyball teams, first as an assistant for the 1968 U.S. men's team, then as head coach of the 1976 Canadian men's team, and finally as an assistant for the gold-medal winning 1984 U.S. men's team. Neville was technical director for the United States Volleyball Association (USVBA) from 1986 to 1988. While with the USVBA, he was responsible for initiating their Coaching Accreditation Program (CAP), which prepared him to put together this guide for more effective coaching.

About the USVBA

The United States Volleyball Association is the nation's governing body for the sport from the youth club level to the Olympics. The objective of the USVBA is to promote volleyball and make playing volleyball accessible to all Americans. To that end, the USVBA established its Coaching Accreditation Program (CAP). CAP accreditation provides volleyball coaches at all levels with standards for effective teaching, organization, drilling, practicing, and planning.